PRIVATE CLIENT

RECENT GLOBAL DEVELOPMENTS

Law Over Borders Comparative Guide 2023

Edited by Joshua S. Rubenstein, Katten Muchin Rosenman

THE
GLOBAL LEGAL POST

Published in 2023 by:
Global City Media
86-90 Paul Street
London EC2A 4NE
United Kingdom
Telephone: +44 (0) 20 7193 5801
www.globalcitymedia.com
www.globallegalpost.com

Editor: Joshua S. Rubenstein
Editorial Director: Mary Heaney
Commercial Director: Maria Sunderland
Editorial and Production Manager: Debbie Knowles
Associate Publisher: Claudia Tan
Digital: Elanganathapillai Sivakanthan

Printed in the UK by:
TJ Books
Trecerus Industrial Estate
Padstow
Cornwall
PL28 8RW
www.tjbooks.co.uk

ISBN: 978-0-9935776-6-6

INTRODUCTION

Joshua S. Rubenstein
Katten Muchin Rosenman

I am pleased and privileged to serve as the editor of Private Client: Recent Global Developments, a new Law Over Borders Comparative Guide. In order to make this project as valuable and informative to the reader as possible, I have selected a number of leading practitioners and firms from around the world that represent the *crème de la crème* of the private client profession. The aim is to make available to you the wisdom and insight of a circle of experts globally in this fast-changing and increasingly important area of law.

I designed this work to be different from the typical multi-jurisdictional guide where each author submits an article on a particular subject that may or may not be of broad interest and that never changes. The pandemic was a perfect storm for the private client profession. Clients found themselves quarantined at home with time on their hands, and were forced to confront mortality, so they renewed their focus on planning with a sense of urgency. Sadly, given the high death rate, there were more estates to administer than ever before. And given the closure, or near closure, of courts around the world – and considering that families were 'cooped up' with each other during this protracted time – private client litigation exploded.

Post-pandemic, the private client landscape is changing faster than ever, as governments seek out ever greater revenue streams from our client base, and cash strapped governments and disappointed beneficiaries find new ways to attack planning structures. In addition, the courts in most countries are struggling with near insurmountable backlogs, creating an unusual incentive to administer estates extra-judicially and to attempt to compromise disputes. This book, and the online guide, will provide an up-to-date jurisdictional comparison of the latest tax and non-tax developments for the private client profession in the areas of planning, administration and litigation. It is our intention to update this work every other year with the latest developments over the prior two years.

I hope you find this to be of value, and I thank the authors of each chapter for their hard work and cogent insights.

Joshua S. Rubenstein
Partner and National Chair, Private Wealth Department
Katten Muchin Rosenman

BERMUDA

Craig MacIntyre & Grace Quinn

Conyers Dill & Pearman

1. TAX AND WEALTH PLANNING

1.1 National legislative and regulatory developments

Bermuda has long been recognised as an attractive and secure jurisdiction with a favourable taxation regime for private wealth management for international private clients.

Taxation

There have been few developments in relation to tax in Bermuda and so the present position is outlined below.

From an international estate planning and trust perspective there are no real taxes applicable to non-Bermudians. There is no income tax, profits tax, capital gains tax, capital transfer tax or inheritance tax applicable to Bermuda residents or Bermuda companies (subject to points below and those outlined at 2.1 Estate administration). There are also no exit or similar taxes based on a resident's wealth when ceasing to be resident and there are no other consequences of leaving the jurisdiction.

Bermuda has an extensive Stamp Duty regime which only applies, for the most part, to Bermudians and Bermuda property. For example, there is no *ad valorem* Stamp Duty applicable to trusts which receive or enter into transactions in non-Bermuda currency or assets. See Section 2.1 Estate administration below in relation to Bermuda Stamp Duty.

Bermuda also has a Land Tax regime which applies to the owners of Bermuda property which is paid bi-annually and based on the ARV (annual rental value) of the property on a sliding scale.

Gifts or transfers of Bermuda currency or property into a trust do attract Stamp Duty at increasing rates to a maximum of 15% on values exceeding BDA 1 million.

Finally, for those businesses with employees in Bermuda there is a system of taxation on payroll. There are various reliefs, including for low earners and job creators.

Wealth Planning

A core part of wealth planning for international clients in Bermuda is by the use of trust structuring (see Section 2).

A corresponding part of wealth planning for international clients may include the preparation of a Bermuda Will, particularly for those who own Bermuda property. The applicable legislation is the Wills Act 1988 (as amended). In order to prepare a Will the individual must be over the age of 18, have testamentary capacity, be in writing and be signed by the testator in the presence of two independent adult witnesses (who must also be of sound mind).

Bermuda has freedom of testamentary disposition and there is no forced heirship regime.

1.2 Local legislative and regulatory developments

There is no localised legislation or regulation.

1.3 National case law developments

Please see Section 3 below.

1.4 Local case law developments

There is no localised case law.

1.5 Practice trends

There is an increased use of Private Trust Company (PTC) and use of Purpose Trusts to facilitate commercial transactions and quasi-philanthropic activities.

1.6 Pandemic related developments

In response to the pandemic the Bermuda Government is now offering one-year, renewable, residency certificates for remote workers aimed at 'digital-nomads'. There were also some tax reliefs available to the hospitality sector.

2. ESTATE AND TRUST ADMINISTRATION

2.1 National legislative and regulatory developments

Estate Administration

Estate administration in Bermuda is similar in many respects to that of England & Wales. An application for a grant of probate is made by the person or persons named as executor in the Will of the deceased and is completed by the filing with the Supreme Court in Bermuda of an 'Affidavit of Value' setting out the value of the estate at death, together with an 'Oath of Executor' whereby the executor undertakes to comply with such directions as the court may give and distribute the deceased's estate according to the Will. The original Will is filed at the court and becomes a matter of public record.

The Affidavit of Value is largely concerned with Bermuda based assets owned by the deceased which are valued in Bermuda dollars and attract Bermuda Estate Duty (for example, Bermuda dollar denominated bank accounts, Bermuda shareholdings and Bermuda real property).

The Stamp Duty applicable on death is on a sliding scale. There are exemptions available on death for gifts to a surviving spouse and a Bermuda registered charity. It is also possible to designate a 'Primary Family Homestead' which enables a person to designate a residential property as a primary family homestead and exempt that property from the applicable Stamp Duty on death. There are provisions to take advantage of this if no designation is made during life.

Trust Administration

Private Trusts

Bermuda's trust law is largely based on English common law, including the doctrine of equity, but it has been enhanced and amended by Bermuda trust related legislation. The Trustee Act 1975 (1975 Act) is, for the most part (but subject to a number of modern amendments and improvements) identical to the England & Wales Trustee Act 1925. There is an emphasis on review and innovation to trust law in Bermuda to ensure it remains a competitive and modern choice for the wealth planning needs of international families and their advisers. There is a collaborative relationship between Bermuda's legislature and private sector associations such as the Society of Trust and

Estate Practitioners to enable regular and innovative reforms of trust laws with legislation that is both modern and facilitative. Below are highlighted some key legislative provisions.

S24 of the 1975 Act provides a statutory power of advancement which can be widely applied (provided it is not specifically excluded by the trust deed). It is generally accepted that this allows incidental benefit to strangers to the trust without resulting in a 'fraud on the power' but the trustee should only exercise their fiduciary powers appropriately for the benefit of the beneficiaries.

Ss47 and 48 of the 1975 Act provide the legislative basis for the variation of trusts and are again based on English law, but modified to suit modern applications. S47 – perhaps the most well-known and innovative feature of Bermuda trust law – requires the court to consider whether it is 'expedient' to confer upon the trustees the power(s) that they request and whether as a matter of law the court can confer those power(s) upon the trustee. One important point to note is that this does not require the consent of all capable beneficiaries, which has proven particularly useful in the context of tax planning in beneficiary home jurisdictions. Case law in relation to s47 has included applications to update modern charging provisions, vary beneficial interests, improve tax efficiency and vary investment powers (amongst other things).

The Perpetuities and Accumulations Act 2009 (2009 Act) and Perpetuities Amendment Act 2015 (2015 Act). The 2009 Act abolished the rule against perpetuities for all trusts settled after 1 August 2009 except for trusts which include Bermuda land. The 2015 Act enables trustees of pre-2009 trusts (and trusts originally established in other jurisdictions which had an applicable perpetuity period or similar limited but are now governed by Bermuda law) to make more simplified, cost effective applications to the Bermuda courts to dis-apply or alter the perpetuity period or similar limitation on duration. The 2015 Act provides that such applications can be made on an *ex parte* basis and are dealt with quickly and cost effectively.

The Trusts (Special Provisions) Amendment Act 2020 came into force in August 2020 and ss.10 and 11 introduced updated 'firewall' provisions. S10 provides a regime for the exclusion of non-Bermuda law in relation to certain questions concerning the creation of Bermuda trusts and the exclusive application of Bermuda law concerning the validity, construction, effects and administration of Bermuda trusts. S11 provides for the exclusion of orders of foreign courts which are inconsistent with the choice of law.

The Trusts (Special Provisions) Amendment No.2 Act 2020 provides that illegitimate children can be excluded from a trust if the trust instrument expressly states a contrary intention. For most other purposes in Bermuda the position of legitimate and illegitimate children was equalised in 2002.

Purpose Trusts

The principal difference in the laws relating to trusts compared to English law are found in the Trusts (Special Provisions) Act 1989 (as amended) (1989 Act). The 1989 Act allows for the creation of non-charitable purpose trusts. These may have both charitable and non-charitable beneficiaries.

A non-charitable purpose trust, for instance, can be used in a number of ways, such as:

- a quasi-philanthropic trust, where the objects are not exclusively within the technical legal definition of 'charitable';
- in structured corporate finance transactions and securitisations;
- to hold voting stock for a specified purpose;
- to own the share of private trustee companies; and
- the creation of 'off balance sheet' orphan companies.

Private Trust Companies
The use of a PTC remains an extremely popular choice to act as the Trustee of a particular trust or group of trusts and the number of incorporations for such companies has increased significantly over the last few years. This enables the Settlor of a trust or group of trusts to retain control and uses corporate solutions to solve clients' organisation and liability problems. In other words such PTC structures are developed to suit the particular client's needs and enable efficient service without the interference and inefficiencies of overly bureaucratic regulation.

Charitable Trusts
The Charities Act 2014 (as amended) regulates charitable trusts. These can be public or private and different regulatory regimes apply depending on the nature of the charitable trust.

Regulation
Bermuda has a robust regulatory and licensing regime for corporate trust providers under the Trusts (Regulation of Trust Business) Act 2019. Bermuda has also enabled the Economic Substance Act 2018 to comply with various EU requests.

2.2 Local legislative and regulatory developments
There is no localised legislation or regulation.

2.3 National case law developments
Please see below Section 3.3 in relation to the case of *Ingham v. Wardman* [2022] CA (Bda) 7 Civ.

2.4 Local case law developments
There is no localised case law.

2.5 Practice trends
There is an increased use of PTCs and use of Purpose Trusts to facilitate commercial transactions and quasi-philanthropic activities.

2.6 Pandemic related developments
Fortunately the pandemic has not impacted upon planning work in this area.

3. ESTATE AND TRUST LITIGATION AND CONTROVERSY

3.1 National legislative and regulatory developments

There have been no legislative or regulatory developments in relation to estate and trust litigation but to provide some context the Supreme Court of Bermuda is the court of first instance in Bermuda with the right of appeal in certain circumstances to the Court of Appeal in Bermuda. The ultimate right of appeal lies with the Privy Council of the United Kingdom. Bermuda has an experienced judiciary and local counsel producing high quality judgements providing useful precedents with global reach. Unlike some other offshore jurisdictions, Bermuda allows KCs to appear in Bermuda courts.

3.2 Local legislative and regulatory developments

There is no localised legislation or regulation.

3.3 National case law developments

Relevant case law to date

In the context of s47 of the 1975 Act, the case of *GH v. KL* [2011] SC (Bda) 23 Civ involved a Will Trust which did not meet the needs of the various family beneficiaries. The application under s47 involved a number of changes, none of which were opposed and some which achieved a better tax outcome for some of the beneficiaries and were neutral for other beneficiaries. The Court ultimately approved all the changes and in the judgment it confirms that the legislation "at least contemplates the possibility of the Court sanctioning a transaction which is expedient for one beneficiary and neutral for the others". The Court also confirmed there was nothing to suggest importing a restriction preventing changes which achieved tax efficiency. A further important judgment in the context of s47 of the 1975 Act is the case of *Re ABC Trusts* [2012] SC (Bda) 65 Civ. Ian RC Kawaley CJ (as he then was) stated in respect of s47: "This power is actually broader than that conferred by the provisions of s48 which explicitly deal with variation alone".

Confidentiality is a key concern for many internationally mobile and wealthy families. It is generally accepted that non-controversial trust cases are private and therefore applications should be held in private and judgments anonymised. In the case of the *BCD Trust* [2015] SC (Bda) 83 Civ, CJ Kawaley stated: "It seems to me that in this type of case it is inherently consistent with the public interest and the administration of justice generally that applications such as these should be anonymised and dealt with as private applications, where there is no obvious public interest in knowing about an internal trust administration matter".

Recent case law

In the context of estate litigation the most recent decided case is *Ingham v. Wardman* [2022] CA (Bda) 7 Civ. This was a decision of the Court of Appeal of Bermuda with Bell, JA, providing the leading judgment. There was a lengthy judicial history to the matter which derived from an estate administration and steps taken in the administration by the executors as well as the grant of a Beddoe Order providing protection to the executors in respect of costs.

The Court of Appeal in this case referred to *Alsop Wilkinson v. Neary* [1995] I All ER 431, which identified three types of disputes in which trustees might find themselves being a trust dispute, a beneficiaries dispute and a third party dispute. The Court of Appeal classified this particular case as that of a beneficiary dispute which therefore required that a trustee's duty is generally to remain neutral, to offer to submit to the court's directions, and to leave the parties that are in dispute to resolve their dispute as they may be advised. The Court of Appeal took the view that the executors had not remained neutral 'but instead chose to engage in hostile litigation'. The Court of Appeal took the view that the executors had acted consistently with the advice provided to them.

The Court of Appeal granted an indemnity costs order against the executors with personal liability and set aside the previously made Beddoe Order. This case highlights the need for executors, and by extension trustees, to remain neutral where such disputes arise.

In the Matter of the X Trusts [2021] SC (Bda) 72 Civ is a recently decided case in respect of the role of the protector. Assistant Justice Dr Ian Kawaley referred, in his judgment, to the role as "a comparatively modern office … yet to be fully worked out by the courts". In this case a dispute arose as to the proper role and function of the protectors, in particular in relation to their power of *veto*. The key issue to be determined was whether the role was akin to a watchdog (that is, to make sure the trustees' decisions were valid and rational) or whether it was fully discretionary (such that the protectors could reach their own conclusions on the issues before them), referred to as the 'Narrow View' and the 'Wider View' respectively. Kawaley AJ held that, based on a contextual reading of the trust deeds, the Narrow View was favoured and, more generally, that unless the trust instrument expressly points to a fully discretionary role, it is likely that the normal inference will be that the role of the protector is one of review.

The other leading Bermuda case law on the topic of Protectors is *Re Information about a Trust* [2014] BDA LR 5, which characterised the role as that of a 'watchdog' or a 'monitoring one'.

3.4 Local case law developments

There is no localised legislation or regulation.

3.5 Practice trends

Beneficiary disputes can take many forms but are often triggered by the death of a patriarch or matriarch meaning that long-standing disagreements come to the fore which make trust restructuring a sensible solution to facilitate harmonious future wealth planning. How these restructurings take place and the division of the assets can often cause disputes. Trustees should remain neutral in such disputes but may wish the 'blessing' of the Court under a *Public Trustee v. Cooper* application.

The extent to which any trustees will be pursued for losses realised either as a result of the pandemic or the current economic down turn has yet to be seen.

3.6 Pandemic related developments

The major pandemic related development is the increased use of virtual hearings.

AUTHOR BIOGRAPHIES

Craig MacIntyre

Craig is a Director in the private client and trust practice in the Bermuda office of Conyers Dill & Pearman. He joined Conyers in 1997. Craig's work encompasses a broad spectrum of trust, company, estate planning and asset protection opportunities.

https://www.conyers.com/people/view/craig-w-macintyre/

Grace Quinn

Grace is an Associate in the private client and trust practice in the Bermuda office of Conyers Dill & Pearman. She joined Conyers in 2020. Grace's work covers the broad spectrum of private client with a particular focus on the creation and ongoing management of international trust structures, trust restructuring and resettlements.

https://www.conyers.com/people/view/grace-quinn/

BRAZIL

**Humberto Sanches, Adriane Pacheco,
Beatriz Martinez & Juliana Cavalcanti**
Humberto Sanches e Associados

INTRODUCTION

The Federal Constitution organizes the country as a Federative Republic, formed by the unbreakable union of the States, Municipalities, and the Federal District. Each of these is competent to legislate on specific matters as determined by the Federal Constitution.

In general, matters of law concerning private clients usually fall within the Federal government's legislative competence. When it comes to taxes, for example, the Federal Union is set by the Constitution as competent to tax income and capital gains. In addition to the Brazilian Constitution, Federal laws such as the Decree-Law No. 4,657/1942 (Law of Introduction to the Brazilian Law) and Law No. 10,406/2002 (Brazilian Civil Code) also rule on matters of international, family, succession, contractual, and corporate law, as well as other relevant topics, serving as the main legal ground for estate and succession planning in Brazil. Nonetheless, the States also have competence to rule on certain relevant matters, as inheritance and gift taxation.

It is also important to point out that, notwithstanding Brazil being a civil law country (i.e., Brazilian legal system is based on statutes rather than on case law), the Law No. 13,105/2015 (the Brazilian Civil Procedure Code) introduced some elements of common law to the local legal system and, as a result, State courts are bound by precedents ruled by both the Brazilian Supreme Court and the Superior Court of Justice over matters regulated by Federal law.

1. TAX AND WEALTH PLANNING
1.1 National legislative and regulatory developments
Taxation of Brazilian individuals

Income Tax (IT) is a Federal tax levied on the economic or legal availability of income to a Brazilian tax resident individual (see Section 1.6 below for the definition of 'tax resident') on a worldwide basis, transferred or not to Brazil, on a monthly basis. Rates vary from 0% to 27.5% on regular income and 15% to 22.5% on capital gains.

Inheritance and Gift Tax (IGT) is a State tax levied on the transmission of assets upon inheritance or donation. Rates vary from 0% to 8% (São Paulo applies 4% and Rio de Janeiro 4% to 8%).

Taxation of foreign investors in Brazil

Foreign investors, as a rule, are subject to the withholding IT at rates varying from 15% to 22.5% on capital gains derived from the sale of assets and rights in Brazil (if the investor is resident in a tax haven jurisdiction, the applicable rate is 25%). Sale of shares in stock exchanges and regulated over-the-counter markets may be exempt. Dividends distributed by Brazilian companies are exempt.

Taxation of Brazilian tax residents on investments abroad

Capital gains (e.g., interest earned or positive exchange variation at the time of sale, redemption, or settlement of any financial assets) will be subject to IT (15% to 22.5%). Gains up to BRL 35,000.00 per month are exempt.

As a rule, there is no taxation of interest earned on investments or exchange rate variation on the disposal, redemption, or settlement of assets until the funds become available to the individual. There is no automatic taxation of foreign controlled companies. Therefore, if the investment is made by the individual through an offshore company, taxes will only be due upon:
- capital reduction (on the positive exchange rate variation if the investment origin is in BRL (15% to 22.5%), otherwise it is not taxed); or
- distribution of dividends (0% to 27.5%).

Redemption of interests in foreign investment funds will be subject to IT on capital gains (15% to 22.5%).

Trust

The trust's characteristics shall be considered to define the legal nature of the amounts transferred by it to Brazilian residents and, therefore, the tax treatment (i.e., whether the transaction is deemed as a donation/inheritance, capital gains, or ordinary income). For instance, when a Brazilian resident transfers assets to an irrevocable trust, such transaction might be qualified as a gift, being subject to IGT — if such transaction is made at cost, IT should not be levied. Notwithstanding, recent tax rulings stated that:
- donations made by Brazilian residents to a trust should be subject to IT at 15% (or 25% if the trust is in a tax haven jurisdiction); and
- distributions from trusts should be subject to IT at 27.5%.

Both rulings are subject to strong criticism by practitioners.

On November 23, 2022, the Bill of Law No. 145/2022 (the "Trust Bill") on the applicable law on trusts and the Brazilian tax consequences of transactions involving trusts was presented to the Brazilian House of Representatives (Câmara dos Deputados).

The Trust Bill provides:
- that trusts shall be governed by the law appointed in the trust deed or settlement, as well as by the rules set forth in any other trust documents (e.g., letter of wishes);
- that Brazilian courts do not have jurisdiction to process and judge lawsuits over trusts that have elected exclusive jurisdiction abroad;
- there would be no need for a probate proceeding with respect to the trusts' assets (except where local laws governing the trust require otherwise);
- that assets transferred from the trust to the beneficiaries during the lifetime of the settlor shall be considered in the Brazilian probate proceeding relating to the assets of the deceased settlor for the confirmation of the compliance with applicable forced heirship rules — the penalty for violation of such rule is the forfeiture of such assets to the other legal heirs;
- for the differentiation between 'Potential Beneficiary' and 'Effective Beneficiary' — a Potential Beneficiary is the equivalent of a discretionary beneficiary as they do not have the right to claim distributions whereas the Effective Beneficiary would have the right to claim distributions from the trust;
- that there is no difference in treatment if the trust is revocable or irrevocable;
- IGT would not be levied on the transfer of assets and rights from settlor to trustee, but rather IT, if the transfer is made at market value of the assets and rights (if the transfer is made based on the acquisition cost, IT would not be levied);

- upon the change of the status of a Potential Beneficiary to an Effective Beneficiary, IGT is levied on the effective value of the trust's assets and rights;
- on the transfer of assets and rights from trusts to the beneficiaries, IT would be levied at progressive tax rates of up to 27.5% or between 15% and 22.5%, as the case may be; and
- upon the transfer of Brazilian real estate directly acquired by the trust, the Transfer Tax on Immovable Properties (v.g., real estate) would also be levied, usually at tax rates between 2% to 4%.

Tax reform
In 2021, the Federal Government proposed fundamental changes to IT legislation through the Bill of Law No. 2,337/2021, which are now under discussion within Brazilian Senate. The main changes are:
- 15% IT on dividend distributions (currently exempt);
- taxation of local close-ended investment funds, which currently allows for tax deferral;
- CFC rules for individuals who control entities located in tax haven jurisdictions (profits would be subject to IT up to 27.5% at the end of the entity's fiscal year);
- limitation on the ability to restructure foreign assets; and
- tax on the sale of Brazilian assets held indirectly by foreign companies.

Recently, there were several attempts to create a wealth tax, but none of them succeeded.

1.2 Local legislative and regulatory developments
Two bills of law are being discussed within the Legislative Assembly of São Paulo to amend the current local legislation on IGT:
- Bill of Law No. 1,315/2019 which proposes progressive tax rates from 3% to 8%, depending on the amount transferred upon death; and
- Bill of Law No. 250/2020 which aims to increase the tax assessment basis and change the treatment provided to donations encumbered with 'usufruto' (a legal type of lien set forth in the Brazilian Civil Code) by progressively increasing the tax rate up to 8%, depending on the amounts involved.

1.3 National case law developments
In 2021, the Brazilian Supreme Court recognized that the transfer of foreign assets by a deceased person to a Brazilian resident by succession should not trigger IGT when based on a State law, since the Brazilian Federal Constitution sets forth that the levy of such tax is a matter of Federal law. As no Federal law has been enacted, Brazilian States are not competent to assess IGT on such case. Thus, any State law providing for such assessment shall be declared unconstitutional.

More recently, in 2023, the Brazilian Supreme Court ruled that taxpayers with final judicial court decisions favourable to the non-payment of continuous collection taxes (e.g., IT) shall automatically lose such right in case a new judicial court decision ruling against it is issued by the Brazilian Supreme Court – in general repercussion or concentrated control of constitutionality (controle concentrado de constitucionalidade). In such event, the tax authorities would be entitled to collect the taxes due as from the calendar year following the date of publication of the new decision, or after 90 days as of the date of publication of such decision, depending on the type of tax.

1.4 Local case law developments
Local case law is not relevant as State Courts' rulings over matters regulated by Federal law are always subject to the Brazilian Federal Courts.

1.5 Practice trends
Asset holding companies
Holding companies are commonly used in Brazil to hold family assets in Brazil and abroad. It is a tax efficient structure, especially for foreign companies as they can currently defer taxes. It also facilitates the management of the assets and the transfer to the next generation. Usufruct is usually involved in such planning alternative, allowing the company's underlying assets to be passed along without giving rise to succession issues – in effect, the legal title to the share is transferred, but its political/economic rights may be reserved to its former holder while still living. Additionally, the family's wishes and mutual agreements may also be consolidated into governance rules established through a shareholders' agreement or by other corporate arrangements (e.g., issuance of ordinary/preferred shares).

Relocation
There has been an increase in the number of Brazilian families relocating to other countries, motivated by job opportunities, family, and even the economic and political instability in Brazil. The relocation should be planned considering Brazilian laws as well as the laws of the jurisdiction of relocation, to ensure the move's efficiency from corporate, tax, civil, and regulatory perspectives. Legal issues shall be addressed in advance by a proper plan of action, which may include the restructuring of the individual's assets.

When verifying the tax residency, Brazilian tax authorities might consider not only if formal procedures have been complied with by the individual, but also the elements of connection with the deemed country of residency (see Section 1.6 Pandemic related developments, below). Therefore, during the pre-immigration planning, a detailed analysis of the individual's wealth and family structure shall be conducted to identify the measures to be taken.

Life Insurance
Motived by succession (see Section 2.5 Estate and trust administration: Practice Trends, below) and tax aspects (below), within the Brazilian insurance market, certain products are used for estate planning:
- **Life insurance:** If the Brazilian insured redeems the life insurance policy during lifetime, the amount shall be subject to IT (regular income: 0% to 27.5%, or capital gains: 15% to 22.5%). Death benefits and premium reimbursements are exempt from IT if paid directly by the insurance company to the beneficiary. IGT does not apply.
- **Free Benefit Generating Life Insurance Plan (VGBL):** It is a personal insurance with survival coverage plan, where IT levies on the income of the:

- amount redeemed;
- value of the single payment; or
- amount received periodically, at regressive rates (35% to 10%) or progressive rates (up to 27.5%).

IGT does not apply as VGBL has the legal nature of an insurance (see below).

- **Free Benefit Generating Plan (PGBL): I**t is a private pension plan (not an insurance). IT will levy on the amount redeemed at regressive rates (35% to 10%) or progressive rates (up to 27.5%). Premium payments are deductible for IT purposes up to 12% on the individual's annual gross income. The assessment of IGT is controversial. Currently, the Brazilian Supreme Court (Extraordinary Appeal No. 1.363.013) is analyzing the constitutionality of certain dispositive of Law No. 7,174/2015 of State of Rio de Janeiro, which provides for the assessment of IGT over VGBL and PGBL. The discussion entails the analysis of the legal nature of both institutes and whether the receipt of resources by beneficiaries upon the contracting party's demise shall be deemed as inheritance. Such a Court decision, when enacted, shall have great impact as the Federal Court recognized its general repercussion.

If inheritance rights over life insurance, VGBL, and PGBL are disputed, this can lead to its inclusion in probates and, consequently, subject to IGT (up to 8%).

1.6 Pandemic related developments

Brazilians who have returned to Brazil with definitive intent to stay after residing abroad, or foreigners that entered the country holding a permanent visa (as from the date of arrival) or a temporary visa (as from the date of residing for 183 days in Brazil), shall qualify as Brazilian tax residents. The "definitive intent" to stay in Brazil is normally analyzed by the local authorities on a case-by-case basis (family domicile, time spent in Brazil, employment relationships, real estate properties and leasing, bank accounts, place of voting registration, etc.). During the pandemic, due to flight restrictions, many Brazilians residing abroad may have spent more than 183 days in Brazil in a period of 365 days, which raises a red flag as tax authorities may use it as an argument to characterize a tax residency in Brazil.

2. ESTATE AND TRUST ADMINISTRATION

2.1 National legislative and regulatory developments

Trusts in Brazil

Despite trusts often being used by Brazilian residents, Brazil is not a signatory to the Hague Convention on Trusts and there is no legal institute that perfectly corresponds to trusts within Brazilian laws. Bill of Law No. 4,758/2020, which is currently under discussions in the Congress, aims to introduce a "fiduciary agreement" in Brazil, a mechanism of asset segregation that resembles a trust. However, the bill only regulates civil matters and the tax treatment of such an institute was left aside. Substantial changes should be made to the bill to enable the new arrangement to work properly and succeed as an alternative succession planning viable in Brazil.

2.2 Local legislative and regulatory developments

Local legislation in Brazil is not relevant as estate and trust administration is not a matter for local State law.

2.3 National case law developments

Courts' intervention in the administration of minors' assets by the surviving parent

Unless otherwise determined by last wills and testaments, parents have the right to manage the assets (including income) inherited by minors (aged 18 and under). Certain law provisions, however, enhance the judicial control over said inherited assets, such as those establishing that a judicial order shall be granted to dispose of immovable assets held by minors or to adopt measures exceeding what is considered mere administration. It is not uncommon to see Courts blocking assets transferred to minor heirs, even without legal provision, under the argument of protecting their interests. When in excess, such judicial control may lead to mismanagement of the property. To avoid such severe interference, the common practice is to include provisions for the administration of minors' inheritance in last wills, or even to contribute the family's assets to holding structures with proper governance rules.

2.4 Local case law developments

Local case law is not relevant as State Courts' rulings over matters regulated by Federal law are always subject to the Brazilian Federal Courts.

2.5 Practice trends

Enduring power of attorney

The enduring power of attorney is not a valid instrument in Brazil and, once someone is incapacitated, any power vested by such individual, either via a private or public deed, shall be considered revoked and null. Representatives of an incapacitated person can only be elected through a Court proceeding. Brazilian Civil Procedure Code lists in order of priority who may be appointed by the Courts as legal guardian, starting with the spouse or companion in civil union, ascendants, and then descendants. However, as the Courts shall consider the individual under custody's wishes and best interest, individuals often use public deeds to list their preferred persons and the reasons they should act as their legal guardian. Wishes concerning wealth management and health and life support may also be included. Although it is not legally binding, the deed serves as a guideline to the Courts.

Investment funds

Under Brazilian law, investment funds are organised as a pool of assets jointly owned by the fund's interest holders as a condominium. Since in Brazil there are no legal structures similar to trusts and the law restricts the power of executors, investment funds have become a great option for individuals who wish to leave to next generations a well-structured and professionally managed entity with a pre-set of investment guidelines and governance. Additionally, investment fund's interests are easier to evaluate for IGT purposes and transfer to successors, and the risk of long-term disputes related to asset distribution or management can be mitigated. However, receiving interest of investment funds can be a disadvantage if the beneficiary is resident in a less tax favourable jurisdiction for this type of entity, such as the United States.

Life insurance
As mentioned above, another trending option for succession planning in Brazil is a life insurance plan, as the insurance proceeds do not enter the probate procedure and the value is automatically transferred to the policy's beneficiaries upon the insured's death. Also, since payment of insurance proceeds is not deemed as inheritance, the insured is not bound by forced heirship rules when appointing beneficiaries. However, if the premium exceeds half of the insured's estate (violating the share reserved to forced heirs ('legítima')), occasionally an heir might challenge the arrangement and succeed. Life insurance plans are a great option to leave more readily available funds to heirs to cover for succession or life expenses while distribution of the estate is not concluded.

2.6 Pandemic related developments
Last wills and testaments
Last wills and testaments are the main tools in local law for succession planning. Considering that Brazil was one of the most affected countries by the pandemic and people of all ages perished due to COVID-19, Brazilian individuals were confronted with the importance of succession planning, causing a rise in the execution of last wills and testaments. Likewise, the demand for more elaborate and complex dispositions became more recurrent, such as clauses regarding custody of minor heirs, administration of assets inherited by minors, indications of specific gifts, distributions per type of asset, etc.

Consequences of the lockdown include the higher number of divorces and disputes over child custody. According to the Brazilian Notarial College, December, 2020 stood out as the month with the highest number of divorces in Brazilian Registry Offices since January, 2007, when extrajudicial divorces were instituted in Brazil.

3. ESTATE AND TRUST LITIGATION AND CONTROVERSY
3.1 National legislative and regulatory developments
In 2017, the Brazilian Supreme Court (Extraordinary Appeal No. 878.694) decided that surviving companions in civil union are subject to the same succession rules applicable to surviving spouses in marriage. The leading case, with recognized general repercussion (topic No. 809), has declared unconstitutional the article 1,790 of the Brazilian Civil Code, which grants to companions in civil union different inheritance rights from those granted to spouses by article 1,829 of the same law. Considering the practical importance and repercussions of such a decision, the Brazilian Supreme Court modulated the effects of said ruling by determining that it should only be applicable to judicial proceedings where a final decision has not been reached and extrajudicial partition proceedings in which a public deed has not been registered yet.

3.2 Local legislative and regulatory developments
Local legislation is not relevant in Brazilian estate and trust litigation as this is not a matter for local State law.

FREQUENTLY ASKED QUESTIONS

1. Would surviving companions be considered forced heirs according to the Brazilian Supreme Court?

In 2017, the Brazilian Supreme Court (Extraordinary Appeal No. 878.694) recognized and declared the unconstitutionality of article 1,790 of the Brazilian Civil Code and declared that companions in civil union and spouses in marriage have the same succession rights. The Brazilian Supreme Court modulated the effects of said ruling by determining that it should only be applicable to judicial proceedings where a final decision has not been reached and extrajudicial partition proceedings in which a public deed has not been registered yet.

2. Could a trust validly established in another jurisdiction be recognized in Brazil?

Brazil, like other civil law jurisdictions, does not recognize the concept of trusts and is not a signatory to the Hague Convention on the Law Applicable to Trusts and on their Recognition, which specifies the law applicable to trusts, lists their characteristics and governs their recognition among its contracting parties. In Brazil, there is no legal institute that perfectly corresponds to

trusts within Brazilian laws and that fact leads to a constant uncertainty on how such contractual relationship will be interpreted by tax authorities and, if challenged, Brazilian courts.

Notwithstanding the foregoing, according to Decree-Law No. 4,657/1942 (Law of Introduction to the Brazilian Law), a valid obligation undertaken by a party pursuant to applicable foreign laws should be recognised in Brazil. This is to say that trusts created abroad that are deemed valid and enforceable pursuant to applicable laws should be respected and complied with in Brazil. Careful consideration should be given to the set-up of the trust as it could give rise to adverse consequences.

3. Would inheritances and donations received from abroad by a Brazilian tax resident be subject to IGT?

In 2021, Brazilian Supreme Court (Extraordinary Appeal No. 851.108/SP) ruled unconstitutional the IGT levied on inheritance of assets located abroad, as long as there is no complementary law regulating the matter, as provided in the Federal Constitution. Therefore, currently, and until a complementary law is enacted, assets located abroad and transmitted as

3.3 National case law developments

Disputes before Brazilian Courts over partition of foreign assets

Brazilian Federal Courts normally abstain from including or considering foreign assets in divorce or probate cases processed under Brazilian law, as the Courts decided that they have no jurisdiction to rule over the partition and distribution of assets located outside of Brazil (Brazilian Supreme Court, Extraordinary Appeal n. 99.230–8 of May 22, 1984, and Superior Court of Justice, Special Appeal n. 1.362.400 of April 28, 2015).

Local State Courts, however, sometimes do not follow such an understanding and consider that, although the partition should be exclusively based on Brazilian assets, it shall not disregard the value and partition of those assets located abroad, inheritance to successors domiciled in Brazil should not be subject to IGT.

Notwithstanding, the Brazilian Supreme Court (Direct Action of Unconstitutionality by Omission 67) determined a period of one year for the enactment of the complementary law regulating the incidence and collection of IGT in cases of inheritance of assets abroad and other cases provided for in the Federal Constitution. Such period will expire in June, 2023.

4. Could a Brazilian tax resident contract a foreign life insurance?

Life insurance companies in Brazil must comply with ordinary and complementary laws, as well as the rules of the National Council of Private Insurance (CNSP) and Private Insurance Superintendence (SUSEP). Insurance companies and intermediaries, when acting and doing business in Brazil, must be licensed with SUSEP. Likewise, insurance products can only be offered in the Brazilian market upon its registration with SUSEP.

As a general rule, Brazilian residents may only contract foreign insurance products (that is, those that have not been subject to registration and approval of the SUSEP and are offered by foreign insurance companies) with non-Brazilian based approved providers under the following specific situations:

- to cover risks for which there is no offer of insurance in Brazil, as long as the contract of such product does not represent a violation to the Brazilian legislation in force;
- to cover risks taken abroad by persons residing in Brazil, as long as this coverage be restricted to the period spent abroad by the Brazilian resident;
- the insurance is subject to international treaties ratified by the Brazilian Congress;
- to secure hulls, machines and civil liability related to vessels; and/or
- if, according to the legislation in force until January 16, 2007, the insurance was validly contracted abroad.

Despite those legal restrictions, we have seen the increase of the use of foreign life insurance policies by Brazilian citizens in the context of their succession planning and/or relocation planning. Careful consideration should be given when examining the form of acquisition of the policy to avoid adverse consequences for the contracting party and the insurance company.

to guarantee fairness in the portions to be attributed to heirs. One recent decision from the São Paulo State Courts, dated as of February 2, 2022, reasoned that the absence of foreign assets would compromise the egalitarian sharing of assets globally and consequently the protection of the reserved portion of mandatory heirs ('legítima').

Nonetheless, as this is a matter of Federal law, local State Courts' decisions can be subject to review by the Brazilian Federal Courts.

3.4 Local case law developments

Local case law is not relevant as State Courts' rulings over matters regulated by Federal law are always subject to the Brazilian Federal Courts.

3.5 Practice trends
Waiver of inheritance rights
The surviving spouse or companion in a civil union, in concurrence with descendants, will either retain their share of the common assets due to marital property regime (universal communion of assets) or inherit a share of the estate (total separation of assets), or both retain their share of common assets and inherit a share of private assets (partial communion of assets).

Brazilian law does not recognize agreements and waivers of inheritance rights related to the succession of a living person. Consequently, there is no matrimonial regime in Brazil that allows couples to maintain their assets separately both in case of divorce and succession. Nevertheless, some couples have been expressing their desire to mutually waive their inheritance rights by executing agreements, which are not enforceable in case of disputes but can be an expression of the couple's intention and useful should the legislation change.

Dating contracts
A civil union is a legal family entity where two individuals hold a public, ongoing, and long-lasting relationship intending to constitute a family. It is a legal fact and does not require formal procedures or documents to legally and validly exist. In view of this, "dating agreements" are an alternative, as contracts where two individuals, in a close relationship, declare that their relationship status is "dating" and does not constitute nor is to be deemed as a civil union. Legally, if the relationship is in fact a civil union and not merely a dating relationship, this contract is not able to avoid the recognition of a civil union if a dispute is brought to Courts. The facts are stronger than the declaration itself. However, since constitution of the civil union relies on relevant facts, circumstances, and behavior of the individuals, dating agreements may be accepted as proof of the lack of desire to constitute family (one of the conditions of the civil union) by the time of signature.

Digital inheritance
Currently, there are no provisions on digital inheritance in Brazilian legislation. However, considering the growing importance of the matter as people are increasingly holding assets in digital format, Brazilian Courts have been determining the inclusion of digital assets in the succession of an individual. There are two types of digital assets, those with and without economic valuation. For the first one (e.g., cryptocurrencies), Brazilian Courts understand that they may be included in the succession equally to other types of assets and under the same terms, as provided for by the applicable law. As for assets without economic value (e.g., social networks and photos), they shall not be included in one's succession, because they are directly related to the individual's privacy. In this respect, heirs are also prevented from obtaining access, for instance, to the deceased's social media account passwords or to the content of private messages.

3.6 Pandemic related developments

Before the pandemic, most of the communication between the parties, Courts trials and hearings were done in person, with the presence of the parties and their counsels. However, since the lockdown, Courts adopted alternative remote communication tools. Exchanges with judges or between parties via telephone and e-mail and Court hearings and trials via video-conferences became more common and efficient. The National Justice Counsel has recently implemented and regulated the possibility and validity of execution of public deeds via videoconference and signatures by digital means.

AUTHOR BIOGRAPHIES

Humberto Sanches

Humberto Sanches has worked for more than 20 years with strategic wealth management for families and with matters involving corporate, tax, aviation, family law, and succession, from a Brazilian law perspective. His practice has earned him recognition in international rankings and publications specialized in this industry, such as Chambers High Net Worth, where Humberto stands on its highest level (band 1), and others such as Who's Who Legal, The Legal 500, and Private Client Global Elite. He is the only Brazilian in international wealth planning academies such as The International Academy of Estate and Trust Law (TIAETL). He is also a member of other relevant international organizations in our practice area, such as STEP and the Editorial Board of the Family Office Journal.

Adriane Pacheco

Adriane Pacheco has been working for about 20 years on matters related to wealth and succession planning for individuals, with emphasis on private international law, family law, succession, real estate, notary and registry law, and tax law involving inheritances and donations. STEP participant, she is usually sought out by families and individuals who are searching for highly-personalized, compassionate, careful, technically-specialized services that, in most cases, involve multiple jurisdictions.

Beatriz Martinez

Beatriz Martinez has been working with family and succession law for over 12 years. She is an expert in wealth and succession planning, even when there are several jurisdictions involved. Beatriz helps clients execute their wills, donations, marriages and civil union agreements, declarations of curatorship and advanced health directives, family and corporate governance, as well as create wealth structures, such as trusts.

Juliana Cavalcanti

Juliana Cavalcanti has experience regarding the creation, organization, and structuring of investments in Brazil and abroad, such as companies, investment funds, and trusts. She also advises clients on various corporate law matters since 2008, usually related to family businesses, shareholders' agreements, and corporate governance.

CANADA

Marilyn Piccini Roy, Ad. E.
Robinson Sheppard Shapiro LLP

INTRODUCTION

Canada is a bilingual, bi-juridical and multi-cultural country. It is a parliamentary system within the context of a constitutional monarchy comprising one federal Parliament, ten provincial legislatures and three territorial legislatures. The division of powers to govern matters is set out in the British North America Act 1867. The legislatures in each province and territory have exclusive rights to make laws in relation to property rights, marriage and matrimonial regimes, but divorce is within the legislative authority of Parliament. Estates and trusts are within the jurisdiction of the provinces and territories. The federal government legislates on tax matters but the provinces and territories also tax income on the same basis as the federal government, except Quebec which has a separate taxation system that is generally harmonized with the federal system. In the area of private law, there are two systems of law in Canada, that is, the civil law in Quebec and the common law prevailing elsewhere in Canada.

1. TAX AND WEALTH PLANNING

Canada is one of the largest countries in the world and also one of the wealthiest. There are three main types of taxes in Canada: income tax, sales tax and property tax.

Canada uses a self-assessment tax system. Under this system, an individual is responsible for filing a tax return by April 30th of each year, or by June 15th for self-employed persons and spouses.

The basis for income taxation in Canada is residency. Canadian residents are taxed on their worldwide income and non-residents only on Canadian-sourced income. An individual is deemed to be a Canadian resident if 183 days or more are spent in Canada.

There are both federal and provincial tax rates which are determined separately and the combined marginal rates for individuals may be as high as approximately 54%. The tax system for individuals is progressive or graduated.

There is a federal sales tax of 5% on goods and services (GST). Some provinces (but none of the three territories) also levy a sales tax (PST), ranging from 6% to 9.975%. Some provinces combine their sales tax with the federal sales tax into a single harmonized sales tax (HST).

Property taxes are levied by local municipalities on land and buildings.

There are no estate, succession, inheritance, gift or wealth taxes in Canada. Instead, Canada has a capital gains regime: there is a deemed disposition at fair market value resulting in capital gains taxes payable by the person making a gift or by the estate of the deceased who is deemed to have disposed of capital property immediately before death.

The deemed disposition rules do not apply to assets transferred to a spouse or common-law partner. The deceased is deemed to have disposed of the assets at their adjusted cost base and the spouse assumes that cost base. No capital gain is triggered until the spouse disposes of the assets, either during their lifetime or at death. This rollover is also available to a testamentary spousal trust that respects certain tax requirements.

There is also a principal residence exemption from capital gains tax. This exemption is only available to a narrow range of trusts who hold a principal residence as part of the trust property.

Canada imposes a "departure tax" on persons relinquishing residency.

Corporations are also subject to tax on their worldwide active business income at combined federal and provincial rates.

Trusts are widely-used vehicles in estate and wealth planning. Personal trusts may be *inter vivos* or testamentary. Qualified alter ego, joint partner and spousal trusts allow for a deferral of tax on any unrealized capital gains in the trust until the death of the income beneficiary or the surviving income beneficiary in the case of a joint partner trust, unless the assets are disposed of earlier.

The top marginal tax rate applies to both *inter vivos* and testamentary trusts, including estates (which are deemed to be trusts for tax purposes). However, graduated rate estates (a maximum duration of 36 months) and qualified disability trusts are taxed at graduated rates.

Except for qualified alter-ego, joint partner and spousal trusts, the 21-year deemed disposition rule applies to trusts. The rule deems a trust to have disposed of all its capital property on the 21st anniversary of the creation of the trust and every 21 years thereafter. Capital gains tax is applicable on the deemed disposition date. Certain planning methods are available to minimize or eliminate the tax.

1.1 National legislative and regulatory developments
Trust reporting requirements
On January 14, 2022, the Government of Canada announced that the legislation proposed in July 2018 expanding the reporting requirements for trusts would be delayed. Following the 2022 Fall Economic Statement, released on November 3, 2022, the new requirements will apply to trusts' taxation years ending after December 30, 2023. These requirements are intended to improve the collection of beneficial ownership information respecting trusts and to enable the Canada Revenue Agency (CRA) to assess tax liabilities for trusts and their beneficiaries.

Speculation and vacancy tax
In response to escalating home prices in urban areas, low rental vacancy rates and high rental prices, British Columbia enacted, in 2018, a speculation and vacancy tax on residential properties in major urban areas.

Luxury tax
The federal government released and approved the Select Luxury Items Tax Act for a new luxury tax regime applicable to certain sales and imports of vehicles, boats and aircraft, which came into effect on September 1, 2022.

Draft tax proposals
On February 4, 2022, the federal government released a package of draft tax legislation, including some announced in the 2021 federal budget.

The proposed mandatory disclosure rules contained in the Income Tax Act address aggressive tax planning through audits and legislative changes and will focus on "reportable transactions", and "notifiable transactions" (such as the avoidance of the deemed disposition of trust property pursuant to the 21-year rule) and uncertain tax positions.

2022 Federal budget highlights

To help individuals purchase their first home, a new Tax-Free First Home Savings Account, an increase to the Home Buyers' Tax Credit, and also a new "anti-flipping" residential real estate tax were announced. On June 23, 2022, Parliament passed the Prohibition on the purchase of residential property by non-Canadians Act which came into force on January 1, 2023.

Personal tax changes were also announced, among which modifications to the existing intergenerational business transfer rules to prevent an individual shareholder from converting dividends into lower-taxed capital gains where there is no genuine intergenerational business transfer, and a new minimum tax regime for wealthy individuals in the 2022 fall economic update.

The budget increases the disbursement quota rate for charities to 5% (from 3.5%) for the portion of property not used in charitable activities or administration that exceeds CAD 1 million.

On June 23, 2022, Canada's Bill C-19, Budget Implementation Act, 2022, No. 1, received Royal Assent and became enacted. It implements certain tax measures announced in the 2022 and 2021 federal budgets, as well as various other measures.

Amendments were made to improve access to the disability tax credit (DTC) and other tax-related measures that require a DTC certificate.

There is an expansion of allowable charitable disbursements by allowing charities to provide resources to organizations that are not qualified donees (charitable partnerships), provided certain conditions are met.

Canada's federal income tax rates for 2023 Tax Year

Tax rate	Tax Brackets	Taxable Income
15%	on the first CAD 53,359	CAD 53,359
20.5%	on the next CAD 53,359	CAD 53,359 up to CAD 106,717
26%	on the next CAD 106,717	CAD 106,717 up to CAD 165,430
29%	on the next CAD 165,430	CAD 165,430 up to CAD 235,675
33%	on any amount of taxable income exceeding CAD 235,675	

1.2 Local legislative and regulatory developments

Provincial and territorial governments develop their own tax laws and policies, but they are generally harmonized with the federal tax legislation. However, the CRA collects and administers income taxes on behalf of the provinces and territories, except for Québec.

1.3 National case law developments

The Supreme Court of Canada granted leave to appeal in *Attorney General of Canada, et al. v. Collins Family Trust, et al.*, 2022 SCC 26, overturned the British Columbia Court of Appeal decision ordering rescission of dividends paid in 2008 and 2009 that became taxable as a result of a subsequent change in case law. The Supreme Court ruled that companies cannot undo transactions that later cause them unintended taxes. The effect of the ruling was that the family trust owed taxes on the dividends.

On December 16, 2021, the Supreme Court of Canada ended nearly six years of legal challenges by refusing leave to appeal from the Federal Court of Appeal's judgment in *Blue Bridge Trust Company Inc. v. Canada (National Revenue), 2021 FCA 62*. The CRA had issued requests for information to Blue Bridge Trust Company Inc. (Blue Bridge) which was the trustee of some opaque Canadian trusts enabling several wealthy French families to save nearly EUR four billion in wealth tax. The Federal Court of Appeal upheld the Federal Court's finding that the requirements for issuing a compliance order under the Income Tax Act had been met and, consequently, Blue Bridge had to provide disclosure to the French tax authorities.

1.4 Local case law developments
In *Menard v. Agence du revenue du Québec*, 2021 QCCQ 3891, the Quebec tax authority denied the taxpayers the capital gains tax exemption in the context of a tax planning device utilizing a discretionary family trust for multiple capital gain exemptions for family members, including minor children.

1.5 Practice trends
The last three years have seen significant changes in tax legislation for private family businesses. Due to the introduction of the tax on split income (TOSI) rules in 2018, the income-splitting benefits of a trust have primarily been eliminated.

A trust continues to be an effective instrument to multiply the lifetime capital gains exemption (LCGE), because trusts can sell shares of corporations that qualify for the qualified small business corporation exemption. The tax payable is minimized as the gain may be shared among the beneficiaries of the trust (multiplication of LCGE).

Trusts continue to be frequently used in succession planning to transfer wealth to future generations in a tax-efficient manner and can result in a deferral of capital gains.

The use of a trust within the context of a private corporation allows for several benefits, including the control of trust assets (i.e., the shares of a private corporation), the reduction of taxes upon death, and the distribution of trust assets to beneficiaries on a tax-deferred basis.

Although the perception about trusts is that they are only created to achieve tax savings, it is critical to note that trusts can offer significant other non-tax benefits, such as:
- avoiding probate fees;
- protecting assets; and
- maintaining confidentiality.

1.6 Pandemic related developments
For COVID-19 benefits received in 2021, such as the Canada Recovery Benefit (CRB), Canada Sickness Recovery Benefit (CSRB) or Canada Recovery Caregiving Benefit (CRCB), a T4A slip was issued. Any one-time provincial payments to help through COVID-19 will not be taxable.

2. ESTATE AND TRUST ADMINISTRATION

2.1 National legislative and regulatory developments

Estate and trust matters are not regulated federally, but fall within the jurisdictional purview of the provinces and territories.

2.2 Local legislative and regulatory developments

Ontario's Succession Law Reform Act, R.S.O. 1990, c.S. 26 (SLRA) was amended to expedite and facilitate the probate procedure in Ontario courts by streamlining the probate application process for small estates under CAD 150,000 and allowing electronic filing of probate.

Many of the SLRA amendments affect spouses, such as the increase in spousal entitlement on intestacy: the preferential share has been raised from CAD 200,000 to CAD 350,000. Prior to the amendments, only testamentary dispositions made to a former spouse (because of divorce or annulment of the marriage) were revoked by the death of the testator. If the spouses were merely separated, the bequests or gifts to the separated spouse remained valid and enforceable. The amendments remove the entitlement of a separated spouse under the will, as well as under an intestacy.

As an antidote to the phenomenon of predatory marriages, the repeal of the SLRA provisions that provide for the automatic revocation of a pre-existing will on marriage is a timely measure. This also brings Ontario in line with similar legislative provisions in Quebec, British Columbia, Saskatchewan and Alberta.

In Alberta, the law on non-revocation of a will by marriage also extends to an adult interdependent partnership or common law relationship.

Similarly, in Saskatchewan, The Wills Act, 1996, SS 1996, c W-114.1 was amended effective March 16, 2020 to provide that a will is not automatically revoked if the testator entered into a new spousal relationship (marriage or continuous co-habitation for two years) unless the will's terms explicitly provided otherwise.

Finally, but possibly the most significant Ontario legislative amendment concerns substantial compliance for the validity of wills. The Superior Court of Justice is authorized to validate a defective document purporting to be a will when the statutory requirements for formal validity or proper execution have not been respected. Priority is given to testamentary intention.

Manitoba enacted the first validating power in Canada and was copied in most common law provinces. Quebec's validating power is a partial compliance provision, giving priority to fulfilment of essential requirements over testamentary intention.

The Legislative Assembly of Alberta updated its current Trustee Act on April 29, 2022 to render the creation and management of trusts more efficient.

All provinces and territories in Canada, except Quebec and Manitoba, have probate fees and their own formula for calculation of the fees. The Manitoba government eliminated probate fees effective as of November 6, 2020, as well as provincial sales tax on the preparation of wills.

In all provinces and territories, a dependant can claim support from the deceased's estate if they have a status recognized by law, such as a spouse or child or was receiving support at the time of death, such as a former spouse.

In *Leblanc v. Cushing Estate*, 2020 NSSC 162, the Nova Scotia court considered a *de facto* spouse as a dependant if the domestic partnership was registered.

De facto spouses have limited and varied rights across Canada. On January 1, 2020, Alberta enacted the Matrimonial Property Act, RSA 2000, c M-8 which provides that property division rules apply equally to married couples and couples in a relationship of interdependence.

2.3 National case law developments

On rare occasions, the Supreme Court of Canada (SCC) grants leave to appeal in estate matters.

In the *Threlfall v. Carleton University*, 2019 SCC 50, the SCC ordered restitution of pension payments amounting to half a million dollars made by Carleton University to a retired professor, resident of Quebec, who went missing for six years but was to found to have died shortly after his disappearance.

In *Sherman Estate v. Donovan*, 2021 SCC 25, the SCC ruled that the open court principle may be limited to protect privacy but only in exceptional circumstances. In a high profile case, a couple were found dead in their Toronto home. The estate trustees obtained sealing orders of the probate files of their respective estates in order to protect the privacy and dignity of the deceased individuals and their family. An investigative journalist successfully appealed the sealing orders, which the Ontario Court of Appeal set aside and which the Supreme Court of Canada upheld. If the protection of an individual's personal information meets the "high bar" required to obtain a confidentiality order, then the constitutional guarantee of open courts may yield to the extent necessary to prevent a serious risk of harm to the individual's dignity.

2.4 Local case law developments

An important accounting issue was before the court in *Duhn Estate*, 2021 ABQB 3, that was affirmed by the Alberta Court of Appeal, 2022 ABCA 360, holding that a competent testator's right to keep pre-death financial affairs private and confidential. Absent a sufficient evidentiary basis for potential abuse, death does not expose a testator's pre-death decisions to scrutiny by the beneficiaries.

The Saskatchewan decision in *Vance (Re)*, 2021 SKQB 320, is a reminder of the importance of updating wills as well as re-affirming the principle of non-retroactivity of legislation.

The Ontario Court of Appeal confirmed the modern approach to cost awards in estate litigation with the release of its decision in *McGrath v. Joy*, 2022 ONCA 119, reinforcing a trend in other provinces.

Fitzgerald v. Fitzgerald Estate, 2021 NSSC was a welcome decision released by the Nova Scotia Supreme Court that reaffirms the primacy of beneficiary designations.

The British Columbia Supreme Court considered the issue of the validity of a bequest to a witness to a will in *Wolk v. Wolk*, 2021 BCSC 1881; under the applicable legislative provision, the court considered testamentary intention to decide in favour of the validity of the gift.

In *Unger Estate (Re)*, 2022 BCSC 189, the British Columbia Supreme Court in the context of a son guilty of murdering his mother and thus disqualified from inheriting, the court determined that his share of the estate passed to his daughter as an "alternate beneficiary" and not to the charities named in the will as alternate beneficiaries, relying on the testatrix's intention in making the will.

The British Columbia Supreme Court in *Bowling Estate (Re)*, 2022 BCSC 369, reduced the legal fees claimed by a dilatory executor with respect to delivering accounts.

The decision in *Pinsonneault v. Courtney*, 2022 BCSC 120 concerned the doctrine of unconscionable procurement which is meant to protect gift-givers from abuse. The court applied the presumption of resulting trust. The recipients failed in rebutting the presumption that the gift-giver did not intend to make the gift.

2.5 Practice trends

The most common devices prevailing in estate planning continue to be trusts, holding companies and multiple wills and *situs* wills.

While the changes in 2016 to the trust tax rules (for example, TOSI) have significantly eroded the attraction of trusts for estate planning purposes, trusts still serve desirable purposes. Discretionary trusts continue to be used in estate freezes and provide a degree of asset protection against matrimonial and creditor claims. Trusts, such as the "alter ego" or "joint partner", also serve as will substitutes, and avoid probate fees and a lengthy probate process. They also provide an effective alternative to a power of attorney in case of incapacity and are useful in planning for disabled beneficiaries.

Holding companies continue to be used to earn investment income at a lower tax rate. Care must be taken to implement appropriate *post-mortem* tax planning to avoid double taxation on death.

Multiple wills strategies enjoy popularity in some provinces such as Ontario and British Columbia where probate fees are high. Nova Scotia's probate legislation has rendered this strategy ineffective.

With a great number of wealthy clients owning property in several jurisdictions, the need for *situs* estate planning has grown exponentially.

In Quebec, practitioners are increasingly using marriage contracts as *situs* will substitutes. Since gifts *mortis causa*, which are assimilated to testamentary dispositions, may be made in a Quebec notarial marriage contract, spouses whose domicile or nationality is not that of Quebec, may make mutual gifts of both movable and immovable property.

Increased real estate values has prompted two initiatives. One concerns the need for farmers to re-evaluate the division of their assets to avoid an inequitable estate plan and the other is the incentive to provide for lifetime gifts to children to enter the real estate market.

The interest in digital currencies such as bitcoin has created new challenges for estate planners.

The digitization of the law and the adoption of new technologies spurred on by COVID-19 reactions are new and continuing phenomena in the estate and trust practice.

Charitable giving has become more prevalent in clients' estate plans whether because of increased wealth or favourable tax benefits or both. A popular option is a gift of publicly traded securities with accrued unrealized gains.

2.6 Pandemic related developments
During the COVID-19 pandemic, most of the provinces and territories, except Nova Scotia, Prince Edward Island, Yukon, Northwest Territories and Nunavut, implemented temporary execution of wills and powers of attorney by audio-visual communication technology. Ontario, Saskatchewan, Manitoba and British Columbia have made remote execution of estate documents permanent.

Quebec was one of the first jurisdictions to authorize the remote execution of notarial acts, such as a will.

British Columbia is the first Canadian jurisdiction to allow electronic wills to be signed and stored completely digitally without need for a printed original paper copy or a wet signature.

3. ESTATE AND TRUST LITIGATION AND CONTROVERSY
3.1 National legislative and regulatory developments
Estate and trust matters are not regulated federally, but fall within the jurisdictional purview of the provinces and territories.

3.2 Local legislative and regulatory developments
See Section 2.2 Estate and trust administration: Local legislative and regulatory developments.

3.3 National case law developments
In *S.A. v. Metro Vancouver Housing Corporation*, 4 SCC 2019, the SCC affirmed the principle that a discretionary trust interest does not count as an asset of the beneficiary receiving government financial assistance.

In *Yared v. Karam*, 2019 SCC 62, the SCC ruled on the interaction of the Quebec rules governing the trust patrimony with the mandatory rules on the "family patrimony".

3.4 Local case law developments
Two cases in British Columbia, *Waslenchuk Estate*, 2020 BCSC 1929 and *Quinn Estate v. Rydland*, 2019 BCCA 91 concluded that "pour over" clauses in British Columbia wills are invalid, illustrating the pitfalls that cross-border situations may engender. Yet, in *MacCallum Estate*, 2022 NSSC 34, the Nova Scotia court held that the pour-over to an amendable secret trust was valid.

In *Walters v. Walters*, 2022 ONCA 38, the Court of Appeal had the opportunity to clarify the limits on powers of an estate trustee granted by the term "absolute discretion". The British Columbia Court of Appeal in *Pirani v. Pirani*, 2022 BCCA 65, overturned the lower court decision that interfered with the trustees' decisions because they were not made in good faith.

Traditionally, both in the common law and the civil law, courts do not interfere in cases where trustees are granted powers to be exercised in their discretion unless the trustees fail to act fairly and in good faith which includes the consideration of extraneous factors. Quebec courts have reinforced the judicial non-interventionist policy with respect to the exercise of discretion by trustees: *Moore v. Moore*, 2021 QCCS 11 and *Corbin v. St. Pierre (Succession de Lelièvre)*, 2021 QCCS 911.

FREQUENTLY ASKED QUESTIONS

1. What are the most important considerations for estate planning for a blended family to ensure my second spouse and my children from my first marriage will receive sufficient inheritances and prevent litigation?

First, consider the economic aspects of interest rates and inflation measured against longer life expectancy. Second, appoint neutral or independent executors and trustees. Consider a professional even though costs may be higher, but not as much as litigation expenses would be.

2. Is it more tax efficient to leave my estate to my adult children in trust rather than outright?

Prior to January 1, 2016, taxable income earned in a testamentary trust (that is, a trust created on the day a person dies and the terms of which are established in the deceased person's will) was subject to the same graduated tax rates as an individual taxpayer. Since the beginning of 2016, testamentary trusts are now subject to the highest marginal tax rate that applies to most *inter-vivos* trusts, subject to two exceptions: a graduated rate estate (an estate that so designates itself will be subject to graduated rate taxation for the first 36 months of its existence) and a trust for a disabled individual who is eligible for the federal Disability Tax Credit where the trust and the qualifying beneficiary have jointly elected for the trust to be a "qualified disability trust" for a particular taxation year.

Peripherally related to the jurisprudence on discretionary powers is *Greenstein v. Mutch*, 2021 QCCS 4228. The issue was whether capital gains resulting from the disposition of shares held by the testamentary trust be considered as capital or revenue. The Superior Court of Quebec concluded that civil law is controlling with regard to trust administration, not tax law. For trust law purposes, capital gains constitute capital while for tax law purposes, they constitute revenue. While the terms of the will conferred upon the trustees a discretionary power to derogate from these generally applicable rules by determining what is to be treated as capital or revenue, the trustees had declined to exercise this discretionary power.

The family paradigm is the centerpiece of Quebec succession law. Recent judicial pronouncements, in the context of divorce and *de facto* spouses, have endorsed the shift in the family paradigm to reflect today's society. The Quebec Court of Appeal in *Succession de Charpentier*, 2022 QCCA 660, recently overturned the lower court's decision that subsidiary legacies to family members of a former husband had lapsed by virtue of Article 764 of the Civil Code of Québec which provides that a legacy to a spouse is revoked by divorce. The holding of the Court of Appeal served to enhance the principles of freedom of willing and actual testamentary intention.

The Superior Court of Quebec in *Succession de Spiric*, 2022 QCCS 3849, on appeal, ruled that a Costa Rican notarial will in Spanish of a Quebec domiciliary was valid and enforceable and had the effect of automatically revoking a prior Quebec notarial will, without the need for any express mention of revocation in the former will. The fact that the testator had not mastered the Spanish language, his comprehension of the language was sufficient and did not affect the validity of the will.

3.5 Practice trends
See Section 2.5 Estate and trust administration: Practice Trends.

3.6 Pandemic related developments
See Section 2.6 Estate and trust administration: Pandemic related developments.

AUTHOR BIOGRAPHY

Marilyn Piccini Roy
Marilyn Piccini Roy is a partner and head of the wealth management group at Robinson Sheppard Shapiro LLP in Montreal, practising in the areas of estates, trusts, regimes of protective supervision and elder law. She is a former adjunct professor and current sessional lecturer at the Faculty of Law of McGill University. She has written numerous articles and presented seminars and conference papers on successions, trusts and elder law, and is currently a member of the editorial board of Estates, Trusts & Pensions Journal. She is an Academician and the Secretary as well as a past executive Councilor of The International Academy of Estate and Trust Law, an active member of the Society of Trust and Estate Practitioners, an International Fellow of the American College of Trust and Estate Counsel, and a past president and now honorary member of the Canadian Bar Association national wills, estates and trusts executive. She is ranked in Chambers HNW, Who's Who Legal Canada and was selected as "Thought Leader" in 2020, and in Best Lawyers since 2008. She was selected as Best Lawyer of the Year, Trusts and Estates, Montreal, Quebec in 2012 and 2020.

ENGLAND & WALES

Patrick Harney & Bethan Byrne

Mishcon de Reya LLP

INTRODUCTION

This chapter provides a general background to the key taxes and the legal framework in the United Kingdom of Great Britain and Northern Ireland (UK). However, it should be noted that strictly, there is no such thing as "UK law", because the UK traditionally consists of three legal jurisdictions:

1) England and Wales;
2) Scotland; and
3) Northern Ireland.

The introduction of devolution means that Wales, Scotland and Northern Ireland are now devolved nations, and limited legislative powers have been devolved to elected assemblies in Cardiff, Edinburgh and Belfast respectively. Further to the public referendums held in September 1997, the UK Parliament passed the three devolution Acts: the Northern Ireland Act 1998, the Scotland Act 1998, and the Government of Wales Act 1998 (later superseded by the Government of Wales Act 2006). These Acts established the three devolved legislatures, giving them certain powers which were previously held at Westminster. Further powers have been devolved since, through the Scotland Act 2016 and Wales Act 2017.

Scotland's chapter features separately in this guide as Scotland has its own distinct legal system (and has its own limited powers to raise and lower income tax). Prior to the devolved assemblies, Wales did not have its own separate law and it is still correct, following devolution, to refer to the law of "England and Wales". Nonetheless, there will now be some minor areas of tax law where the law in Wales will be different to that in England. For example, the Welsh parliament has some control over income tax, stamp duty and landfill tax (the latter is not examined in this chapter). Nonetheless, it is still standard practice in precedent English legal documents to refer to the law of England and Wales.

Devolution in Northern Ireland is distinct and government powers have been divided into three categories. Legislative powers relating to capital transfer taxation rest with the UK Parliament.

For the avoidance of doubt, the law discussed in the rest of this chapter refers just to the law of England and Wales, unless specifically stated otherwise.

Residence, domicile and the remittance basis

Domicile is a common law concept that seeks to identify an individual's "home". Domicile must not be confused with nationality. A "domicile of origin" is acquired at birth. This is normally the domicile of the father if the individual's parents are married.

Domicile of origin may, with varying degrees of difficulty, be replaced by a "domicile of choice". In general terms, a person may be said to be domiciled in the place where they have made their permanent home. An individual cannot have a generic 'UK' domicile, they will have a specific domicile within the UK, in England and Wales for example, or in Scotland or in Northern Ireland, as appropriate.

Domicile and tax residence are separate and distinct concepts under English law. An individual can be tax resident and not domiciled. UK (all nations) tax residence is determined by a statutory residence test. A person will be regarded as UK resident if:

- They stay in the UK for more than 182 days in any tax year.
- They meet any of the automatic UK tests or the sufficient ties tests under the UK's statutory residence test (SRT).
- Additionally, UK tax law imposes a further category for tax purposes whereby residents in the UK for 15 out of the previous 20 UK tax years become "deemed domiciled" for tax purposes. UK deemed domiciled individuals are subject to UK tax on their worldwide income and gains and, on death, their worldwide estate is chargeable to UK inheritance tax (IHT).

One of the distinguishing factors of UK taxation is the remittance basis. It enables non-domiciled individuals, to move to the UK whilst being taxed only on the post arrival income or gains they remit to the UK, in addition to any UK source income or capital gains.

The remittance basis needs to be claimed, but it is one of the most attractive features of UK immigration for high-net-worth individuals. The remittance basis charge (RBC) is an annual charge which is paid by UK residents claiming the remittance basis. The remittance basis is free for the first seven years of UK fiscal residence. Thereafter the RBC is charged at:

- GBP 30,000 for non-domiciled individuals who have been resident in the UK for at least 7 of the previous 9 tax years immediately before the relevant tax year; and
- GBP 60,000 for non-domiciled individuals who have been resident in the UK for at least 12 of the previous 14 tax years immediately before the relevant tax year.

Those claiming the remittance basis will lose their entitlement to personal allowances and the capital gains tax annual exempt amount.

There are limited exceptions where taxpayers may use the remittance basis without making a formal claim or paying the RBC if certain conditions apply, one of which is that the amount of their un-remitted foreign income and gains for the relevant tax year is less than GBP 2,000.

Taxation of individuals in the UK is mostly administered on a self-assessment basis. Whilst employers often deduct income tax at source, the majority of high-net-worth UK tax resident individuals will be required to provide a self-assessment tax return, reporting their taxable income and capital gains to HMRC.

UK tax years run from 6 April of one year to 5 April of the next. When filed online, tax returns must be filed by 31 January following the end of the tax year – so for example, an individual's return for the 2023/24 UK tax year must be filed by 31 January 2025.

1. TAX AND WEALTH PLANNING

Income Tax

Applies in England and in Northern Ireland (Scotland and Wales have had partial income tax powers devolved, although the Welsh system differs only very slightly from the English system).

The income tax rates for the current tax year from 6 April 2023 to 5 April 2024 are as follows:

Band	Taxable income (GBP)	Tax rate*
Personal Allowance	Up to 12,570	0%
Basic rate	12,571 to 37,700	20%
Higher rate	37,701 to 125,140	40%
Additional rate	over 125,140	45%

* Broadly, an extra 1% rate applies in Scotland.

Capital Gains Tax (CGT)
Applies across all devolved nations.
   For the current tax year from 6 April 2023 to 5 April 2024, the standard personal allowance is GBP 6,000, and the prevailing rates are as follows:

Band	Residential property (not a main residence) and carried interest	Non-residential property
Basic rate taxpayers*	18%	10%
Higher or additional rate income taxpayers	28%	20%

* Note that above this threshold, taxpayers will pay 20% or 28% on any amount above the basic tax rate.

Inheritance Tax (IHT)
Applies across all devolved nations.
   The nil rate band (NRB) tax free amount is GBP 325,000 per estate. NRBs are transferable between spouses and civil partners. Transfers of assets between spouses and civil partners are IHT exempt. Following the Spring Budget in March 2023, charitable legacies will only be IHT exempt if made to UK charities as opposed to UK, EU and EEA charities. However, this is subject to a transitional period until 1 April 2024 for EU and EEA charities.
   The residence nil rate band (RNRB) of GBP 175,000 per estate is available where an estate is below GBP 2,000,000 and a qualifying residence is left to one or more direct descendants. The RNRB tapers down over GBP 2,000,000 and estates over GBP 2.35m are not eligible. The RNRB is also transferable between spouses and civil partners.
   IHT remains at 40% above the balance of available NRBs and RNRBs. Although, if 10% or more of a net estate is left to charity, then the estate benefits from a reduced rate of IHT at 36% on the balance.

Annual Tax on Enveloped Dwellings (ATED)
Applies across all devolved nations.
   ATED is an annual tax payable mainly by companies that own UK residential property valued at more than GBP 500,000. ATED, which was introduced on 1 June 2013, and associated measures have heavily discouraged the acquisition and holding of residential property through companies.

Property value (as at 1 April 2023) (GBP)	Annual Charge (GBP)
500,001 to 1m	4,150
1,000,001 to 2m	8,450
2,000,001 to 5m	28,650
5,000,001 to 10m	67,050
10,000,001 to 20m	134,550
More than 20m	269,450

Stamp Duty Land Tax (SDLT)
Applies in England and in Northern Ireland (Scotland and Wales have their own equivalent land transaction taxes).

The current SDLT threshold for residential properties before SDLT becomes payable is GBP 250,000. There were different thresholds for residential properties before 23 September 2022. The threshold for non-residential land and properties is still GBP 150,000. There are numerous SDLT rates depending on the circumstances, type of property and value. SDLT is charged according to a slice system, as set out below.

Importantly, if a purchaser of UK property is not present in the UK for at least 183 days (6 months) during the 12 months before purchase they are 'not a UK resident' for the purposes of SDLT.

Non-resident purchasers will usually pay a 2% surcharge if buying a residential property in England (or Northern Ireland) on or after 1 April 2021.

All purchasers will usually pay a 3% surcharge on top of these rates if they already own another residential property, and the purchase is not to replace their main residence.

Residential property rates:

Property/Lease Premium value (GBP)	SDLT rate
Up to 250,000	0%
The next 675,000 (from 250,001 to 925,000)	5%
The next 575,000 (from 925,001 to 1.5m)	10%
The remainder over 1.5m	12%

Commercial property rates:

Property/Lease Premium value (GBP)	SDLT rate
Up to 150,000	0%
The next 100,000 (from 150,001 to 250,000)	2%
The remainder over 250,000	5%

1.1 National legislative and regulatory developments

The Register of Overseas Entities came into force in the UK on 1 August 2022 through the Economic Crime (Transparency and Enforcement) Act 2022. This introduces a 'Register of Overseas Entities' to ensure that the identities of the beneficial owners of UK property are no longer obscured behind privacy screening offshore companies, as the global push towards ownership transparency continues. This change had been tabled for some time.

Foreign companies owning UK property will now need to openly identify their beneficial owners, and register them with Companies House, bringing them into parity with UK companies owning UK property, and UK companies generally under the PSC register. This was introduced by The Small Business, Enterprise and Employment Act 2016 (implemented under The Companies Act 2006 as amended) and supplemented by The Register of People with Significant Control Regulations 2016, as of 6 April 2016, UK companies are required to keep a register identifying people who retain significant control over them, as a way to target a perceived lack of transparency over who controls companies doing business in the UK. The rules will also apply to individuals who have significant control over the foreign entity, for example if they hold 25% minimum of the voting rights or shares, they will be caught.

There are high financial penalties and criminal sanctions for failure to register where required on the 'Register of Overseas Entities'.

1.2 Local legislative and regulatory developments

There have been no local legislative and regulatory developments.

1.3 National case law developments

The case of *A taxpayer v. Revenue and Customs* [2022] UKFTT 133 (TC) (see *www.bailii.org/uk/cases/UKFTT/TC/2022/133.html*) explored HMRC's approach to the exceptional circumstances limb of the SRT, and the conditions that must be met in order to qualify for this status, to prevent certain days spent in the UK counting towards the day count thresholds for UK tax residence. The appellant argued that her visits to the UK were exceptional, as she was required to care for her twin sister, and minor children, as a result of the twin's alcoholism.

HMRC did not consider these circumstances to be exceptional, on the basis that:

1) the condition of the sister was known and the issue was therefore foreseeable when the appellant chose to take up residence outside of the UK, so would need to come back to visit;

2) the exceptional circumstances test does not apply to someone who has entered the UK under a moral obligation or as a matter of conscience to care for someone; and

3) the exemption can only apply to someone who was already in the UK, and whilst they were there were 'overtaken' by exceptional circumstances which prevented them being able to leave (it is noted that this argument in particular was contradictory to HMRC's guidance that someone who came to the UK due to exceptional circumstances and was then prevented from leaving due to the same circumstances should qualify).

On these particular facts, the appellant had use of a private jet, which HMRC argued could have been used to fly in and out each day. There was also a separate history of dispute between the appellant and HMRC. The Tribunal subsequently rejected all of these arguments, considering HMRC's approach to statutory interpretation in this case to be clearly wrong.

The Tribunal found that Parliament had quite clearly intended to avoid injustice as to how the SRT is applied, by allowing for such exceptional circumstances, and that it cannot have been Parliament's intention for that test to be failed if the taxpayer independently thought it necessary to be present due to some illness, or other serious health issue, suffered by a close relative. The Tribunal also criticised HMRC's comments that the circumstances should be 'highly exceptional, not merely unusual, and out of the ordinary in the extreme', and that a sibling could not be within the exemption – the legislation is silent on who that person must be. Given the history between the parties, HMRC's approach here appears unusually strict, but it is worth noting the comments both of the Revenue and the Tribunal in attempting to foresee the direction of decisions in future on the subject.

The case of *Jonathan Oppenheimer v. HMRC* [2022] UKFT 00112 (TC) considered in depth the tiebreaker test to ascertain treaty residence within the double taxation agreement between the UK and South Africa. Jonathan Oppenheimer (of the family controlling the De Beers company) retained permanent homes in both the UK and South Africa, and a thorough investigative exercise was necessary to ascertain whether Mr Oppenheimer would be classed as treaty resident in the UK or in South Africa. He had received large sums from a family trust between 2010 and 2017, and whilst he accepted that he was tax resident in the UK, he did not accept that he was treaty resident in the UK. HMRC had argued that Oppenheimer was indeed treaty resident in the UK between 2010 and 2017, but Oppenheimer appealed, and ultimately won the dispute, with the First Tier Tribunal ruling that he was in fact treaty resident in South Africa during the relevant time period, despite holding extensive business interests and a long term residence in the UK. The decision was reached on the tiebreaker principle, and in the matter of Mr Oppenheimer's centre of vital interests, it was decided that throughout the relevant period, his economic and personal relations critically remained closer to South Africa than to the UK. The Tribunal also found that Mr Oppenheimer had a habitual abode in South Africa. Since he was also a national of South Africa, this would have been determinative had it not been possible to determine his centre of vital interests, and he was found therefore to be treaty resident in South Africa. It is clear for practitioners that a wholly holistic approach was taken in arriving at this decision, and that a thorough and comprehensive analysis of the taxpayer's lifestyle including previous family history and past relationships, interests and hobbies, economic connections, charitable and political activity, amongst other factors, all played a role in the final outcome. This demonstrates that each case in this arena will be entirely dependent on its own facts, and that in particular, it should be noted that length of tenure in one jurisdiction is not necessarily the key factor, especially where ties to prior jurisdictions have not been cut.

1.4 Local case law developments

There have been no local case law developments.

1.5 Practice trends

The UK has experienced a period of political upheaval. The period commencing with the former English Prime Minister, Boris Johnson's resignation on 7 July 2022 was followed by a leadership battle for the new Prime Minister and was won by Liz Truss, who was appointed on 6 September 2022. Her Late Majesty Queen Elizabeth II passed away on 8 September but by 20 October 2022, Liz Truss had been replaced as Prime Minister by Rishi Sunak. A large part of Liz Truss' short tenure was due to a "mini budget" delivered on 23 September 2022 by the then Chancellor, Kwasi Kwateng. The mini budget dramatically cut taxes in a bid to spark economic growth and introduced measures such as planning the abolishment of the 45% income tax rate and reversing the plan to increase corporation tax from 19% to 25% from April 2023. The mini budget was negatively received by global markets and caused the value of the GBP to plummet. Despite the fact that the UK government reversed nearly all measures soon after, the Bank of England was forced to stablise the economy by raising base interest rates to the highest recent levels, which has increased the cost for UK borrowing and mortgages exponentially. The UK is experiencing rising inflation and a cost-of-living crisis, amidst an economic recession and a large UK Government deficit, caused partly by the COVID-19 pandemic. There has been much speculation that the UK Government will seek to repay the deficit by raising CGT rates and review the favourable remittance basis for non-UK domiciliaries. Whilst the Government have yet to increase CGT rates, from 6 April 2023, the CGT personal allowance has been halved to GBP 6,000. Practitioners will be considering ways to "lock in" the current GGT rates for clients and will be closely monitoring any proposed reforms to the remittance basis.

1.6 Pandemic related developments

UK restrictions at the pandemic's peak forced practitioners to seek guidance on permissible methods of witnessing deeds, signing wills and the validity of electronic signatures.

Deeds

Prior to the pandemic, it was accepted that deeds may be signed electronically by all parties (as confirmed by the Law Commission on 4 September 2019), however the witness must physically be present and have sight of the person making the deed.

Wills

On 7 September 2020 The Wills Act 1837 (Electronic Communications) (Amendment) (Coronavirus) Order 2020 SI 2020/952 was laid before Parliament. It amends The Wills Act 1837 to allow video-witnessing and execution of wills through a live-action video-link. It applies to wills made on or after 31 January 2020 and on or before 31 January 2024. Government advice remains that where people can make wills in the conventional way, they should continue to do so.

Making a will where video witnessing will be performed, or obtaining probate where a will was video-witnessed or said to be video-witnessed, introduces a further level of risk which practitioners and their firms need to assess and manage. We can expect to see cases heard in the UK Courts in due course.

Statutory Residence Test – expansion of COVID-19 exceptional circumstances
HMRC recognised that COVID-19 prevented some people from going to and from the UK and may have resulted in unexpected days in the UK. Guidance in the Remittance and Domicile manual expanded on pandemic specific exceptional circumstances such as:
- quarantining or official advice to self-isolate;
- official Government advice not to leave the UK;
- closure of international borders preventing leaving the UK; and
- employer's request to return to the UK temporarily.

2. ESTATE AND TRUST ADMINISTRATION

Estate administration within England & Wales is regulated by the Probate Registry, part of His Majesty Courts and Tribunal Service (HMCTS).

The type of grant of representation issued to a deceased's estate depends on whether the deceased left a valid will. If there is a valid will, the executors apply for a grant of probate. If there is no will (or the will is invalid) the estate is "intestate", and an application is made for a grant of letters of administration which appoints administrators. Both types of grant ultimately enable an estate to be administered, however executors' powers to deal with assets of the estate are derived from the will itself, whereas administrators' powers are conferred by the grant of letters of administration. Having made this important distinction and for the purposes of the rest of this section, all further references to a grant of probate and a grant of letters of administration have been shortened to the "Grant".

Property held jointly in the UK passes by operation of the law (survivorship) to the surviving joint owner. A Grant may not, therefore, always be needed.

2.1 National legislative and regulatory developments
Estate administration
HMCTS has digitalised the Grant application process, which for solicitors is now via an online portal. Initially the portal was limited to applications by individual executors however it is now possible to use the online portal for trust corporations acting as executors. Certain applications must still be made on paper (for instance where there is a non-UK will that is held in a foreign court and only a certified copy is available or the deceased was not UK domiciled or it is desired to re-seal a Grant obtained in another jurisdiction).

HMCTS increased the Grant fee from GBP 155 to GBP 273 per application. There is no fee if the estate is valued below GBP 4,999. The cost for copies of Grants remains at GBP 1.50 per copy. There was some discussion around introducing a fee on a sliding scale, however this was abandoned amidst concern that this would introduce a second-tier inheritance tax by stealth. There are no current proposals to increase fees.

In an attempt to simplify the application process, and effective 1 January 2022, significantly more non-inheritance tax paying estates will be "excepted estates". For deaths after that date it is no longer necessary to submit form IHT205 for excepted estates where the deceased died domiciled in the UK. Applications where the deceased died up until 31 December 2021 remain unchanged.

Trusts – and the new Trust Registration Service
The Trust Registration Service (TRS) was introduced in 2017, aimed at taxable trusts. The Money Laundering and Terrorist Financing (amendment) (EU Exit) Regulations 2020) was extended to include non-taxable UK trusts as well as some non-UK trusts with some specific exclusions. Taxable trusts are registrable by 31 January (or 5 October where there is first time liability to CGT/income tax) following the end of the tax year in which the trust had a UK tax liability. Non-taxable trusts (UK or non-UK) in existence on or after 6 October 2020 require registration by 1 September 2022.

Non-taxable trusts created on or after 4 June 2022, and those created from 1 September 2022, are registrable within 90 days of creation. Some non-UK trusts are also subject to reporting requirements. There are certain exclusions but tax tends to trump the exclusion. Practitioners need to have regard to the TRS's wide net. Trusts of land will require registration if the beneficial and legal owners are not the same.

2.2 Local legislative and regulatory developments
There have been no local legislative and regulatory developments.

2.3 National case law developments
Case law of note is addressed in detail below in Section 3. Estate and trust litigation and controversy. However, it is worth noting the key case of *Re Bhusate* [2020] which enabled a widow to bring a claim for financial provision 25 years and nine months after the limitation period in the Inheritance (Provision for Family and Dependants) 1975 Act. The High Court granted the deceased's widow permission to make a claim. The appeal brought by the defendants was dismissed. The significance of this case shows that such applications may succeed even when brought out of time.

2.4 Local case law developments
There have been no local case law developments.

2.5 Practice trends
Trusts
In light of the TRS's new and more onerous requirements, practitioners and trust corporations ought to audit trusts to ensure compliance. Record keeping and maintenance is key. As a general rule, UK express trusts and certain types of non-UK express trusts liable to UK taxation, or with interests in UK land, are required to keep detailed records on those trusts.

2.6 Pandemic related developments

Administration

HMCTS experienced severe delays during the pandemic. Practitioners will recall that correspondence to obtain financial information from banks and authorities took significantly longer. All HMRC officers, including those answering the IHT queries helpline started working from home which created further delays.

In recognition of social distancing regulations and avoiding unnecessary contact, HMRC now permit IHT accounts to be signed electronically. This has continued since pandemic restrictions were lifted.

3. ESTATE AND TRUST LITIGATION CONTROVERSY

3.1 National legislative and regulatory developments

The area of trust and estate litigation is not one subject to significant legislative change, whether nationally (affecting the United Kingdom) or locally by jurisdiction.

As touched on above, one statute of note however is the Wills Act 1837 (Electronic Communications) Amendment (Coronavirus) Order 2020. This varied the execution requirements for a will, in view of the COVID-19 pandemic, to permit the remote witnessing of wills as covered earlier in the chapter. From a litigation perspective we have not seen reported cases, but have concern about undue influence as noted below.

3.2 Local legislative and regulatory developments

There have been no legislative and regulatory developments.

3.3 National case law developments

Such is the volume of case law developments in the past 12-18 months that it is helpful to consider some of the themes arising from the cases.

Capacity and vulnerability both continue to be areas of significant litigation. The decision in *Clitheroe v. Bond* [2021] EWHC 1102 (Ch) confirmed that the correct test for establishing testamentary capacity remained the case of *Banks v. Goodfellow*, not the test set out in the Mental Capacity Act 2005, a matter which has been considered on a number of occasions in recent years. The Court also considered how to determine whether someone is suffering from a delusion (applying the fourth limb of *Banks v. Goodfellow*) and that a false belief needs to be irrational and fixed in nature.

Subsequently in *Hughes v. Pritchard* [2022] EWCA Civ 386 the Court of Appeal overturned the trial judge's decision that a testator lacked testamentary capacity. In this case, the evidence of the solicitor who drafted the will (and followed the 'golden rule'), a medical professional, and a retrospective expert report had supported a finding of capacity.

In January 2021 the Court considered capacity to litigate (applying the test in *Masterman-Lister v. Brutton*) in the case of *Ruhan v. Ruhan* [2021] EWFC 6 and confirmed that capacity to litigate could not depend on whether the party received no legal advice or the quality of that advice. If a party could make decisions with the benefit of advice, they had capacity whether or not they had the benefit of that advice.

FREQUENTLY ASKED QUESTIONS

What is the difference between 'residence' and 'domicile' under the law of England and Wales?

Generally speaking, an individual is domiciled in the jurisdiction with which they are most closely connected (which may be different from the country in which they are resident for the time being).

Unlike in the case of residence, an individual must, under common law, at all times be domiciled somewhere, but can only be domiciled in one jurisdiction at any one time.

The UK's residence rules are outlined in various statutory rules and it is possible to determine in any given year if a person is UK tax resident. This, combined with domicile, determines an individual's exposure to income tax, CGT and IHT. Domicile is also crucial for many non-tax purposes, which include aspects of succession, family law, and civil jurisdiction.

Closely connected to the question of capacity, 2021 and 2022 saw a number of will dispute cases alleging want of knowledge and approval. In *Skillett v. Skillett* [2022] EWHC 233 (Ch), DJ Mott noted at para 71 that "The lack of mathematical equality at the time of death does nothing to undermine the rationality of the provisions which [the Testator] was instructed to incorporate at the time of making the Will." However in *Reeves v. Drew* [2022] EWHC 153 (Ch) in January 2022, it was found that the Testator did not know and approve the contents of his will which dealt with his estate worth over GBP 100m, but that he had not been unduly influenced by his daughter. In the same month, similar allegations of undue influence (in this case fraudulent calumny) ran alongside a want of knowledge and approval claim in *St Clair v. Farrel* [2022] EWHC 40 (Ch). The claimant daughter of the testator failed on all grounds.

Claims for reasonable provision for a deceased's estate under the Inheritance (Provision for Family and Dependants) Act 1975 included interesting analysis of the overlap with the Family courts. In *Tucker v. Purle* [2021] EWHC 3485 (Ch) the Court found that a financial remedy order made in 2013 was insufficient to meet the needs of the deceased's 15 year old daughter up to finishing university and consequently increased her share of the estate. *Sismey v. Salandron* [PT-2020-BHM-000090] was the first case to consider s11 of the 1975 Act (contracts to leave property by will) and considered the enforceability of a divorce agreement to leave a property to the deceased's son, which the deceased's wife was seeking as part of a claim for reasonable financial provision. The son was successful in his claim.

In relation to trust litigation, many of the key decisions continue to be offshore, although their impact is of importance nonetheless for English practitioners. The two cases of *In the Matter of the X Trusts* [2021] SC (Bda) 72 Civ (Bermuda) and the subsequent *Piedmont Trust* [2021] 248 (Jersey) on the role of Protectors — whether wide or narrow, a watchdog or decision maker and their interaction with the trustees is of great interest to English advisors.

Similarly the Privy Council decision *Webb v. Webb* [2020] UKPC (Cook Islands), on reserved powers and the validity of a trust in the context of matrimonial assets, provided guidance on assessing trust validity and the equitable approach the Court might take when considering the ability of divorcing spouses or creditors to access trust assets.

Blessing applications (for example, *Public Trustee v. Cooper*) continue to come before the Court and in one recent case — *Brown v. New Quadrant Trust* [2021] EWHC 1731 — the Court 'blessed' a trustee's decision to dispose of a shareholding in a company in relation to which a principal beneficiary had sought an injunction to prevent the sale.

3.4 Local case law developments

There have been no local case law developments.

3.5 Practice trends

We have noted above some of the key themes we have seen in the reported decisions.

We have seen the issue of protection for vulnerable parties and witnesses also become a key area of concern. In April 2021, new Practice Direction 1A to the Civil Procedure Rules came into force which recognised (as the Family Courts have for some time) that the vulnerability of a party or witness could impede participation and diminish quality of evidence, and that directions may need to be made to make suitable adjustments.

The question of costs continues to be an area of considerable judicial commentary and reference to alternative means by which to settle disputes (mediation, ENE, FDR), a regular theme. Further, in *Hirachand v. Hirachand* [2021] EWCA Civ 1498, the successful adult child claimant bringing a claim under the 1975 Act was able to recover, as part of her award, a contribution towards a success fee under a Conditional Fee Agreement (CFA). Whilst specific to the facts of the case, we watch with interest how this may be applied in future 1975 Act cases.

We anticipate that the coming months or years will see an increase in litigation stemming from pandemic related changes, whether allegations of undue influence in relation to remote witnessed wills or challenges to trustee decision making at a time of uncertainty. Digital assets (including cryptocurrencies, NFTs etc.) will undoubtedly be potential source of controversy.

3.6 Pandemic related developments

In terms of case law related specifically to the pandemic, there have been a number of reported decisions by the Court of Protection on the question of capacity to consent to the COVID-19 vaccine or booster. These cases involved the Court considering the best interests test set out in the Mental Capacity Act 2005 and balancing this against the wishes of one of more family members or, in some cases, the incapacitated individual themselves. In *Re E (E v. Hammersmith and Fulham LBC)* [2021] EWCOP 7 the Court found it to be in the best interests of the patient to have the vaccine, however in *SS (by her accredited Legal Representative) v. London Borough of Richmond Upon Thames* [2021] EWCOP 31 the Court found that the patient's autonomy should be respected.

One development which will remain for the foreseeable future is that of remote hearings (and electronic bundles). The pandemic led to a transition to remote hearings, requiring both legal representatives and clients to adopt a radically new way of progressing hearings of a case and to ensure the justice system continued to operate. There were existing plans to digitise the Courts, but the pandemic expedited the process. This had some advantages in terms of time and cost but there was concern about the impact on vulnerable parties in particular, who may be best served by in person hearings (see Report by HM Courts and Tribunals Service (HMCTS) at *www.gov.uk/government/publications/hmcts-remote-hearing-evaluation#history*). The mode of hearings ultimately remains a matter of judicial discretion. In March 2022 a new Video Hearings Platform was introduced into some Business and Property Courts designed for use in hybrid and remote hearings.

AUTHOR BIOGRAPHIES

Patrick Harney

Patrick is a Partner in Mishcon de Reya. A market leading international private client lawyer who has worked in Dublin, London and New York, Patrick specialises in cross border tax advice with a particular focus on US-UK and UK-Irish tax, trust and estate planning and UK resident non-domiciled tax planning.

His wide range of clients include high profile individuals, family offices and hedge funds spanning the UK and Ireland, the US and Latin America. He has a particular expertise in the use of family partnerships and family investment companies as a tax efficient wealth holding vehicle.

Patrick has been consistently ranked by the private wealth industry and professional directories as a leading expert in tax law. He is a Chartered Tax Adviser, an International Fellow of the American College of Trust and Estate Counsel (ACTEC) and in November 2019 he was admitted as an Academician of The International Academy of Estate and Trust Lawyers.

He is a STEP member and lectures on International Estate Planning at the STEP/ Irish Law Society Diploma Course on Trust and Estate Planning.

Bethan Byrne

Bethan is a Managing Associate for Private Wealth Disputes at Mishcon de Reya.

Bethan provides technical support to the team and assists in fee earner training, professional development as well as working with the team on strategy and practice development initiatives. She is also responsible for centralising know-how, risk management and best practice. Bethan has a wealth of experience, specialising in advising lay and professional clients on all types of contentious trust and succession matters from private practice.

Bethan is a member of ACTAPS and STEP.

FRANCE

Line-Alexa Glotin
UGGC Avocats

INTRODUCTION

The French civil law system has protected family members and family assets for centuries.

The transfer of assets through generations can be structured so that the tax erosion is mitigated and, thus, the family wealth protected. The French legal system favors family governance and shareholders' agreements, which offer business and asset protection.

Thanks to EU Regulations and a substantial network of Tax Treaties, families and entrepreneurs enjoy some flexibility for transferring their wealth and business to younger generations — transfers and succession planning can be easily and properly organised.

Worth mentioning is the implementation of the European Succession Regulation in 2015, the objective of which is to avoid the fragmentation of successions and enable people living in, or investing in, multiple jurisdictions to organise their succession in advance.

Taxwise, France has become more attractive since the election of Emmanuel Macron as President of the Republic in 2017. In particular, his promised reforms in tax law have largely become a reality. The key changes include the following reforms:

- the wealth tax basis is limited to real estate assets, thus excluding financial assets and investments;
- the taxation of capital gains, dividends and interest is now subject to a flat tax of 30% for residents of France and 12.8% for non-residents; and
- more generally, more opportunities now exist for efficient personal and estate planning for individuals, although some of the new rules still require clarification.

1. TAX AND WEALTH PLANNING

1.1 National legislative and regulatory developments

The current government is urging reforms, notably of the French tax system. This is triggering reactions and protest movements but can offer opportunities to refresh the tax system.

Tax considerations for French and non-French resident individuals

Individual residents in France are subject to income tax on their worldwide income, wealth tax and gift/inheritance tax on their worldwide assets, subject to tax treaties. Non-residents of France are subject to the same taxes on their French source income and French assets, as qualified under internal rules and tax treaty provisions. The French tax system provides multiple income tax, wealth tax and gift/inheritance tax exemptions as regards business assets, works of art and family assets transferred between spouses, civil partners and among family members.

Income tax

Dividends and interest received by residents and non-residents from French corporations are subject to a flat tax of 12.8%. French taxpayers are subject to social contribution taxes (referred to below as the "social tax") that operate as a personal income tax; social contribution taxes, added together, are levied at the flat rate of 17.2%. Specific personal income tax rates apply (75%) when so-called "non-co-operative jurisdictions and territories" (états et territoires non coopératifs) are involved.

Residents of France are subject to personal income tax according to a progressive brackets system with a marginal rate of 45% above EUR 169,000 on their worldwide income (wages, bonus, professional fees, rental income, etc.) plus social tax.

An additional tax is due:
- at the rate of 3% between EUR 250,000 and EUR 500,000 and 4% above EUR 500,000 for a taxpayer who is single; or
- at a rate of 3% between EUR 500,000 and EUR 1 million and 4% above EUR 1 million for married couples and members of a PACS (civil pact between different or same sex couples).

Specific rules apply to income generated within life-insurance vehicles as well as income withdrawn by the policy owner during the life of the policy.

Capital gains realised by tax residents of France on the sale of securities are subject to a levy of 12.8% or to the progressive brackets system, plus social tax. Non-residents of France are fully exempt on the condition that they have not held, during the five years preceding the sale, directly or indirectly, alone or with certain close relatives, more than 25% of the share capital of the relevant French entity. Some tax treaties can provide different rules for qualifying "substantial" or controlling participation in a French entity.

Capital gains realised on the sale of French real estate are taxed at a rate of 19% when the vendor resides in an EU member state, 33.3% otherwise and 75% when non-co-operative jurisdictions and territories are involved. Social contributions of 7.5% are due in addition to capital gains tax, plus a surtax of between 2% and 6% depending of the amount of the gain.

Gift taxes and Inheritance taxes

Between parents and direct descendants, the tax is computed in accordance with a brackets system. The marginal rate is 45% above EUR 1.8 million subject to a basis reduction of EUR 100,000 (available every 15 years).

There is no inheritance tax between spouses or members of a PACS. Lifetime gifts between such couples are subject to tax at the marginal rate of 45% above EUR 1.805 million subject to a basis reduction of EUR 80,000.

Other rules apply to siblings (45% above EUR 24,000) and non-relatives (60%).

Wealth tax

Wealth tax is payable every year on the basis of a person's total real estate value. Wealth tax was heavily reformed as from 2018.

The applicable wealth tax rates are progressive. For instance, it amounts to 0.5% of net wealth between EUR 800,000 and EUR 1.3 million and 1.5% above EUR 10 million.

As regards a tax resident of France, the taxable basis is made up of the individual's worldwide properties, less local taxes and the wealth tax itself. Non-residents are liable to wealth tax only as to their French-*situs* properties. Non-residents are not subject to wealth tax on their financial investments in France (for example bank accounts, receivables from French-based persons, assets held in a

French life insurance vehicle and controlling or non-controlling participation in the share capital of companies).

Wealth tax is subject to certain limitations other than those mentioned above, such as a 30% rebate on the individual's residence.

1.2 Local legislative and regulatory developments

On regulatory matters, beyond the modernisation of a number of bilateral treaties, France has entered into a number of tax information exchange agreements, which, subject to some specifications, are in line with Article 26 of the OECD Model, notably with Andorra, the British Virgin Islands, Belize, Gibraltar, Guernsey, Liechtenstein, Jersey and Uruguay.

In parallel, rules similar to the US Foreign Account Tax Compliance Act, are in force in the EU territory and codified in France, submitting financial institutions to annual or occasional reporting obligations to the EU tax authorities regarding individuals owning, directly or indirectly, bank accounts or financial investments. French internal rules also provide strict controls and substantial penalties for hidden bank accounts.

The EU Council has revised several times the 2018/822 MDR Directive (DAC6) imposing reporting obligations to intermediaries and taxpayers. Recently, the impending European directive DAC 8, on the taxation of digital assets, will require exchanges and crypto-related service providers to report their customers' transactions to European authorities

Recent decisions rendered by the European Court of Justice in November/ December 2022 state that these rules cannot impose on lawyers to disclose confidential information and documents to the tax authorities and that the UBO registry cannot be public.

1.3 National case law developments

The French administrative Supreme Court has recently ruled that the spontaneous communication by a taxpayer during an audit of a document covered by professional secrecy can be interpreted as a tacit agreement to the lifting of the professional secrecy (Conseil d'Etat 9 December 2021, no. 446366).

1.4 Local case law developments

Different Courts have authority and competence on the French territory, but no specific local case law system exists. Court decisions are therefore rendered for the whole state.

1.5 Practice trends

Families and entrepreneurs tend to use French legal vehicles, shareholders agreements and dismembered ownership rights in order to mitigate taxes due at the occasion of assets transfers to the next generation but in retaining partly or fully the control of the family wealth and/or business assets.

1.6 Pandemic related developments

Flexibility and dematerialization have developed considerably during and since the pandemic and became the rule in terms of work organization and relations with clients and administrations. This has notably changed the process for signing legal acts, whether notarized or not, relations with the Administrations as well as the judges and the Court proceedings.

2. ESTATE AND TRUST ADMINISTRATION

2.1 National legislative and regulatory developments

France has a civil law system which provides forced heirship rules and limits testamentary freedom. If French succession law applies, then the issue of the deceased and, in the absence of descendants, certain close relatives enjoy special protection so that they receive a minimum portion of the succession. This depends on the number of children. When a child dies, the same rules apply to the descendants.

In an international context, Regulation (EU) No 650/2012 of the European Parliament and of the Council of 4 July 2012 on jurisdiction, applicable law, recognition and enforcement of decisions and acceptance and enforcement of authentic instruments in matters of succession and on the creation of a European certificate of succession has applied since 17 August 2015, and offers testators the option of adopting the law of their nationality, which therefore allows the right to circumvent French succession law and therefore heirship rules.

Article 913 of the French civil code, amended in 2021 provides, however, a new rule which circumvents the EU Succession Regulation in offering a claim to heirs (being French/EU citizens or residents) who are disinherited in application of a foreign legislation. That new rule needs to be implemented by the practitioners and will certainly be challenged in Court.

As regards Trusts, France signed the 1985 Hague Convention on Trusts and their Recognition in 1991 but never formally ratified it. Nonetheless, France has bound itself to recognise the essential validity of foreign trusts that were the subject of the Convention.

In a fiscal context, for decades, French internal law has referred directly to trusts and similar vehicles. In addition, the revised Finance law for 2011 introduced transparency rules for wealth tax and inheritance/gift tax, as well as imposing substantial disclosure obligations on trustees.

Trusts will be deemed transparent for gift and inheritance tax purposes. If the beneficiaries are identified individually, the relevant standard gift (inheritance) tax rate will apply. If they cannot be so identified but are all in the line of descent, the tax rate will be 45%. Otherwise, the tax will be levied at a rate of 60%.

France also has in place a substantial number of bilateral treaties for the avoidance of double taxation, notably with the United States, Canada and the United Kingdom, which often contain references to matters affecting trusts.

2.2 Local legislative and regulatory developments

France is not a federal state, its legislation applies over the national territory.

2.3 National case law developments

With the law of May 17, 2013, on marriage for all, France has become the 9th European country and the 14th country in the world to authorize same-sex

FREQUENTLY ASKED QUESTIONS

1. How to protect a surviving spouse and transfer family assets without conflict or tax erosion?

We assist many couples, being married or not, French or international, to protect the surviving of the two as well as anticipate the transfer of their family assets to their descendants, collaterals or third parties and charitable institutions. In order to avoid conflict among members of the family and persons involved in any businesses (for instance), it is important to anticipate governance rules. This does not only concern business assets but also family and dynastic assets. Anticipation may indicate modifying the matrimonial property regime, preparing wills and proper succession planning. Transfer assets among generations may also imply contributing these assets to (family) legal entities, being French or not, with by-laws duly customized in consideration of the patriarch and/or matriarch wishes in terms of governance and benefit/use of the family assets. It is also important to anticipate tax implications, and we may organise and document transgenerational gifts and bequests, directly or through legal vehicles of these family transfers, enjoying favourable tax treatments in France and in other states where clients, heirs and legatees may reside.

2. Can non-French nationals or residents arrange for their Estate/Tax planning arranged elsewhere to be implemented in France?

Working for non-French nationals or residents in order that their Estate / Tax planning crafted by practitioners of their state of residence is implemented in France, where they acquired or inherited assets, sometimes requires adjusting this Estate and Tax planning, so that it becomes efficient from a legal and tax viewpoint. The best approach is to work directly and in advance with all the estate practitioners engaged by the clients in the different states where they own assets or have an heir or legatee.

3. How to anticipate charitable gifts?

Transnational gifts and bequests are frequent points discussed with clients. Assisting international families as well as Foundations, Museums, Hospitals and any legal entities registered in multiple jurisdictions for collecting funds indicates action to anticipate the legal qualification of the gift and bequest, secure the tax treatment from a national and international viewpoint, and also to provide documents and justifications, the beneficiary or the donor/testator being subject to civil or common law rules, as well as Sharia law.

marriage. This law opened up new rights for marriage, adoption and succession, in the name of the principles of equality and the sharing of freedoms.

The evolution of families have been again recently considered by the French Parliament which gave, thanks to the law on bioethics published in the Official Journal on August 3, 2021, access to medically assisted procreation (MAP) for couples of women and single women, right of access to the origins of children born from a PMA, conservation of gametes without medical reason, research on embryos and stem cells.

Adoption law was the subject of a major reform on February 21, 2022 (Law no. 2022-219, 21 Feb. 2022), the new law being applicable from February 23, 2022. As an extension of this reform, an ordinance of October 5, 2022, re-codified the title of the Civil Code devoted to adoption, which will come into force on January 1, 2023. It is quite common for a child to be adopted by the spouse of one of its parents, but this option was only open to the spouse of the parent of the child. The law of February 21, 2022 now opens this option to the PACS partner and the cohabitant, both for simple adoption and for full adoption.

2.4 Local case law developments
Different Courts have authority and competence on the French territory, but no specific local case law system exists. Court decisions are therefore rendered for the whole state.

2.5 Practice trends
Under the Civil Code, an individual interested in estate planning can ask for an heir's consent to waive irrevocably the right to challenge violations of their "reserved portion", the advantage being, for instance, not to dilute the shareholding and the control of a family business. The heir(s) excluded from the family business could receive other family assets.

Using "gradual" and "residual" gifts or bequests is also a planning opportunity for asset protection, the lifetime gift or bequest being in this case subject to the conditions that the transferee on their death leaves the gift or bequest to a named third party or what remains of (residual gift or bequest).

The tax system applicable to gradual and residual gifts and bequests is also attractive.

2.6 Pandemic related developments
Flexibility and dematerialization have developed considerably during and since the pandemic and became the rule in terms of work organization and relations with clients and administrations. This has notably changed the process for signing legal acts, whether notarized or not, relations with the Administrations as well as the judges and the Court proceedings.

3. ESTATE AND TRUST LITIGATION AND CONTROVERSY
3.1 National legislative and regulatory developments
The 2022 Finance Law, applicable since 1 January 2022, establishes a presumption to facilitate the application of Article 123 *bis* of the Tax code to settlors of trusts. To facilitate the application to trusts of the provisions of this article, which allow the administration to tax in the name of a natural person domiciled in France the income received through the intermediary of a controlled entity located in a State with privileged taxation rules, the law presumes that the condition of holding at least 10% of the shares, financial rights or voting rights of the entity is satisfied when the taxpayer is a settlor or beneficiary deemed to be a settlor of a trust.

It is further provided that the reversal of this presumption "cannot result solely from the irrevocable nature of the trust and the discretionary power of management of its administrator."

3.2 Local legislative and regulatory developments
France is not a federal state, its legislation applies over the national territory.

3.3 National case law developments
Aside from these significant European Court decisions, that impact all EU Member states, one of the most relevant national case laws for private clients refers to forced heirship and trust: the French Supreme Court ruled that a trust constituted in fraud of the rights of the heirs is unenforceable against the succession when the deceased had retained overall control until their death of the entities to which these funds had been transferred (Cass. 1e civ. 18-5-2022 no. 20-20.609 FS-D).

3.4 Local case law developments
Different Courts have authority and competence on the French territory, but no specific local case law system exists. Court decisions are therefore rendered for the whole state.

3.5 Practice trends
Anticipating and preventing litigations among family members are relevant for French and international clients, notably at the occasion of the transfer to the next generations of substantial assets and businesses.

Particularly in the context of complex international disputes, lawyers must have experience in dispute resolution, arbitration or mediation/conciliation in order to propose efficient settlement options.

3.6 Pandemic related developments
Flexibility and dematerialization have developed considerably during and since the pandemic and became the rule in terms of work organization and relations with clients and administrations. This has notably changed the process for signing legal acts, whether notarized or not, relations with the Administrations as well as the judges and the Court proceedings.

AUTHOR BIOGRAPHY

Line-Alexa Glotin
Line-Alexa Glotin is a partner and head of the private client and tax department at UGGC Avocats in Paris. She advises private clients and institutions in a domestic and international context. She has experience in assisting individuals, family businesses, family offices, charities, trustees and foundations (including art foundations), notably in regard to the transfer and restructuring of private assets, tax planning and estate planning. Ms Glotin also advises on voluntary disclosures and assists clients in tax litigation. She studied law at the Panthéon-Assas University, where she received an advanced studies degree in business law and tax. She is notably a member of the International Academy of Estate and Trust Law (IAETL), STEP and the International Bar Association. She publishes regularly and is a lecturer in her field of experience abroad in private client forums, she also teaches at the University Paris Dauphine PSL.

GERMANY

Dr. Andreas Richter &
Dr. Katharina Hemmen
Poellath

INTRODUCTION

Private wealth and private client law in Germany is characterised by a high number of tax and legal regulations on the one hand, and a high level of judicial review on the other. Not only the civil and finance courts, but also the state and federal constitutional courts, ensure the consistent and proportionate application of German civil and tax law.

In recent decades, private wealth and family-owned enterprises have been growing and also become more international.

1. TAX AND WEALTH PLANNING

The worldwide income and assets of individuals whose tax residence is in Germany are subject to:

- income tax; and
- inheritance and gift tax.

If real estate located in Germany is acquired, the following taxes apply:

- real estate transfer tax; and
- (annual) real estate tax.

Corporations with its effective place of management or statutory seat in Germany are subject to:

- corporate tax; and
- trade tax.

1.1 National legislative and regulatory developments

The EU's Anti-Tax Avoidance Directive (ATAD) obliges all Member States to implement a minimum standard for additional taxation in national tax law. Based on the Directive, the rules of the Foreign Tax Act (FTA) have been amended. The amended law is in force from 1 January 2022. In particular, the taxation of hidden reserves for departing natural persons with capital shares was tightened (exit tax). If an individual has owned more than 1% of shares in a corporation within the past 5 years and has been subject to unlimited tax liability in Germany for at least 7 of the 12 years prior to departure, the disposal of the shares is feigned. The increase in the value of the shares is taxed without realization ("dry income"). Any deferral and returner rules were tightened as a result of the amendment. Payment of the exit tax is now due immediately. Upon request, payment can be made in 7 annual instalments. Usually, a deferral is granted only upon the provision of collateral. In practice, tax offices often do not accept shares in the tax-triggering company as a collateral. Often this is also not possible due to the articles of association. Violation of certain rules of conduct may lead to the immediate maturity of the tax payment. The tax claim expires if the taxpayer returns to Germany within 7 years and has not transferred their shares in the meantime. An intention to return has to be made credible in the tax return.

In contrast to German family foundations, foreign family foundations are not liable to pay substitute inheritance tax. Further, according to a ruling of the German Federal Fiscal Court from 2021, distributions from foreign family foundations to German resident beneficiaries are only subject to gift tax if they do not comply with the statutory purposes of the foundation or if the beneficiaries have an enforceable entitlement to distributions. However, the undistributed income of a foreign family foundation may be attributed to the personal income of the founder or the beneficiaries if they are resident for tax purposes in Germany (Section 15 FTA).

Comprehensive changes will be implemented in the law of foundations in the near future. At the end of June 2021, the German Parliament and the Federal Council passed the reform of the law on foundations. The two main objectives of the reform are to bundle the hitherto federally fragmented foundation law in a uniform and conclusive manner in the German Civil Code and to establish a centrally managed foundation register. The new regulations will come into force on 1 January 2023. The public foundation register will be introduced on 1 January 2026.

1.2 Local legislative and regulatory developments

The relevant areas of law are all governed at the federal level, so there are no local developments.

1.3 National case law developments

A recent decision by the Hamburg Fiscal Court attracted considerable attention and is particularly relevant in the area of non-German family foundations. The court ruled that Section 15 of the FTA did not violate higher-ranking law. Section 15 is an anti-abuse provision intended to prevent tax evasion and tax avoidance as well as exploitation of the shielding effect of foreign foundations for purposes of taxation. Therefore, Section 15 of the FTA attributes the assets and income of the foreign family foundation to the founder subject to unlimited tax liability or, alternatively, to the beneficiaries. The court also stated that the criterion of withdrawal of legal and factual power of disposal under Section 15 (6) No. 1 of the FTA has to be interpreted broadly, excluding the attribution of income if the foundation has its registered office or its management in an EU Member State or an EEA Treaty State. The persons referred to in subsections 2 and 3 have to prove that they are legally and factually deprived of the power of disposition. The possibility of proof requires that the tax authorities have a possibility of verification through mutual agreement by means of exchange of information. The taxation of foreign sourced income under Section 15 of the FTA is an expression of the scepticism of German law towards foreign family foundations. In practice, the desired tax effect of foreign family foundations can only be achieved if the founders are also willing to place their assets in the hands of third parties. The family foundation has to be able to provide evidence of the lack of legal and actual power of disposal.

1.4 Local case law developments

Local case law developments are included above in Section 1.3 National case law developments. Court decisions of local courts are usually relevant beyond the borders of the individual federal state and should therefore be considered nationwide.

1.5 Practice trends

Two structures are commonly used in Germany to hold assets: corporations and partnerships.

Corporations

A corporation is subject to German corporate tax on its worldwide income if its effective place of management or statutory seat is located in Germany. The corporate tax amounts to 15% plus the solidarity surcharge. In addition to corporate tax, a trade tax is also levied. The trade tax due depends on the rates determined by the local authorities. A participation exemption may apply, however, for dividends and capital gains. Profits distributed to shareholders of the corporation are subject to withholding tax at a flat rate of 25% plus the solidarity surcharge.

A foreign corporation with income from German sources might be subject to German corporate tax. If a foreign corporation has a branch in Germany that constitutes a permanent establishment, the corporation will be subject to German corporate tax and trade tax on all income effectively connected to this permanent establishment.

Partnerships

Partnerships are fiscally transparent in Germany for income tax purposes. The partners are subject to income tax at their individual tax rates (plus the solidarity surcharge, if applicable). If the partnership is engaged in trade or business, the partnership itself is subject to trade tax. Trade tax levied from the partnership is (to a large extent) credited against the income tax of the partners if they are individuals.

1.6 Pandemic related developments

Wealth tax has not been levied in Germany since 1997. Since then, there have already been numerous impulses in the political landscape for either reintroducing the tax or introducing a one-time wealth fee. This demand could even be found in some of the parties' election programs for the 2021 federal election. Given the current coalition in the federal government, the introduction of a wealth tax is considered unlikely.

2. ESTATE AND TRUST ADMINISTRATION

2.1 National legislative and regulatory developments

Unlimited inheritance or gift tax liability is triggered if either the decedent/donor (hereinafter both referred to as transferor) or the successor/donee (hereinafter both referred to as transferee) is resident in Germany, regardless of whether the assets received are effectively connected to Germany. If neither the transferor nor the transferee is resident, inheritance and gift tax is only due on certain assets situated in Germany (e.g., real estate and business property). The transfer of a German bank account between non-residents generally does not trigger inheritance or gift tax.

Concerning inheritance and gift tax, each transferee is liable for the tax on the value of the assets received, regardless of their personal wealth. The inheritance and gift tax rates range from 7% to 50%, depending on the relationship between the transferor and the transferee, and on the value of the assets received. Spouses and descendants pay inheritance and gift tax at a rate of 7% to 30%. Spouses receive a personal allowance of EUR 500,000 and a maintenance allowance of up to a maximum of EUR 256,000. Children receive a personal allowance of EUR 400,000 and an age-dependent maintenance allowance of up to EUR 52,000; grandchildren in principle receive a personal allowance of EUR 200,000. Transfers between most other relatives are taxed at a rate of 15% to 43%. Between unrelated persons, the applicable tax rate is 30% or 50% (for a transfer of more than EUR 6 million).

Besides income tax and inheritance and gift tax, only a few other taxes are relevant for private clients. A real estate transfer tax with different regional rates ranging from 3.5% to 6.5% applies to the acquisition of real estate or a substantial shareholding (at least 90%) in a company holding real estate. Furthermore, real estate tax is levied annually and is calculated on the basis of rates determined by the local authorities, and property values, which were last assessed in 1964 or 1935. However, the German Federal Constitutional Court found that these obsolete valuation methods are inconsistent with the constitutional principle of equality of taxation. In October 2019, the German Parliament passed a law that is supposed to change how the assessment of property values is conducted by local authorities from 1 January 2022 onwards. Due to the new tax law, more than 30 million properties have to be reassessed. For this purpose, property owners will have to submit tax returns as early as 2022. For this, each state will require different information from taxpayers, which further complicates the matter.

Trusts are generally not recognised in Germany. The use of trust structures in connection with German resident settlors or beneficiaries or German assets can therefore trigger inheritance and gift tax in several ways. The establishment of a trust by residents or of a trust comprising assets located in Germany is considered to be a transfer of assets that is taxable in accordance with the Inheritance and Gift Tax Act. Distributions to beneficiaries during the trust period or on the trust's dissolution may trigger income tax and gift tax as well, if the beneficiary is a German resident or if German *situs* assets are distributed. The relationship between gift tax on the one hand and income tax on the other with regard to trust distributions has not yet been ultimately clarified by the courts. According to a recent ruling of the German Federal Fiscal Court (BFH II R 6/16), distributions from foreign family foundations to German resident beneficiaries are only subject to gift tax if they do not comply with the statutory purposes of the foundation or if the beneficiaries have an enforceable entitlement to distributions. Even though the ruling referred to foreign family foundations, it should also be applicable to trusts.

In addition, corporate tax can be triggered if income is received by a foreign trust from German sources. The worldwide income of a foreign trust may be subject to corporate tax if the trust's management is in Germany and if certain other conditions are met; for example, if the effective management of a trust is vested with a trustee resident in Germany.

Undistributed income received by a foreign trust can be attributed to the settlor or the beneficiaries if they are German residents. In this case, it can be subject to the settlor's or the beneficiary's personal income tax.

FREQUENTLY ASKED QUESTIONS

1. What are possible structuring options with regard to shares held in a corporation (>1%) that prevent the triggering of exit taxation under Section 6 FTA?

Two possible solutions are the implementation of a foundation or a management holding company in the legal form of a partnership.

Both options can have the effect that the shares in the corporation are not withdrawn from the German tax base and are therefore not subject to exit taxation under Section 6 FTA.

However, it should be noted that both structuring options have certain other tax consequences themselves.

2. How can I best set up my philanthropic project in Germany?

Clients who wish to implement a philanthropic project in Germany often feel overwhelmed by all the bureaucratic burden. They are often concerned not only with maximizing tax savings that certain structuring options can bring, but more importantly with making the philanthropic project sustainable. Within the framework of a variety of options, a charitable foundation or a non-profit limited liability company are often the most suitable vehicles.

Both options have their advantages and disadvantages and depend on the goals of the philanthropist.

If the philanthropist intends a more flexible solution and a moderate capital outlay, this argues in favour of the non-profit limited liability company.

If, on the other hand, it is important to the philanthropist to pursue the charitable goals they have set for a long time, even after their death, this speaks in favour of a charitable limited liability company.

2.2 Local legislative and regulatory developments

The relevant areas of law are all governed at the federal level, so there are no local developments.

2.3 National case law developments

Recent decisions by the German Federal Fiscal Court on matters of inheritance and gift tax with regard to foreign trusts resolved some previous ambiguities about the gift tax treatment of trusts in Germany. The Court has clarified and confirmed criteria under which a trust qualifies as opaque or transparent for inheritance and gift tax purposes. The crucial factor is how much power over the transferred assets still lies with the settlor. Generally speaking, a trust is transparent if the settlor can access its funds or assets like their bank account. Whether a settlor can freely dispose of the trust's assets or whether a beneficiary has a sufficient legal claim to demand distributions is to be determined by the applicable foreign trust law. The burden of proof lies with the taxpayer. Transparent trusts are effectively considered non-existent by German tax law. Therefore, the trust's assets are attributed to either the settlor or the beneficiaries (depending on the specific circumstances). Opaque trusts, on the other hand, are treated in a similar way to foreign foundations. For income tax purposes, distributions made by an opaque trust are treated as capital income (similar to dividends). An additional gift tax may only be levied if distributions are made in violation of the provisions of the trust deed or if the recipient is legally entitled in any way to receive the distributed funds (i.e., has a claim to receive distributions as a beneficiary or remainderman). In such cases, trust distributions may trigger both inheritance and gift tax and income tax.

2.4 Local case law developments
See above Section 2.3 National case law developments. Court decisions of local courts are usually relevant beyond the borders of the individual federal state and should therefore be considered nationwide.

2.5 Practice trends
The most recent rulings of the Federal Fiscal Court as outlined above provide more clarity, but some uncertainties remain. It remains to be seen what conclusions and practice trends will be drawn from this.

2.6 Pandemic related developments
No pandemic-related developments are to be highlighted.

3. ESTATE AND TRUST LITIGATION AND CONTROVERSY

3.1 National legislative and regulatory developments
No national legislative and regulatory developments concerning trusts are to be highlighted here.

3.2 Local legislative and regulatory developments
The relevant areas of law are all governed at the federal level, so there are no local developments.

3.3 National case law developments
The above-mentioned decisions of the Federal Fiscal Court also have an impact on inheritance tax in the area of trusts. The assets of an opaque trust are no longer attributable to the settlor and can therefore, under domestic inheritance law, be subject neither to statutory succession nor to a disposition upon death (non-transparent trust). If, as described above, the settlor of the trust has reserved for himself so many powers of control over the trust assets that he can deal with them in a manner comparable to a bank deposit, the trust is a transparent trust. The assets of a transparent trust can be inherited and are therefore subject to inheritance tax.

3.4 Local case law developments
Local case law developments are considered above in Section 3.3 where national case law developments are outlined. Court decisions of local courts usually have a relevance beyond the borders of the federal states and can therefore not be considered separately.

3.5 Practice trends
In the private sector, a transfer of assets subject to usufruct is a suitable option.

Usufruct (Sections 1030 *et seq.* of the German Civil Code (BGB)) is a form of easement and entitles the usufructuary to draw the benefits from the encumbered property himself. The usufruct is often used in the transfer of real estate. The advantage is that the asset substance is transferred and the allowances are used, but the income remains with the donor. For inheritance tax and gift tax purposes, a separate property value is determined and the usufruct burden with its capitalized value is deducted from this.

3.6 Pandemic related developments

No pandemic-related developments are to be highlighted in this field.

AUTHOR BIOGRAPHIES

Andreas Richter

Dr. Andreas Richter LLM is a partner at Poellath. He has outstanding experience in business and wealth succession, estate planning, legal and tax structuring of private wealth and family offices, corporate governance for family-owned businesses, expatriation taxation and charities, as well as in trust and foundation law. Some of Germany's leading family offices, family businesses and foundations, as well as their peers abroad, form the client base for Andreas's work as a legal and tax adviser. Clients in common law jurisdictions often engage Andreas owing to his background in English law (BA Hons, Trinity College, Cambridge) and US law (LLM, Yale Law School). He is listed in domestic and international rankings as one of the leading lawyers in his practice areas. Among others, Who's Who Legal: Germany 2021 lists Andreas as one of the 'Most Highly Regarded Individuals' in the practice area 'Private Client'. Andreas is the managing director of the Berlin Tax Policy Forum (Berliner Steuergespräche), chair of the executive board of the inheritance law and business succession postgraduate programme at the University of Muenster and a member of the International Academy of Estate and Trust Law. He serves as a member on boards of family offices, foundations and family businesses and acts as executor. Andreas is the editor of the leading German compendium on foundations and trusts and related tax issues. He is also the author and editor of numerous other publications, commentaries and compendiums, in particular on family offices, foundation law, business succession and all tax-related matters.

Katharina Hemmen

Dr. Katharina Hemmen LLM is admitted as an attorney-at-law and tax adviser. As a partner at Poellath in Frankfurt, she focuses on legal and tax advice with regard to domestic and international tax law, inheritance law and succession planning, as well as trust and foundation law. She regularly speaks at conferences, such as those of the International Bar Association, on private client topics, and has been ranked as 'One to watch' in the Private Client Global Elite by Legal Week. She has authored many publications in her practice areas. In 2023 she was admitted as a member of the International Academy of Estate and Trust Lawyers.

GUERNSEY

Matt Guthrie

Ogier (Guernsey) LLP

INTRODUCTION

Guernsey is an independent and self-governing island of some 63,000 or so inhabitants and a total area of around 63 square kilometres. The Bailiwick of Guernsey is made up of three main islands, being Guernsey, Alderney and Sark. Guernsey was part of the Duchy of Normandy before the conquest of England by William the Conqueror in 1066 and became annexed to the English crown through that conquest. When the French King Phillipe-Auguste conquered continental Normandy in 1204, Guernsey remained loyal to the English crown and has been a crown dependency ever since.

As such, Guernsey legal roots lie in Norman customary law but with the passing of time the island has been increasingly influenced by its links to England and English law. It is these links together with an attractive tax environment which originally led to the growth of the private wealth industry in Guernsey. Today, Guernsey offers far more than that and it is access to world class services and an experienced court system which lead clients to choose Guernsey as a destination to both relocate to and to hold their wealth through.

Guernsey is now a world leader in the provision of private wealth services and is recognised internationally as being one of the leading jurisdictions on the implementation of tax transparency and international co-operation. At the same time, Guernsey has adopted data protection legislation to ensure that individual's legitimate rights to privacy are respected at all times.

1. TAX AND WEALTH PLANNING

Guernsey does not impose any inheritance or wealth taxes and has no capital gains tax. The principal tax for individuals is income tax which is paid at a flat rate of 20% on a Guernsey resident individual's worldwide income. High net worth individuals can elect to pay a tax cap which will be set at GBP 150,000 for non-Guernsey source income and GBP 300,000 for qualifying Guernsey source income for 2023. The tax year runs from 1 January to 31 December for any given year.

Guernsey companies are subject to income tax at between 0 and 20% depending on the nature of the source of their income. Investment holding companies are generally taxed at 0%.

Non-residents are generally not subject to tax on Guernsey-source income save in certain limited circumstances – these are primarily income from real property in Guernsey and profits from a business with a permanent establishment in Guernsey.

1.1 National legislative and regulatory developments

As Guernsey is a small self-governing Island, it is not necessary to draw a distinction between national and local legislative developments. As such, all relevant developments are noted below under the local legislative heading.

1.2 Local legislative and regulatory developments

Lasting powers of attorney

The States of Guernsey has, through the Capacity (Bailiwick of Guernsey) Law, 2020 (the Capacity Law) and The Capacity (Lasting Powers of Attorney) (Bailiwick of Guernsey) Ordinance, 2022 (the LPA Ordinance), introduced into Guernsey law lasting powers of attorney (LPAs), similar to those which have existed under Jersey and English law for some time.

Whilst it is already possible to grant a power of attorney (POA) under Guernsey law, unlike an LPA, a POA ceases to be valid upon the grantor losing capacity.

A Guernsey LPA can be made in relation to details regarding health and welfare, or property and financial affairs, or both.

The principal requirements for granting a valid LPA are as follows:

- the grantor must be over 18 at the time of registration of the LPA;
- the grantor must have capacity and not be under any undue influence;
- the attorney(s) must be over 18 and, if the LPA is in respect of property and financial affairs, they must be over 18 or be a Guernsey licenced fiduciary. There are also eligibility restrictions relating to the bankruptcy and insolvency of a proposed attorney;
- the LPA can provide for successor attorney(s) to be appointed and if a grantor's spouse or civil partner is the attorney and they divorce or legally separate, then, unless expressly stated in the LPA, their appointment ceases;
- the LPA must be in a prescribed form available online from the Royal Court of Guernsey or otherwise meet the requirements of the Law and Ordinance but be immaterially different to the prescribed form;
- the LPA must be executed in line with execution guidance provided by the Royal Court of Guernsey; and
- a grantor has to register the LPA in person with HM Greffier and pay a fee.

The LPA requires the attorney to act in the best interests of the grantor, and there are safeguarding restrictions in the Capacity Law and Capacity Ordinance that prevent the LPA from being used to change the grantor's will or to make gifts of the grantor's property. In relation to health and welfare LPAs, the new legislation includes provisions relating to advance decisions to refuse treatment and advance care plans, as well as any wishes expressed before the LPA is activated.

In certain circumstances it is possible to amend, terminate or revoke a LPA. Once activated upon the grantor losing capacity (or beforehand if so provided for in the case of a property and financial affairs LPA), there are specific capacity, treatment and assessment requirements for the attorneys to adhere to and submissions to be made to HM Greffier.

Beneficial ownership information

In 2017 the States of Guernsey (the States) approved the Beneficial Ownership of Legal Persons (Guernsey) Law which introduced a non-public register of beneficial ownership of all legal persons domiciled in Guernsey (the UBO Register). It requires resident agents of such legal persons to obtain and submit relevant information to the Guernsey Registry (the Registry), and imposes duties on the beneficial owners to provide the requisite information.

At present the information on the UBO Register is not public, unlike the property register in the UK, and only specified individuals at the Guernsey Financial Services Commission (GFSC), the Financial Intelligence Unit and the Registry can access the information.

Guernsey and the other Crown Dependencies published a joint announcement on 19 June 2019 in respect of their commitment to bring each of their registers in line with EU standards (the Commitment). The legislative framework has not been fully fleshed-out and this is a developing area to monitor over the coming years. In October 2022, the States published a consultation paper in respect of one aspect of the Commitment; namely, to open up access to the UBO Register to "obliged persons". Obliged persons are those subject to AML/CFT requirements and the intention is that they will be able to gain access to certain information held on the UBO Register by way of notification to the Registry. The consultation covers aspects of the mechanics of such access and the scope of any exemptions. In response to a recent decision of the Court of Justice of the European Union (Joined Cases C-37/20) on the incompatibility of public registers with the right to respect for private life, the States announced on 22 December 2022 that the introduction of access to registers for obliged entities would be delayed pending further advice being taken.

1.3 National case law developments
As noted above, Guernsey does not distinguish between national and local case law.

1.4 Local case law developments
There have been no relevant local case law developments in this area.

1.5 Practice trends
Guernsey's status as a leading international finance centre, committed to meeting all applicable global standards, means that it continues to attract high value and complex structures for international families. The increasingly high regulatory burdens (and associated costs) means that the structures which are being established now tend to be higher value and fewer in number. Advisors in Guernsey now need to be well versed not only on how to structure wealth for clients but also as to how that wealth will be reported under the Automatic Exchange of Information (AEOI) framework.

1.6 Pandemic related developments
There were no relevant laws which were changed as a result of the pandemic. There was, however, a recognition by the Guernsey Revenue Service that restrictions on international travel may have made it more difficult for companies to comply with the economic substance requirements in Guernsey and this was taken into account when assessing compliance with such legislation.

2. ESTATE AND TRUST ADMINISTRATION
2.1 National legislative and regulatory developments
As noted above, all relevant developments are set out under local legislative developments below.

2.2 Local legislative and regulatory developments
New charities legislation
Guernsey has introduced new charities legislation to further strengthen the regulatory position of charities in the jurisdiction.

The Charities etc. (Guernsey and Alderney) Ordinance, 2021 (the Charities Ordinance) and The Charities etc. (Amendments, Exemptions, Governance and

Specified Amount) (Guernsey and Alderney) Regulations, 2022 (the Charities Regulations) set out which charities and non-profit organisations (NPOs) are required to register on the Register of Charities and provide governance guidelines.

NPOs are organisations that are established solely or principally either for the non-financial benefit of their members or for the benefit of society. On the other hand, a charity is a NPO that meets the following two additional requirements:

1) all the purposes of the entity are charitable in nature, or incidental to any of its charitable purposes; and
2) the entity provides or intends to provide benefit to the public or a section of the public locally or internationally to a reasonable degree in giving effect to its purposes.

A non-exhaustive list of charitable purposes have been set out in the Charities Ordinance and include the prevention or relief of poverty, education and religious causes. Both NPOs and charities benefit from preferential income tax rates on profits. Charities also receive tax rebates on the donations that they receive, subject to certain limitations.

NPOs must register on the Register of Charities if they reach a certain financial threshold (essentially having gross assets of GBP 100,000 or more – subject to a few exemptions) or they reach the international threshold, meaning they raise and distribute assets abroad.

There are certain concessions from some of the more onerous governance requirements under the Charities Ordinance afforded to NPOs that are administered, controlled or operated by a person regulated by the Guernsey Financial Services Commission (the GFSC), meaning that the NPO <u>need not</u> comply with the following requirements:

- the board must consist of a chair, secretary and treasurer each filled by a separate person;
- a majority of the board is Guernsey or Alderney resident; and
- that board members must be persons of integrity and probity who have suitable and appropriate skills and experience.

The Charities Regulations introduced fairly stringent and prescriptive provisions for NPOs and their governance requirements. In addition to the board requirements as detailed above, further detail is required in the constitutional documents, meaning that certain registered charities and NPOs will need to amend their constitutional documents within the timeframes described in The Charities etc (Commencement and Transitional Provisions) (Guernsey and Alderney) Regulations, 2022. Further, NPOs will also be required to keep financial records and to file annual these annually. There are also requirements to keep minutes and records of meetings and other records to ensure providence, financial probity, and transparency.

Recent and upcoming deadlines in relation with the changes introduced by the Regulations and the Ordinance are:

- from 1 August 2022, registered NPOs must identify donors and beneficiaries if they receive a donation from outside the Bailiwick or provide assets to a beneficiary outside the Bailiwick of GBP 15,000 or more in any one year, or if they receive a donation which they consider to be unusual;
- any international payments over GBP 100,000 made on or after 1 August 2022 must be reported to the Registrar (excluding the donation of physical items,

payments that are incidental to the purposes of the NPO to support a person from the Bailiwick who is residing elsewhere for reasons connected to the payment, or payments to an affiliated organisation in the UK, Jersey, or the Isle of Man);
- all NPOs must carry out a risk assessment and put in place mitigating measures where necessary — internationally focussed NPOs must have completed this by 30 November 2022 and domestic NPOs by 31 March 2023; and
- internationally focussed NPOs must also have a written anti-financial crime policy in place and filed with the Registrar by 30 November 2022.

New fiduciary legislation
A new suite of comprehensive Regulatory laws have recently been introduced and are now in force, the most relevant of which are:
- the Banking Supervision (Bailiwick of Guernsey) Law, 2020 (the Banking Law);
- the Protection of Investors (Bailiwick of Guernsey) Law, 2020 (the POI Law); and
- the Regulation of Fiduciaries, Administration Businesses and Company Directors, etc (Bailiwick of Guernsey) Law, 2020 (the Fiduciary Law), which was accompanied by the Fiduciary Rules and Guidance, 2021 (the Rules).

The primary aims of this overhaul were to consolidate the existing framework and to ensure compliance with international standards ensuring effective overall supervision.

The Rules
The Rules are much more detailed than the previous code of conduct, and include new requirements on handling client money that ensure Guernsey's regulatory regime is in line with the Standard on the Regulation of Trust and Corporate Service Providers issued by the Group of International Finance Centre Supervisors.

Lending
With Guernsey's executive, the States approval of the Lending Credit & Finance (Bailiwick of Guernsey) Law, 2022 separate licensing requirements will be introduced in relation to the provision of credit services. The primary aim of the legislation is to improve consumer protection but, with the public consultation on the guidance and implementation of the law having closed in September 2022, details of the extent of any impact on the provision of lending within trust arrangements are expected imminently.

Updated probate procedure
On 3 June 2020, the States passed a resolution approving the transfer of jurisdiction for grants of representation from the Ecclesiastical Court to the Royal Court. However, by 2021 these plans had been abandoned by agreement between the Dean of Guernsey and the States, whereby the Ecclesiastical Court retained responsibility for the probate service but committed to transferring any net surplus of the Court's fees to the States Social Investment Fund. As a result of the revised plan, the probate service has now been rebranded as the Guernsey Probate Registry and a more structured and efficient procedure put in place to receive applications for grants.

2.3 National case law developments

As noted above, all relevant developments are set out under local legislative developments below.

2.4 Local case law developments

In the *Matter of the K Trust* [2020 GLR 312] the Court of Appeal clarified the meaning of the term 'share' as used in a trust instrument. The K Trust instrument directed the trustees to, at their discretion split the Trust Fund equally between the Settlors' two daughters. If a daughter was to die with no issue, then her 'share' of the K Trust property was to be split, with half going to the other daughter and half to another trust. One of the daughters died in infancy and, thus, the Trustees applied for directions as to the true construction of the instrument.

The Court of Appeal found that the deceased daughter did have a share as the term was not a defined legal term in Guernsey trust law. It could refer to both a present and future interest. The Court thereby directed the Trustee to follow the directions in the instrument and split her share.

2.5 Practice trends

None.

2.6 Pandemic related developments

There were no pandemic related legal developments in this area.

3. ESTATE AND TRUST LITIGATION AND CONTROVERSY

3.1 National legislative and regulatory developments

As noted above, all relevant developments are set out under local legislative developments below.

3.2 Local legislative and regulatory developments

New summary civil forfeiture procedure

The Forfeiture of Money etc. in Civil Proceedings (Bailiwick of Guernsey) (Amendment) Ordinance 2022 amends the Forfeiture of Money etc. in Civil Proceedings Law, 2007 by:

- introducing a summary forfeiture procedure for cases where the law enforcement authorities have refused to consent to a transaction involving particular assets;
- reversing the burden of proof in standard civil forfeiture applications, so that where the court has frozen assets that are suspected to be linked to criminality and His Majesty's Procurer then applies for a forfeiture order, the court must make the forfeiture order unless satisfied on the balance of probabilities that the assets are not linked to criminality;
- giving the Committee for Home Affairs the power to make Regulations to introduce a procedure under which a forfeiture order can be reconsidered if new evidence comes to light;
- exonerating law enforcement authorities for costs or damages in respect of a civil forfeiture application, except for loss caused by an act or omission made in bad faith.

FREQUENTLY ASKED QUESTIONS

1. My client would like to establish a trust in Guernsey – what information will be publicly available in relation to the proposed trust?

As trusts are not entities (they are a fiduciary relationship), the trust itself is not registered anywhere and there is no register of trusts. Information about the settlor and beneficiaries would be held by any Guernsey licensed trust company in order to comply with their anti-money laundering and regulatory obligations. That information would be kept confidential save where it is required to be shared with tax authorities, regulators or law enforcement.

2. My client wants to set up a Private Trust Company (PTC) or Private Trust Foundation (PTF) to act as trustee of several family trusts – can they or their family members form part of the board of directors of the company?

It is possible for settlors and their family members to form part of the board of directors of the PTC or council of the PTF but advice should be taken in the jurisdictions in which they are tax resident before appointing them to the role to ensure they do not onshore the PTC or PTF. It is important to also consider whether they are subject to domestic legislation that could be used to obtain detailed information about the PTC/PTF, its underlying trusts and their assets.

3. My client would like to retain some control over investment decisions – what options are there?

The settlor can reserve a power to direct the trustee in relation to investments, or a power to appoint or remove an investment advisor or investment manager. The settlor could even be appointed as an investment advisor or investment manager himself.

Under Guernsey's anti-money laundering regime, it is possible for a person to request consent from the Financial Intelligence Unit (FIU) prior to undertaking a relevant act which they anticipate could result in them committing a money laundering offence. If the FIU consents, then the consent acts as a defence. The refusal of consent has to date served as an informal freezing of the assets because the person generally will not proceed with the activity for fear of committing a money laundering offence.

The new summary procedure will enable the court to make an order for the forfeiture of assets in a Bailiwick bank account where a relevant consent request has been refused at least 12 months previously.

A summary forfeiture notice with details of the court hearing will be served on the bank account holder and the bank at which the account is held. If the account holder does not attend the hearing, the court may make a forfeiture order without further notice to the recipient. If the account holder does appear, they will have to satisfy the court that the funds are not the proceeds of unlawful conduct or intended by any person for use in unlawful conduct.

3.3 National case law developments

As noted above, all relevant developments are set out under local legislative developments below

3.4 Local case law developments

Equity Trust (Jersey) Ltd (Respondent) v. Halabi (in his capacity as Executor of the Estate of the late Madam Intisar Nouri) (Appellant) (Jersey); *ITG Ltd and others (Respondents) v. Fort Trustees Ltd and another* (Appellants) (Guernsey) [2022] UKPC 36.

On 13 October the Privy Council handed down judgment in respect of appeals from the courts of appeal of both Guernsey and Jersey. Both cases concerned the rights of indemnity of successive trustees against trust assets and the ranking of the consequent indebtedness where the trust had become insolvent. The judgment addressed four outstanding questions resulting from the numerous prior judgments at first instance and on appeal concluding as follows:

- a trustee's right of indemnity confers a proprietary interest in the trust assets;
- such proprietary interest survives a change of trustees;
- a trustee's proprietary interest ranks *pari passu* with the proprietary interests of other trustees of a trust without regard to when such interests arose; and
- a trustee's indemnity extends to the costs incurred by such trustee in proving its own claim against the insolvent trust.

3.5 Practice trends

The Guernsey courts continue to be busy with trust and estate disputes. The decision in *Equity Trust* and *ITG Ltd* by the Privy Council has conclusively answered a number of questions as to priorities between trustees and creditors in insolvent trusts which is an area of law unique to Guernsey and Jersey on account of the jurisdictions' limited recourse provisions in their respective trust laws.

3.6 Pandemic related developments

The global COVID-19 pandemic has demonstrated the resilience of the financial services sector in Guernsey, with fiduciary services providers, the regulator and the Courts all adopting remote working practices. This has enabled business to continue very much as usual with little to no disruption for the end clients. Ironically, the shift away from travel and international mobility has made it easier for those in Guernsey to do business internationally, as video calls have replaced the necessity to meet clients face to face, at least, for the time being.

AUTHOR BIOGRAPHY

Matt Guthrie

Matt is frequently engaged by clients to design and implement bespoke cross border structures, to restructure existing trusts and to advise trustees in relation to complex matters and disputes. Matt also advises clients in relation to their international reporting requirements, economic substance and automatic exchange of information between jurisdictions. Matt is a member of the International Academy of Trust and Estate Practitioners and a member of STEP. Matt is the co-author of "Guernsey Trust Law" the only book dealing exclusively with trust and foundations under Guernsey law, which was published by Hart in 2020.

ISRAEL

Lyat Eyal

Aronson, Ronkin-Noor, Eyal, Law Firm and Notary

INTRODUCTION

Israel is a small State in the Middle East, established as a State in 1948. Its form of government is a democracy led by an elected prime minister with a 120-seat parliament known as the Knesset.

The legal system is based on the common law in which the Supreme Court is the highest judicial authority serving as an appellate court and a 'constitutional' court. Although there is no formal constitution, there are 13 main Basic Laws which have been legislated to serve as a type of constitution, such as the Basic Law- Knesset; Basic Law- Government; Basic Law- Judiciary; Basic Law- freedom of Occupation; and Basic Law- Human Dignity and Freedom.

Notwithstanding its mere 74 years of statehood, it is an international technological hub with extensive ongoing interest by the international business and investment communities. The track record of many start-up companies that have either gone public (mainly trading on NASDAQ) or have been merged with or into large international companies has proven to be a driving force to the local economy over the past decade.

Israel has been a member of the Organisation for Economic Cooperation and Development since 2010 (OECD), and was admitted as a full member of the Financial Action Task Force (FATF) in December 2018. The membership in these international organizations demonstrates the confidence of the international community in the country's economy and government.

The booming high-tech industry mentioned above has resulted in the creation of high net worth and ultra-high net worth individuals. These are added to existing HNW and UHNW families that have been well established mainly through conventional and industrial businesses. While the culture of estate planning and inter-generational wealth transfers remains to be developed, there is a need for these services, especially involving cross-border expertise. The generational transfers in a few families over the past few years resulting from the death of the patriarchs/matriarchs and the court family feuds has proven just how much planning is lacking and is crucial.

The main legislative authorities in the estate planning field relevant for this chapter include the Succession Law-1956; the Trust Law 1979; the Tax Ordinance [New Version]. A number of relevant governmental agencies include the Tax Authority, the Anti-Money Laundering Authority, the Inheritance Registrar and the family courts. (Note: There is extensive legislation pending that, if passed, is likely to change much of the existing legislation. The information contained in this chapter may not be relied upon without independent professional advice.)

1. TAX AND WEALTH PLANNING

Israel's tax system for Israeli tax residents is based on worldwide taxation. For foreign tax residents, as a general rule, Israeli taxes are imposed on their Israeli source income and gains. Further, contrary to tax systems in many jurisdictions internationally, the Israeli tax system is based on withholdings and while there is an annual tax reporting obligation, there are many exceptions to said obligation. As a result, many Israeli residents do not file annual tax returns.

In addition, new immigrants and long-term returning residents are subject to a special tax regime as mentioned further below.

As of 2022, the personal income tax rates are as follows:

- Employment income: 10-47% based on progressive rates, depending on the income amount.
- Interest income: 15-25%.
- Capital gains: 25-30% (depending on the % of ownership in the company which is the source of the capital gain).
- Surtax: An additional tax at the rate of 3% over taxable income in the approximate amount of USD 195,000 is imposed annually on individuals.
- In addition, there are compulsory payments to the national insurance agency which also covers health insurance. The amounts differ depending on a few factors such as an individual's employments status, age, marital status and the number of children.
- Wealth transfer taxes: no estate or inheritance taxes are imposed in Israel. Also, no gift taxes are imposed unless the gift is in kind to foreign residents resulting in capital gains taxes.

1.1 National legislative and regulatory developments

Taxation

A public committee in the field of international taxation was appointed by the Israel Tax Commissioner in 2021 and comprised governmental tax experts and private sector tax experts, including from the Bar and CPA associations. The purpose of this committee was to simplify as well as grant certainty and efficacy to the Israeli tax system.

The committee's report was submitted to the Tax Commissioner in November 2021 and covered various areas including residence, exit taxes, new immigrant tax benefits, CFC rules, relief from double taxes on foreign source income, foreign residents and their tax obligations in Israel and other areas relevant to international taxes.

This chapter will address a few key points of the report that may be relevant to an international audience with an emphasis on the fact that these are recommendations that have not yet been legislated.

Current legislation: residence

As of January 1, 2003, generally, the tax system in Israel taxes Israeli resident individuals on their worldwide income subject to credits granted in Israel for certain taxes paid in a foreign country in accordance with the provisions of the Tax Ordinance [New Version] (Ordinance) and any relevant tax treaty.

The Ordinance provides that Israeli residence of individuals is determined based on a qualitative and a quantitative test as set forth below:

- An individual whose center of life is in Israel will be considered an Israeli resident. Criteria reviewed in a determination of one's center of life includes, but is not limited to, a permanent residence/home of the individual and the individual's family members, the individual's place of business or employment, the individual's place of vital financial interests and activity in organizations or various institutions (the "qualitative test").

- A rebuttable presumption (the presumption may be rebutted by the Tax Authority or the taxpayer) of Israeli residence is created where an individual is present in Israel for at least 183 days in any tax year or is present in Israel for at least 30 days in a tax year and a total of at least 425 days cumulatively together with the immediately preceding two tax years (the "quantitative test"). A 'day' includes any part of a day

In addition, there is a subjective test of where an individual <u>views</u> their center of life. While this is not a strong test, in some cases it can be a 'tie breaker'.

The Ordinance further provides the definition of a foreign resident by two options:

- Any individual who is not an Israeli resident.
- An individual is a foreign resident if, over a period of four years, two of the four cumulative tests are satisfied:
  - In the first and in the second year, the individual was present abroad at least 183 days in each year.
  - In the third and fourth year the individual's center of life was not in Israel.

The center of life test has resulted in disputes between the Tax Authority and taxpayers, some of which have led to extensive litigation and high-profile precedents. As a result, the committee's objective was to create certainty in the determination of residence by way of irrebuttable presumptions/conclusive determinations of residence, in Israel or abroad. Notwithstanding, the Committee decided to maintain the center of life test, as a rebuttable presumption, where the definitions of an Israeli resident or a foreign resident do not apply.

The Committee's Recommendations

The Committee's Recommendations relating to Israeli residence of individuals for tax purposes are set forth below. These are each, as a stand-alone, conclusive evidence of Israeli residence:

- An individual is present in Israel at least 183 days per year during two consecutive tax years. Residence will commence in the first year in which the individual was present at least 183 days.
- An individual is present in Israel at least 100 days in any tax year and a total of at least 450 days cumulatively together with the immediately preceding two tax years. This presumption will not result in the individual being an Israeli resident if the individual was present in a treaty country at least 183 days in each of the relevant tax years reviewed subject to providing a residence certificate for tax purposes in the treaty country for the relevant tax years.
- An individual is present in Israel at least 100 days in any tax year and the individual's spouse or cohabiting partner is an Israeli resident.

In addition, the Committee's Recommendations include the presumptions listed below which will be irrebuttable/conclusive evidence of the individual's residence abroad:

1) An individual present in Israel less than 30 days in every tax year during the last 4 consecutive tax years will be considered a foreign resident from the first tax year.

2) An individual present in Israel less than 30 days in every tax year during the last 3 consecutive tax years will be considered a foreign resident from the second tax year.
These irrebuttable presumptions (1 & 2) will apply if the individual is not present in Israel at least 15 days in the first month of the first tax year or the last month in the final tax year.

3) An individual and spouse, present in Israel less than 60 days in each tax year during a period of 4 consecutive tax years, will be considered foreign residents from the first tax year.

4) An individual and spouse, present in Israel less than 60 days in each tax year during a period of 3 consecutive tax years, will be considered foreign residents from the second tax year.
These irrebuttable presumptions (3 & 4) will apply if the individual and spouse are not present in Israel at least 30 days in the first 2 months of the first tax year or the last 2 months in the final tax year.

5) An individual and spouse, present in Israel less than 100 days in each tax year during a period of 4 consecutive tax years, will be considered foreign residents from the first tax year provided that the individual and spouse were present in a treaty country in each tax year at least 183 days and provided a residence certificate for tax purposes in the treaty country for the relevant tax years.

6) An individual and spouse, present in Israel less than 100 days in each tax year during a period of 3 consecutive tax years, will be considered foreign residents from the second tax year provided that the individual and spouse were present in a treaty country in each tax year at least 183 days and provided a residence certificate for tax purposes in the treaty country for the relevant tax years is presented.
These irrebuttable presumptions (5 & 6) will apply if the individual and spouse are not present in Israel at least 50 days during the first 100 days of the first tax year or the last 100 days of the final tax year.

New immigrants/Israeli citizens returning to Israel
The Ordinance provides special rules for certain residence categories. These include the new immigrant, the long-term returning resident and the returning resident. For the purpose of this chapter, an individual who has never been an Israeli resident in the past and moves to reside in Israel for the first time will be referred to as a "new immigrant".

The Ordinance provides, as a general rule, that an individual who has become an Israeli resident for the first time after 2007 is entitled to a tax exemption in Israel for a period of ten years, on all such individual's foreign source income. This includes income such as active or passive income and capital gains; all as long as the income is derived abroad (the "New Immigrant Benefits"). In addition, new immigrants are not required to file tax returns in Israel in connection with their foreign source income during the 10-year exemption period. The reporting exemption is a topic of great concern to the Tax Authority and a constant demand for its abolishment is voiced, including internationally. The committee's recommendation is that the reporting exemption for new immigrants be abolished while maintaining the tax exemption.

The Taxation of Trusts
The committee recommended further deliberations and recommendations specifically on the taxation of trusts.

The Ordinance sets forth the following five categories of trusts.

1. Israeli residents trust (IRT)
The IRT, at the time of its settlement, requires that:
- at least one settlor and one beneficiary are Israeli residents; and
- during the tax year, at least one settlor or one beneficiary is an Israeli resident.

The IRT is the default category for any trust that does not match the definition of any other trust under the Ordinance.

The IRT is subject to annual reporting in Israel and is taxable on its worldwide income. Distributions to beneficiaries are not subject to taxes once the tax payments are made by the trustee.

2. Foreign beneficiary trust (FBT)
The FBT is settled by an Israeli resident for the benefit of individual foreign residents.

The trust must meet all of the following:
- it is irrevocable;
- all of the beneficiaries are identified individuals and are foreign residents; and
- at least one settlor is an Israeli resident.

If all above conditions are met upon the settlement of the trust, the trust deed must provide that no Israeli beneficiary can be added as a beneficiary of the trust and the settlor must declare that there is no Israeli resident beneficiary or an Israeli resident who may be appointed a beneficiary if they cease to be an Israeli resident.

If the assets and income of a FBT are derived from sources abroad, there is no taxation in Israel. If the assets and income are derived from sources within Israel, the trust is taxable in Israel. The trust is subject to reporting obligations upon its settlement and annually as confirmation of the beneficiaries' residence abroad. Exit tax may be applicable upon the settlement of assets in the trust.

3. Foreign resident trust (FRT)
All settlors and all beneficiaries of a FRT are and have always been non-residents of Israel. Recognized Israeli charitable organizations, as beneficiaries, do not change the trust categorization.

The FRT is treated as a foreign resident for tax purposes and is subject to reporting and tax obligations in Israel only to the extent that it holds Israeli assets or derives income from Israeli sources.

4. Israeli resident beneficiary trust (IRBT)
The IRBT is settled by a non-resident of Israel where at least one beneficiary is an Israeli resident.

Two additional criteria must be met for an IRBT to be an Israeli relatives' trust. First, the settlor and the beneficiaries must be immediate family members. Second, the settlor must be living.

If all criteria are met the IRBT is subject to tax obligations as follows:

- The default option – distributions to Israeli resident beneficiaries are taxed at the rate of 30% of the distribution unless the trustee provides evidence of the income and capital portions of the distribution. A distribution of capital is not taxable. Note that the Tax Authority's position is that income is distributed first.
- The trustee may opt to subject trust income allocated to an Israeli resident beneficiary to tax at the rate of 25% in the tax year in which the income is accrued. If the tax payment is made annually, distributions to beneficiaries are not taxable.

Either option chosen by the trustee, either actively or by default, is irreversible.

If even one of the above additional criteria is not met, the IRBT trust will be taxed as an IRT.

5. *Testamentary trust*

A testamentary trust is settled under an Israeli resident's last will and testament and subject to the categories above.

Anti-Money Laundering

The Anti Money Laundering Law 2000 (AML Law) is aimed at the prevention of money laundering, through means such as the imposition of due diligence and know your client requirements on professionals in the private sector. These professionals include banks, credit card companies, investment institutions and lawyers and accountants who provide a business service to clients. The AML Law provides for AML offences to result in criminal prosecutions with between at least 5-10 years of imprisonment as well as fines and asset confiscation if the assets are obtained through criminal activity under the AML Law. The AML Law allows for international cooperation between Israel and foreign authorities in the area of money laundering and terrorist financing.

In March 2022, the Ministry of Justice published a draft bill amending the AML Law (AML Proposed Amendment) seeking to grant the Anti-Money Laundering Authority supervisory and enforcement authority over financial service providers in the area of money laundering and terror financing. This is not yet legislation but is expected to be passed in the next few months.

1.2 Local legislative and regulatory developments

Israel is a small country where there is no division between a federal/state or a national/local system but rather one national government and a national court system.

1.3 National case law developments

There have been court precedents relating to the question of tax residence over the past few years. The case of *Babachanov* issued in 2021, reviewed the question of tax residence where the family unit and thereby the center of life is split between spouses in different jurisdictions. The case involved a wife and children residing in Israel and a claim by the husband to his center of life in a different country, including a cohabitation relationship in said country with another woman.

The court, not impressed by the facts, found the husband to have had his center of life in Israel due to factors such as business activity in Israel, presence in Israel, a close relationship with his wife and children in Israel and therefore taxable in Israel.

1.4 Local case law developments
Israel is a small country where there is no division between a federal/state or a national/local system but rather one national government and a national court system.

1.5 Practice trends
The issue of residence and the rebuttable presumptions under the current legislation has resulted in litigation over the past few years. If passed as drafted, the Ordinance will provide clearer guidance and certainty on this point.

1.6 Pandemic related developments
Questions of residence in Israel during the COVID-19 pandemic by those that were unable to travel have been arising and will continue to arise. One of the areas where this issue will be most relevant relates to new immigrants. As mentioned above, the Ordinance provides that new immigrants are entitled to a tax exemption on their foreign source income.

Ethics- Attorney Duty of Confidentiality
While not specifically connected to private client practice, an important ethics opinion was issued by the Ethics Committee of the Bar Association in January 2022 impacting the legal profession at large. The main recommendations of the Ethics Committee are:
- The requirement that attorneys review the service providers and the licenses of their computer software programs and the security of email servers.
- Protection and security of all digital activities including email, internet and desktop stations.
- Review of all software used by the attorney and the relevant security updates.
- Review and updates of passwords including remote access.
- Confirmation that video conferences and meetings are adequately secure to avoid access by third parties and/or unauthorized recoding without the knowledge of the participants.
- Regular participation in seminars on cyber security during 2022 and thereafter at least bi- annually.
- Maintaining firm policy/guidelines for employees.
- Having a cyber-attack and/or privacy breach plan for a quick recovery therefrom, including a policy of client updates.

2. ESTATE AND TRUST ADMINISTRATION
2.1 National legislative and regulatory developments
There is no recognition of foreign probate proceedings in Israel and orders granted by such proceedings abroad are invalid in Israel (*The Attorney General v.*

Agam; C.A. 970/93). As a result, probate proceedings must be filed in Israel for the distribution of a foreign resident's Israeli estate. For administrative purposes, it is advisable for foreign residents, during their planning, to execute a separate Israeli will to govern Israeli assets. Such a will is generally shorter than foreign wills as Israel does not impose estate or gift taxes and will allow probate in Israel to commence with the Israeli will without the need to obtain exemplified court copies of the foreign will from abroad.

2.2 Local legislative and regulatory developments
Israel is a small country where there is no division between a federal/state or a national/local system but rather one national government and a national court system.

2.3 National case law developments
The appointment of an executor is not obligatory for Israeli estates. The appointment process requires the consent of all heirs and a specific application for such appointment. While a named executor in a will is relevant, it is not a determinative factor in an appointment, in general, or in the appointment of the named individual. A court decision from July 2022 affirmed the court's authority not to appoint an individual named in a will as the executor of the estate under the specific circumstances of the case. These facts included a complicated and untrustworthy relationship between the parties and the concern for no cooperation, conflicts and controversies and the need to have the court involved on a regular basis to resolve these conflicts.

2.4 Local case law developments
Israel is a small country where there is no division between a federal/state or a national/local system but rather one national government and a national court system.

2.5 Practice trends
Where a decedent executed a separate Israeli will, probate proceedings can commence in Israel more efficiently. In addition, the translation of a foreign will to Hebrew for the Israeli proceedings will be more expensive than the translation of a shorter Israeli will. Foreign estate planners advising clients owning assets in Israel should advise that clients receive local advice.

2.6 Pandemic related developments
Amendments in the areas of document execution were adopted during the pandemic by the Ethics Committee of the Israel Bar Association, initially as emergency and temporary solutions but thereafter remained valid for powers of attorney, affidavits and durable powers of attorney. There is no remote witnessing for wills or notarization of documents (which the Israeli Bar strongly opposes).

Execution of Durable Powers of Attorney
The completion, execution and filing of a durable power of attorney (DPA) are governed by the Legal Capacity and Guardianship Law 1962. The DPA allows a competent adult to appoint an agent to act on behalf of said adult in the event of

FREQUENTLY ASKED QUESTIONS

1. As a foreign resident, will the last will executed in my country of residence be recognized in Israel?

As no foreign probate order is recognized in Israel to transfer assets owned by a foreign decedent, the foreign last will will be submitted to probate in Israel. While it will be valid in Israel, if valid in the country of residence, the process will be simpler with a separate will relating only to Israeli assets.

2. As a grantor/settlor of a foreign trust, what should I consider if one of my children, a beneficiary of the trust immigrates to Israel?

Any trust in which there are foreign resident beneficiaries together with Israeli resident beneficiaries will ultimately create an unwanted tax result. A separate trust for Israeli resident beneficiaries should be created prior to immigration to Israel.

the loss of legal capacity. The forms are completed by a duly qualified attorney who also witnesses and confirms the signatures of principals and agents. The executed forms are filed in a database of the Guardian General.

As part of the remote signature witnessing passed during the pandemic, the attorney must witness and confirm the signature of a principal in person. The signature of agents may be witnessed remotely and a specific procedure must be followed when filing a DPA witnessed remotely.

Execution of Powers of Attorney

Unlike the DPA, the validity of a power of attorney that is not a DPA will lapse upon the loss of capacity by the principal. The remote execution of a power of attorney in favor of an attorney, as agent, may be permitted if the client is an existing client of the attorney and both are present in Israel at the time of the remote execution. Any power of attorney in favor of third parties requires an in-person signature before an Israeli notary as mentioned above.

Execution of Affidavits

The remote execution of affidavits is permitted pursuant to guidance issued by the Ethics Committee of the Israel Bar Association under the circumstance below:

- The client must be identified through an identification process via a website managed by the government (the Governmental Identification System).
- Both the client/affiant and the attorney are present in Israel at the time of the video call.
- The affiant presents an identification document during the video call.
- The attorney reads a warning to the client which the affiant confirms.
- The attorney must record the meeting pursuant to the affiant's consent. The recording should include a declaration of the date, time, subject matter and the attorney's identifying details.
- The attorney receives a copy of the affiant's identification document and the client's signature on the document (whether by scan or signed digitally) and confirms said signature.

3. ESTATE AND TRUST LITIGATION AND CONTROVERSY

3.1 National legislative and regulatory developments

No foreign probate order is recognized in Israel to transfer assets owned by a foreign decedent. As such, a separate will relating solely to assets in Israel will simplify the local probate process.

3.2 Local legislative and regulatory developments

Israel is a small country where there is no division between a federal/state or a national/local system but rather one national government and a national court system.

3.3 National case law developments

An important decision in the area of trusts, gifts, corporate laws, contract laws and other legislation was issued by the Tel Aviv District Court (*Markus et al v. Pat*; Tel Aviv Financial Court 20569-07-17). The case involved the applicant, David Markus, Deceased (the "Deceased"), whose heirs succeeded him in the procedure as of June 3, 2018 when he passed away (the "Applicants") who filed a claim for the court to assert that the respondent, Ms. Pat, had no proprietary rights in certain shares of the Applicants (the "Corporate Shares") despite the formal registration thereof in her name. Following a long and arduous court process, the court found that the Corporate Shares were registered jointly in the Deceased's and Ms. Pat's name for the purpose of Ms. Pat holding said shares in trust without granting her proprietary rights in the Corporate Shares.

3.4 Local case law developments

Israel is a small country where there is no division between a federal/state or a national/local system but rather one national government and a national court system.

3.5 Practice trends

There is a trend for a separate will referring to Israeli assets.

3.6 Pandemic related developments

As mentioned above, foreign probate court orders are not valid in Israel. Pursuant to the Succession Law 1965 (Section 137), (Succession Law), as a general rule, the governing law of the distribution of a foreign resident's estate is the law of the decedent's jurisdiction of residence.

Also, the Succession Law (Section 140) provides that a last will will be recognized as a valid will in Israel under the following circumstances:

- If the will is valid under Israeli law.
- If the will is valid under the laws of the country where it was executed.
- If the will is valid under the laws of the country of domicile or residence of the testator at the time of its execution or at the time of the testator's death.
- If the will is valid under the laws of the testator's country of citizenship at the time of its execution or at the time of the testator's death.

As to the legal capacity to execute a last will, it will be recognized if the will is valid under the laws of the testator's country of domicile at the time of its execution.

As part of the probate proceedings, a legal opinion is submitted in Israel opining on the validity of a non-resident's foreign will and the distribution of the Israeli estate. The issues of remotely executed wills and their validity in Israel will likely appear before the Israeli courts during local probate proceedings over the next few years when non-resident testators pass away with a valid remotely executed foreign will.

AUTHOR BIOGRAPHY

Lyat Eyal

Lyat Eyal is a partner at Aronson, Ronkin-Noor, Eyal, Law Firm and Notary where she manages the firm's private client practice with a focus on international families, multi-jurisdictional cross border estate planning issues including trusts, wills, taxation of trusts and pre-immigration planning. Lyat also provides probate and estate administration services. Lyat was admitted to the New York State Bar in 1998 and to the Israel Bar in 2005. Lyat is a member of the Society of Trust and Estate Practitioners (STEP) and the New York State Bar Association Trusts and Estates Law and International Sections. Lyat is a Fellow at the American College of Trust and Estate Counsel (ACTEC) and an Academician at the International Academy of Estate and Trust Law (TIAETL). Lyat publishes regularly in distinguished professional publications and speaks at seminars and conferences internationally in her areas of expertise.

ITALY

Raul-Angelo Papotti, Giovanni Cristofaro,
Gian Gualberto Morgigni & Camilla Culiersi
Chiomenti

INTRODUCTION

In recent years, the matter of private wealth planning has played an increasingly central role in Italy, particularly as a result of the climate of uncertainty exacerbated by the COVID-19 pandemic. People felt the need to manage and transfer their wealth in order to avoid being caught unprepared in exceptional scenarios. Italian law has always provided several wealth planning tools in order to structure and transfer estates, however the culture of assets organisation and succession planning has shown an increase only in the last few years. A sign of such increased awareness has come from the increase in the number of wills and donations. Also the settlement of trusts has increased in the last few years because of the growing interest for this instrument and, therefore, Italian jurisprudence had to become familiar with complex scenarios of settlors, multiple beneficiaries, and assets held under a legal arrangement governed by foreign law. Now we have established case law that — due to the lack of trust domestic legislation — plays a decisive role in the definition of the trust instrument, as better detailed below. Due to the acknowledgment by the Italian tax authorities of the interpretation put forward in recent years by the Italian Supreme Court concerning the indirect tax regime applicable to the settlement of trusts, trusts are expected to be even more used by individuals for tax planning purposes.

1. TAX AND WEALTH PLANNING

1.1 National legislative and regulatory developments

Italian domestic rules on the tax residence of individuals

According to Italian tax law, an individual is considered to be an Italian tax resident when, for the greatest part of the tax period, they:

- are enrolled in the registry of the Italian resident population; or
- has their domicile in the Italian territory (the place where the person usually physically stays and where they appear to be willing to stay); or
- has their residence in the Italian territory (the main centre of their economic and personal ties).

The three mentioned requirements are alternatives and not concurrent. The tax period corresponds to the calendar year. No split-year treatment is provided by the domestic legislation

Ordinary personal income tax regime

Items of income

Italian tax resident individuals are subject to personal income tax (IRPEF) in Italy on the basis of their worldwide income. Conversely, non-resident individuals are taxed only on income realized in Italy.

Individual income is classified into the following six categories:

- income from real estate;
- income from capital;
- employment income;
- self-employment income;
- business income; and
- miscellaneous income.

Applicable rates

As a general rule, the overall taxable income concurs to the IRPEF taxable basis and is subject to the following progressive rates (that have been updated starting from the 2022 tax period):

- up to EUR 15,000: 23%;
- over EUR 15,000 and up to EUR 28,000: 25%;
- over EUR 28,000 and up to EUR 50,000: 35%;
- over EUR 50,000: 43%.

Certain regional and municipal surcharges apply to the overall taxable income up to a 4% rate.

The great majority of investment and trading income is generally subject to a flat 12.5% or 26% substitute tax. In addition, certain deductions and exemptions are provided (e.g., sale of real estate assets held for more than 5 years).

Italian tax law does not provide for any exit tax for individuals.

Italian inheritance and gift tax regime

The Italian tax law provides for inheritance and gift taxes (IHT), which apply to transfers of assets and rights as a result of death, gifts, or other gratuitous transactions.

Italian resident individuals are subject to IHT on transfers upon death or gifts of all assets, wherever located, while non-Italian resident individuals are subject to IHT only on Italian *situs* assets.

IHT applies at rates ranging from 4% to 8% depending on the relationship between the deceased/donor and the heir/donee. Certain allowances are provided for close relatives.

As a general rule, the IHT taxable basis is the fair market value of the transferred assets, but different rules apply to specific assets (e.g., real estate assets).

Cadastral and mortgage taxes would be levied on any transfer of Italian-*situs* real estate at a 3% aggregate rate, regardless of whether such transfers are exempt for IHT purposes.

Exemptions from IHT are provided for certain assets (e.g., transfers of controlling shareholdings if certain conditions are met, insurance policies, and certain government bonds).

Wealth taxes

In principle, no general "net worth tax" is levied in Italy. However, any individual or entity owning Italian real estate assets is subject to a local property tax, regardless of their tax residence. The ordinary rate is 0.86% to be applied to the cadastral value of the real estate asset. Non-Italian *situs* real estate assets owned by Italian tax resident individuals are subject to an annual wealth tax at a 0.76% rate; the taxable basis varies depending on the State where the property is located.

Italian tax resident individuals are subject annually to a 0.2% wealth tax on Italian and foreign financial assets (e.g., bonds, shares, other securities, etc.). The current accounts are subject to the wealth tax at the fixed amount of EUR 34.20.

Annual tax monitoring obligations on assets held abroad apply.

Beneficial tax regimes for new residents

Italian flat tax regime

Since the 2017 tax period, individuals wishing to move their tax residence to Italy may benefit from a favorable regime provided that they have been considered non-Italian tax residents for at least 9 out of the 10 tax periods before their relocation.

The regime provides for the application of a yearly EUR 100,000 substitute tax (increased by EUR 25,000 per year for each additional family member opting for the regime) on any foreign-sourced income received by new Italian residents. Any Italian-sourced income will be ordinarily subject to IRPEF.

The main features of the Italian flat tax regime are the following:
- no IHT is due on transfers of non-Italian *situs* assets upon death or gifts;
- exemption from wealth taxes and tax monitoring obligations on assets held abroad;
- capital gains upon disposal of qualified participations in foreign companies are out of the scope of the substitute tax if incurred within 5 years from the first year of the regime's validity (the anti-avoidance rule);
- the individuals are entitled to benefit from Double Tax Treaties for income tax purposes entered into by Italy, save that the specific Double Tax Treaty provides otherwise;
- possibility to file an advance ruling request to obtain confirmation of the applicant's eligibility for the regime, confirmation that a specific item of income is covered by the substitute tax, and the possibility to disapply the anti-avoidance rule.

Italian pensioners regime

Since the 2019 tax period, non-Italian tax resident individuals holding foreign pensions and moving their tax residence to certain Italian Municipalities may opt for the Italian pensioners' regime, which provides for the application of a flat 7% substitute tax on any foreign-sourced income, provided that they have not been Italian tax resident for at least 5 tax periods before their relocation and other conditions are met. Any Italian-sourced income will be ordinarily subject to IRPEF.

The regime provides for the exemption from wealth taxes and Italian tax monitoring obligations on assets held abroad.

Italian inpatriate workers regime

Non-Italian resident workers who – irrespective of their citizenship and State of residence – transfer their tax residence to Italy, may opt for the Italian inpatriate workers regime that provides for the application of IRPEF, for five tax periods, on a portion equal to 30% of their employment income, quasi-employment income (i.e., directorship fees), self-employment income, and business income (with an effective tax rate of approximately 14%), provided that they have been non-Italian tax resident for at least 2 tax periods before their relocation and they work predominantly in Italy. The personal income tax basis is reduced to 10% if the workers transfer their residence to certain Southern Italian Regions and is increased to 50% for sportsmen.

1.2 Local legislative and regulatory developments

From a tax perspective, trusts are recognized as taxable entities, to the extent that they are not regarded as interposed under Italian tax law. The Italian tax authorities have provided several guidelines dealing with the direct and indirect tax aspects related to trusts.

Italian resident trusts are subject to tax in Italy on their worldwide income, while non-Italian resident trusts are subject to tax in Italy on their Italian-sourced income only.

Italian law provisions distinguish between opaque trusts (i.e., discretionary trusts) and transparent trusts (i.e., trusts whose beneficiaries are identified). Income realized by an opaque trust is subject to corporate income tax in the hands of the trust itself, income realized by a transparent trust is directly attributed to the beneficiaries on an accrual basis and taxed in their hands.

As regards taxation of the beneficiaries, any distribution made by a non-resident opaque trust should not be subject to income tax in the hands of the beneficiaries, unless the trust is established in a low-tax jurisdiction. In this latter case, the income distribution is subject to IRPEF in the hands of the Italian tax resident beneficiaries according to a tax provision that is in force from the 2019 tax period.

On 20 October 2022, the Italian tax authority released Circular Letter No. 34/E, concerning direct and indirect taxation applicable to trusts and beneficiaries, as well as tax monitoring obligations.

In particular, with respect to indirect taxes (IHT and mortgage and cadastral taxes), the guidance acknowledged the position of the Italian Supreme Court provided in several judgments in the last years, according to which the transfer of assets to a trust does not entail an immediate and actual transfer of the ownership of such assets and then is not subject to indirect taxes at proportional rates. Indeed, the indirect taxes will be due in case of distribution of the assets settled in the trust to the beneficiaries.

1.3 National case law developments

In the past 4/5 years, the indirect taxation of trusts has been addressed in several decisions of the Italian Supreme Court. Indeed, the judges stated that the transfer of an asset to a trust does not produce an immediate and actual translational effect, but shall rather be considered as a mere impoverishment of the settlor, not linked by default to a correspondent enrichment of the beneficiary which is, in turn, the event giving rise to the application of inheritance and gift tax. Such interpretation is now consolidated and has also recently been agreed upon by the Italian tax authorities, which in the past called upon the application of indirect taxes (including IHT) upon the transfer of assets by the settlor to the trust (irrespective of the effective enrichment of the beneficiaries).

1.4 Local case law developments

In recent judgments, the Italian local tax Courts dealt with the tax regime applicable to financial life insurance policies (e.g., unit-linked policies), outlining the factual and contractual elements relevant to the disapplication of the beneficial tax regime applicable to life insurance policies.

The elements taken into account by the Courts are, *inter alia*, the following:

- no minimum return guarantee and obligation to return the invested capital;
- no coverage from demographic risk, as there was no premium for the occurrence of death (i.e., in case the company only has the obligation to liquidate the value of the financial instruments included in the policy);
- option to request early redemptions, either total or partial, making the contract term irrelevant;
- the policyholder provides instructions concerning the specific investments underneath the policy; and
- the insurance company does not bear any effective risk concerning the insured event.

In a nutshell, life insurance policies are subject to the following tax treatment:

- a 26% substitute tax on the difference between the amounts transferred to the policy and the amounts received upon redemption;
- the postponement of taxation upon the redemption;
- exemption from income taxes for the amounts payable by the insurance company for the coverage of the insured event; and
- exemption from IHT.

If a financial policy is disregarded, the assets under the policy are considered to be held by the policyholder and the income arising from such assets would be subject to tax on a cash basis according to the relevant tax regime.

1.5 Practice trends

Due to the acknowledgment by the Italian tax authorities of the interpretation put forward in recent years by the Italian Supreme Court concerning the indirect tax regime applicable to the settlement of trusts, trusts are expected to be even more used by individuals for tax planning purposes.

Indeed, the new guidance of the Italian tax authority confirms that IHT shall apply at the moment of the transfer of the trusts' assets to the beneficiaries as a final transfer. The guidance further confirms that:

- in order to determine the different applicable IHT rates the line of kinship existing between the settlor and the beneficiary of the trust at the moment when the assets are transferred to the beneficiaries should be considered; and
- the moment when the assets are settled to the trust should be considered in order to the determine whether such transfer falls within the territorial scope of IHT or not.

According to this new interpretation, the IHT might never be due in case no capital distribution is made to the beneficiaries.

1.6 Pandemic related developments

Italy has not issued any law or regulation concerning this issue. The Italian government has entered into specific agreements with certain foreign States concerning the taxation of frontier employees working in home offices due to the continuance of the COVID-19 pandemic.

Also, the Italian tax authorities focused their attention on the possible configuration of permanent establishments in Italy of foreign companies as a result of the fact that certain employees were forced to work from their homes in Italy due to the restriction to movements as a result of the pandemic.

2. ESTATE AND TRUST ADMINISTRATION

2.1 National legislative and regulatory developments

The matter of estate administration is provided in Italy by the second book of the Italian Civil Code, which was adopted by Royal Decree No 262 on 16 March 1942. Since then there have been no particular legislative developments on the matter. In general, Italian law provides for various figures who have the task of administering the assets of the estate from the moment of the opening of the deceased's succession until the moment of the acquisition of the assets by the relevant heirs. Specifically, under the will a testator can appoint a third person in whom they place particular trust as executor of their will: it is understood that the appointment of an executor is not mandatory. The subject appointed as executor shall administer the deceased's estate to ensure that the provisions of the deceased's will are executed accurately: estate administration can involve selling real estate, preparing tax returns, paying debts, and preparing and furnishing accountings to beneficiaries, all of which must be handled appropriately before bequests are given to the beneficiaries. While performing his office, the executor may perform acts of extraordinary administration, subject to the authorisation of the judge, after hearing the heirs.

With reference to trust administration, Italian law does not provide for domestic legislation concerning trusts; trusts are recognized and enforced in Italy pursuant to the provisions of the Hague Convention of 1 July 1985 on the law applicable to trusts and their recognition, which was ratified in Italy with Law No 364 of 16 October 1989. Due to the lack of domestic legislation, trusts can only be established in Italy subject to a foreign governing law that provides for trusts (and in accordance with the Convention provisions). As a consequence, the trust administration is also regulated by the foreign law chosen as the governing law of that trust together with the relevant Convention provisions.

2.2 Local legislative and regulatory developments

Italy has no local legal provisions on estate and trust administration; therefore, there have been no regulatory developments in this regard.

2.3 National case law developments

There have been no significant developments in the national case law of recent years in regard to estate administration and many decisions recently adopted by the Italian Supreme Court have merely reaffirmed long-established principles.

In particular, with reference to the role of the executor of an Italian will, the Italian Supreme Court has clarified in several recent judgments that the executor of a will acts in its own name but in the exclusive interest of executing the will's provisions, under the control of the judicial authority (*inter alia*, Italian Supreme Court, decision No. 24147 dated 26 November 2015) at the same time, the executor is required to manage the estate of the deceased, taking possession of the assets included in the estate, as a fair *pater familias*, and can perform all necessary acts of management with no time limits (*inter alia*, Italian Supreme Court, decision No. 12241, dated 14 June 2016).

With reference to trust administration, Italian case law decisions played a decisive role in the definition of the terms of powers and legal qualification of such activity. In the past few years, there have been several disputes among, *inter alia,* whether the assets conferred in trust should be considered as a separate fund or part of the trustee's estate. In such perspective, recent decisions have expressly recognized that the trustee's ownership of assets in the context of a trust settlement has a mere "temporary nature", and it has been clarified that the effective transfer of the ownership shall occur when such assets are transferred to the beneficiaries of the trust. More specifically, Italian Supreme Court, with decision No. 19558 dated 17 June 2022, has ruled that the transfer of assets on trust settlement does not consist of an effective transfer of ownership to the trustee. The trust assets are placed by the settlor under the control of a trustee for the benefit of a beneficiary or a specified purpose. Therefore, such assets constitute a separate fund and are not a part of the trustee's own estate, so that the trustee's creditors cannot impair them. The Supreme Court has also recently recognised the validity and effectiveness of the self-declared trust, i.e., a trust in which the trustee and settlor are the same person (*inter alia*, Italian Supreme Court, order No 734, dated 7 November 2018).

2.4 Local case law developments
As mentioned, the executor of a will must comply with provisions of the will in order to execute the wishes of the testator exactly, carrying out for this purpose mere material fulfilments. It follows that they are entitled to take part in legal proceedings involving the deceased only in order to duly implement the will's provisions. The Court of Appeal of Genova, with decision No. 440 dated 16 April 2021, has reiterated this principle. The Court has stated that – should the deceased be involved in legal proceedings during their lifetime claiming their rights against third parties – the heirs of the deceased are the sole persons entitled to take part in these proceedings after death, even if the deceased appointed an executor of the will.

By contrast, with reference to trust administration, due to the absence of domestic legislation, local case law decisions played a decisive role in the definition of such activity. In particular, the Court of Bologna, with decision No. 2209 dated 2 September 2022, has stated that – since the trust does not have a legal personality – the trustee represents the sole centre of imputation of subjective legal situations pertaining to the trust. Pursuant to the Convention provisions, the term "trust" merely refers to the legal relationship created – *inter vivos* or on death – by a person, the settlor, when assets have been placed under the control of a trustee for the benefit of a beneficiary or a specified purpose. Therefore, the trustee, having the exclusive power to dispose of the rights on the trust assets, shall be the sole person entitled to enforce them in relations with third parties. In this respect, the Court of Cassino, with decision No. 17 dated 8 January 2009, has qualified the trustee as the party entitled to take part into a proceeding commenced by a settlor's creditor in order to obtain the revocation of the deed of trust harming to his interests, since the title to the trust property stands in the name of the trustee and the latter is the sole party authorised to intervene for the protection of it.

2.5 Practice trends
Traditionally, the appointment of an executor of a will was not a widespread practice. Nowadays, in line with a more general intention of people to plan the generational transfer of their estate, this figure seems to be more valued. The appointment of an executor may take place, for instance, if the testator has no confidence in the heirs, especially when the latter's interest is at odds with certain

provisions of the will or due to the presence of disputes between those entitled to the estate or the existence of objective difficulties in executing the testator's wishes. With reference to the trust administrator, the practice of assigning such a role to legal persons – whether or not belonging to banking groups – operating on a professional basis is becoming increasingly widespread in Italy, in order to ensure continuity over time and competence in performing the task.

2.6 Pandemic related developments

Given the growing climate of uncertainty caused by the pandemic, the use of asset protection instruments continued. In particular, because of the pandemic, people felt the need to manage their wealth in order to avoid being caught unprepared in front of exceptional scenarios. The careful choice of an administrator to ensure full implementation of the testator's will or the proper execution of the trust program defined by the settlor ensure a greater sense of protection.

3. ESTATE AND TRUST LITIGATION AND CONTROVERSY

3.1 National legislative and regulatory developments

Certain reforms occurred in family law matters which have had a significant impact on matters of estate. These include the regulation of filiation (as per Law of 10 December 2012, No 219, which sought to achieve complete equality of treatment of all children with regard to the filiation relationship) and the amendment introduced under Law of 20 May 2016 No 76 (the so-called "Cirinnà Law" that has introduced the possibility in Italy for two persons of the same sex to enter into an arrangement similar to marriage, called "civil union", recognizing them – in case of death of one of the partners – the same inheritance rights provided for married couples by the Italian Civil Code). Moreover, the recent entry into force of the European regulation. No. 650/2012 can be considered a turning point in terms of the law applicable to the successions of citizens of European Union states.

With reference to trusts, as anticipated, Italian law does not provide for comprehensive domestic legislation; however, the Italian legislator has enacted some law provisions concerning trusts over the years. In particular, under Law No 112 of 22 June 2016 – better known as "Dopo di Noi" and containing provisions on assistance for persons with severe disabilities without family support – the Italian legislator has recognized the use of trust as one of the instruments that can be used as measures of assistance, care and protection for disabled persons.

3.2 Local legislative and regulatory developments

Italy has no local legal provisions on estate and trusts.

3.3 National case law developments

Traditionally, family disputes among heirs in Italy mainly arise from the violation of the reserved shares committed by means of testamentary dispositions or donations made by the deceased during their lifetime. Such traditional disputes have combined with the complexity of the current family structures: civil unions, *de facto* cohabitation and more marriages per person. New disputes have also arisen with regard to the widespread use of additional estate planning tools and in connection with the

FREQUENTLY ASKED QUESTIONS

1. Are there beneficial tax regimes for new Italian tax resident individuals?
The Italian legislator has implemented in the past years three main beneficial regimes that are applicable to individuals relocating to Italy. The three regimes are aimed at attracting, respectively, HNWIs, pensioners and workers (employees, directors, freelance and entrepreneurs).

2. Could an Italian will remain valid even if it is not compatible with the Italian forced heirship rules?
Please consider that, as per the Italian succession law, a will remains valid even if it does not comply with the reserved share rule, but in such a case it may be challenged by the forced heirs (or their descendants) alleging that their reserved shares were infringed by the will.

3. Would it be possible to set up a trust which disregards the rights of forced heirs?
Article 549 of the Italian Civil Code provides that the forced heir is entitled to receive and enjoy their reserved share immediately upon the opening of the succession, without any restriction, lien and condition. Therefore, a trust preventing the forced heir to receive or enjoy their reserved share would not comply with the above mentioned law provisions, even in the case in which the forced heir is a beneficiary of the trust.

transnational natures of many situations. With reference to trusts, thanks to the national case law developments, doubts on the validity of the instrument of trust are overcome. Therefore, if compliant with the Convention and the relevant foreign governing law, trusts are now recognized as enforceable in Italy subject only to the Italian public order principles. Even trusts 'interni' (i.e., trusts established by Italian individuals with regard to assets located in Italy and where the sole foreign element is the governing law) are now fully recognized as valid by the Italian case law (*inter alia*, Italian Supreme Court, decision No. 10105, dated 9 May 2014; Italian Supreme Court, decision No. 15804, dated 16 April 2015). In addition, since trusts 'interni' are regulated by foreign governing law, should a dispute pertaining to a trust be conferred to the jurisdiction of an Italian court, the latter shall be required to apply the relevant trust foreign governing law. In this perspective, in a recent decision adopted by the Court of Ancona (decision No. 414, dated 29 January 2014), the judges – applying the provisions of Article 51 of the law of Jersey – have come to issue a measure (not known in the Italian legal system) similar to the one that could have been issued by the Court of Jersey. Finally, as of today, the Italian Supreme Court (decision No. 9637 dated 19 April 2018) has definitely overcome the theory according to which a trust was an "atypical contract" and therefore subject from time to time to judicial review as to its merits: such assessment is to be considered to have already been made with Italy's ratification of the Convention which recognised the circumstance that the trust instrument is intended to realise interests worthy of protection under the Italian legal system.

3.4 Local case law developments
The first two judgments issued by Italian Courts concerning "digital inheritance" should be highlighted. In particular, the Court of Bologna on 25 November 2021

(following a single ruling in such matter by the Court of Milan in the same year), has ruled on the transfer *mortis causa* of digital data belonging to a deceased person in favour of their heirs. The decision addresses, for the first time in Italy, the issue of the access to personal data of a deceased person, as well as the ways in which the rights of the deceased can be exercised by their heirs. In the Court's opinion a specific will expressed by the *de cuius* may exclude the possibility of their heirs having access to their digital data. With reference to trusts, local case law has mainly reaffirmed the same principles provided for by national case law. In particular, local Courts have also affirmed the validity of trusts 'interni' compliant with the Convention and the relevant foreign governing law. In the decision of the Court of Bologna dated 1 October 2003, the Court has clarified that the only limit to the validity of trusts 'interni' is that they must be able to pursue legitimate interests, which is to say interests not prohibited by Italian mandatory rules. Moreover, local courts are increasingly faced with trusts set up for a wide variety of purposes. In particular, trusts are increasingly used in the context of divorce proceedings. In this respect, the Court of Turin, with a decree dated 31 March 2009, has provided for the first time the establishment of a trust in a divorce decree. The Court considered the trust instrument as the most suitable tool to segregate the economic resources to be used for their children until they achieve economic independence. In connection with the adoption of Law No 112 of 22 June 2016 (better known as "Dopo di Noi"), trusts are often used as a measure to assist persons with severe disabilities. A first relevant example of the use of a trust instrument in this sense can be found, among others, in the decree issued by the Court of Florence on 8 April 2004, by which the Court has authorised the parents of a minor child affected by disabilities to set up a trust with the assets of the child himself.

3.5 Practice trends
Also with a view to ensuring freer transfer of inheritance assets, there are now persistent voices calling for a renewal of the principles concerning the rights of the forced heirs in such a way as to free the assets of donative inheritance from the constraints of possible legal action and to overcome the prohibition of agreements on renouncement of inheritance. With reference to trusts, the use of such an instrument is now widespread and continuous. Trusts are now used in Italy for new specific purposes and are frequently established not only for the purpose of passing wealth and control from generation to generation but also for the benefit of individuals with disabilities or for charitable initiatives (both by public entities and individuals).

3.6 Pandemic related developments
Given the growing climate of uncertainty caused by the pandemic, the use of asset protection instruments has continued. A sign of such increased awareness has come from the increase in the number of wills and donations, the latter often involving only bare ownership of real estate and company's shares, thus allowing the donor to retain full disposal of them. In the same perspective, the trust instrument is now considered one of the best arrangements to ensure legitimate preservation and transfer of the wealth, but also a flexible tool that can satisfy the economic needs of the settlor and their family according to actual circumstances.

AUTHOR BIOGRAPHIES

Raul-Angelo Papotti

Raul-Angelo Papotti is Head of Chiomenti Tax practice and co-head of Advisory department. Raul-Angelo advises on all areas of tax law, with particular emphasis on international tax law. He has a special expertise in the taxation of trusts and tax planning structures, and in estate planning, advising corporate and private clients alike. Clients include investment banks, private banks, corporates as well as high net worth individuals, families and family offices. He is author of many publications on international tax and estate planning matters and is a frequent speaker at the most prestigious domestic and international congresses.

Raul-Angelo is ranked as a leading expert in the foremost international legal guides such as Chambers, Legal 500 and Who's Who Legal.

Giovanni Cristofaro

Giovanni Cristofaro is a Partner and Head of Private Wealth at Chiomenti in Italy. He has completed his studies in Rome and has been admitted to the Italian Bar Association. He advises Italian and international clients on matters concerning planning, management and use of family assets (including company shareholdings and artworks) with a focus on family wealth planning, including succession, intra-family wealth transfers and trusts. He is author of many publications on private wealth matters and is a frequent speaker at domestic and international congresses. Giovanni is a member of IBA (International Bar Association), of the Board of Directors of STEP (Society of Trust and Estate Practitioners) Italy and of the Italian Association of Trust. He is ranked as a leading expert in private wealth law in the foremost international legal guides such as Chambers, Legal 500 and Who's Who Legal.

Gian Gualberto Morgigni

Gian Gualberto Morgigni is a senior associate of the Tax and Tax Planning department at Chiomenti. He obtained his law degree from Lu.i.s.s. Guido Carli University of Rome in 2010 and his master's degree in tax law from Sole24Ore Business School in 2011. He joined Chiomenti in 2011 and was admitted to the Italian Bar Association in 2013. His expertise covers, among others, estate planning, taxation of HNWIs and trusts, taxation of corporate transactions, and structuring of incentive plans for key managers with regard to both domestic and international aspects. Gian Gualberto has authored several publications on tax matters and participates as speaker at tax conferences and seminars.

Camilla Culiersi

Camilla Culiersi is a senior associate of Private Wealth at Chiomenti. She obtained her law degree from Lu.i.s.s. Guido Carli University of Rome in 2012. She joined Chiomenti in 2013 and was admitted to the Italian Bar Association in 2016. She regularly advises Italian and international clients on matters concerning planning, management and use of family assets (including company shareholdings and artworks) with a focus on family wealth planning, including succession, intra-family wealth transfers and trusts.

JAPAN

Tomoko Nakada
Tokyo Heritage Law Firm

INTRODUCTION

Japan adopts a civil law system. Japan is a unitary state, and has only a national law. The Japanese Civil Code follows the concept of universal succession. The heirs automatically receive the ownership of the assets of the deceased and also inherit debts of the deceased (Article 896 of the Civil Code). Therefore, no probate proceeding, similar to other common law countries, exists in Japan.

1. TAX AND WEALTH PLANNING

Basics of the Japanese inheritance tax

Japan imposes an inheritance tax on an heir/devisee who receives assets (i.e., the beneficiary) (Article 1-3 of the Inheritance Tax Act). Neither the estate itself nor the executor is taxed.

The basic exclusion amount (which is deducted from the amount of the total taxable assets held by the decedent to calculate the tax base) for inheritance tax is: (1) 30 million Japanese yen (JPY), plus (2) the amount obtained by multiplying JPY 6 million, by the number of legal heirs under the Japanese Civil Code (= JPY 30 million + (JPY 6 million × number of legal heirs)) (Article 15 of the Inheritance Tax Act). For example, if a husband dies leaving a wife and two children (three heirs), the basic exclusion is JPY 48 million (JPY 30 million + (JPY 6 million x 3)).

The calculation of the inheritance tax amount is complicated. The inheritance tax rate, from 10% to 55%, is applied not to the decedent's estate as a whole but to the amount each heir assumptively receives pursuant to their intestacy share under the Japanese Civil Code (Article 16 of the Inheritance Tax Act). For example, 55% is applied if assets which an heir assumptively receives pursuant to their intestacy share is over JPY 600 million. The objective behind this method is to calculate the total inheritance tax, regardless of how assets are actually divided by the heirs/ devisees.

1.1 National legislative and regulatory developments

Recent legislative developments (2018 and 2021 Tax Reform)

Because of the beneficiary-based tax in Japan, a beneficiary who is a resident of Japan is subject to Japanese taxation on worldwide assets (Article 1-3, Paragraph 1 (1) and Article 2, Paragraph 1 of the Inheritance Tax Act). The legal residency for inheritance tax purposes is the "principal place of living" under Article 22 of the Civil Code. It is determined by objective factors such as the length of the person's stay, the person's occupation, the location of the person's spouse and other family members and the person's assets/property.

A beneficiary who is a non-resident of Japan can also be subject to the same worldwide taxation (excluding the case where the decedent falls within certain exceptions), to prevent tax avoidance (Article 1-3, Paragraph 1 (2) and Article 2, Paragraph 1 of the Inheritance Tax Act).

Since wealthy Japanese individuals have tried to avoid taxes by having a beneficiary reside outside Japan and transferring their assets overseas, the Japanese tax agency has been expanding the scope of the taxes on overseas assets under the 2000, 2013 and 2017 Tax Reforms. The 2017 Tax Reform, however, widened the scope of worldwide taxation too much by taxing non-Japanese citizens who left Japan with respect to their non-Japanese assets inherited by non-Japanese citizens who are non-residents of Japan. In order to encourage highly skilled non-Japanese citizens to come to work in Japan and to transform Japan into a global financial city, the 2018 and 2021 Tax Reforms provided them relief.

Under the 2018 Tax Reform, after non-Japanese citizens leave Japan, their overseas assets will no longer be subject to Japanese inheritance tax (excluding the case where the beneficiary is subject to worldwide taxation).

Further, under the 2021 Tax Reform, the requirement of a limited stay (10 years or less within the past 15 years) for a decedent who is a non-Japanese citizen but resident in Japan in order to avoid worldwide taxation was abolished. If the decedent is a non-Japanese citizen residing in Japan with a Table 1 visa under the Immigration Control and Refugee Recognition Act (Act), such as a work visa, at the time of his death, even if he has resided in Japan for more than 10 years, his overseas assets will not be subject to Japanese inheritance tax (excluding the case where the beneficiary is subject to worldwide taxation).

Scope of Japanese Inheritance and Gift Taxation (after the 2021 Reform)
See diagram, "Scope of Japanese Inheritance and Gift Taxation", opposite.

Please note, however, that the requirement of a limited stay (10 years or less within the past 15 years) for a beneficiary who is a non-Japanese citizen but resident in Japan with the Table 1 visa in order to avoid worldwide taxation remains. If a beneficiary is a non-Japanese citizen residing in Japan for more than 10 years, even if they stay in Japan with the Table 1 visa, the worldwide assets which they inherit (from US-based parents, for example) will be subject to the Japanese inheritance tax.

1.2 Local legislative and regulatory developments
Not applicable, because Japan has only a national law.

1.3 National case law developments
Not applicable, because Japan has adopted a civil law system and codified statutes predominate.

1.4 Local case law developments
Not applicable, because Japan has only a national law.

1.5 Practice trends
The type of visa held by non-Japanese would have an impact on Japanese inheritance and gift tax.

Some of non-Japanese citizens residing in Japan choose a Table 1 visa such as a work visa rather than a Table 2 visa such as a spouse visa, because, in some cases, they can avoid worldwide taxation of the Japanese inheritance and gift tax.

1.6 Pandemic related developments
No developments.

SCOPE OF JAPANESE INHERITANCE AND GIFT TAXATION

Decedent/Donor ↓ \ Heir/Devisee/Donee ("Beneficiary") (Taxpayer) →	Residence in Japan	Residence in Japan — Non-Japanese Citizen	No residence in Japan — Japanese Citizen	No residence in Japan — Japanese Citizen	No residence in Japan
		Temporary Resident (*B)	Had Residence in Japan within past 10 years	No Residence in Japan within past 10 years	Non-Japanese Citizen
Residence in Japan	Worldwide	Worldwide	Worldwide	Worldwide	Worldwide
No residence in Japan — Non-Japanese Citizen Resident (*A)	Worldwide	Japanese-situs only	Worldwide	Worldwide	Japanese-situs only
No residence in Japan — Japanese Citizen — Had Residence in Japan within past 10 years	Worldwide	Worldwide	Worldwide	Worldwide	Worldwide
No residence in Japan — Japanese Citizen — No Residence in Japan within past 10 years	Worldwide	Japanese-situs only	Worldwide	Worldwide	Japanese-situs only
No residence in Japan — Non-Japanese Citizen	Worldwide	Japanese-situs only	Worldwide	Worldwide	Japanese-situs only

Key:
- (light) Tax on worldwide assets
- (dark) Tax on Japanese-*situs* assets only

To determine whether assets are taxable in Japan, find the resident status of the beneficiary at the time of death or gift in the top row, and then find the resident status of the decedent/donor at the time of death or gift in the left-hand column.

"Residence" in the above table means a "principal place of living" (*jusho*).

Definitions:
(*A): Non-Japanese Citizen Resident: A resident with residence status listed in Table 1* of the Immigration Control and Refugee Recognition Act at the time of death or gift.
(*B): Temporary Resident: A resident (i) with residence status listed in Table 1* of the Immigration Control and Refugee Recognition Act at the time of death or gift; and (ii) whose total period of residence in Japan is 10 years or less within the past 15 years prior to death or gift.
*Table 1: For example, a highly-skilled professional, business manager, legal/accounting service provider, medical service provider, engineer/specialist in humanities/international services, or intra-company transferee, temporary visitor, or dependent.
Table 2: For example, a permanent resident, spouse or child of a Japanese citizen, or spouse or child of a permanent resident.

2. ESTATE AND TRUST ADMINISTRATION
2.1 National legislative and regulatory developments
National legislative developments in inheritance law
2018 Amendment of Civil Code (Inheritance Law)

The inheritance law chapter of the Civil Code (Code) was amended in July 2018 for the first time in 38 years, most of which took effect in July 2019. Since Japan is aging fast, the amendment aims to protect elderly widows and widowers, and to encourage people making wills.

- **Creation of spousal right to live in an inherited residence.** The amendment created the right for a widow or widower (hereinafter "widow") to continue living in an inherited residence. When a widow has lived in a home that belonged to her deceased spouse at the time of the spouse's death, the widow will have the right to keep living there for free, if the spouse has devised such a right to the widow in his will, or if the right is given pursuant to the estate division agreement among all of the heirs (or a court order) (Article 1028, Paragraph 1 of the Code). This right lasts until the widow dies, but can end sooner than that (Article 1030 of the Code). By registering this right in the real property registry, the widow can claim her right against a third party (Article 1031, Paragraph 1 of the Code).

- **Relaxing the requirement of a holographic will.** The forms of the wills under the Code includes a holographic will. The testator must handwrite the entire text, the date and their name and affix their seal. It could be difficult for the testator to handwrite the details of assets. To make it easier for the testator to make a holographic will, the amendment enabled the testator to attach a list of assets not handwritten to their holographic will. The testator must sign and affix their seal on each page of the list in order to prevent forgery (Article 968, Paragraphs 1 and 2 of the Code).

- **Creation of governmental system to safekeep a holographic will.** A new law, the Act on Storage of Wills in the Legal Affairs Bureau, was enacted in 2018, and the Legal Affairs Bureau has started to safekeep originals of holographic wills since July 10, 2020. The testator must bring the original of their holographic will and visit the Legal Affairs Bureau in person. A lack of deposit does not impact the validity of the holographic will, but if a holographic will is deposited with the Legal Affairs Bureau, there will be no need of the will's procedure named kennin in family court after the testator's death.

- **Right to legally reserved portion as monetary claim.** A certain portion of the estate is reserved for certain heirs. Eligible heirs are the spouse, descendants (including adults) and ascendants, but not siblings (Article 1042 of the Code). The legally reserved portion is generally one-half of the decedent's estate. Certain lifetime gifts (evaluated as of death) are added to the estate (Article 1029, Paragraph 1 of the Code). For example, assuming that a Japanese citizen dies leaving his wife and two children, each legally reserved portion of the heir is: wife, 1/4 (=1/2 ×her intestacy share of 1/2); each child, 1/8 (=1/2 ×each child's intestacy share of 1/4). Under the old law, a will becomes void to the extent it infringes a claimant's legally reserved portion when an heir claims their right. This often makes business succession difficult. To ensure the testator's testamentary freedom, the amendment changed the right to the legally reserved portion into a monetary claim against the devisee (Article 1046 of the Code). A will remains valid even after an heir claims their right.

National legislative developments in trust law
2006 Amendment of Trust Act
Trusts were incorporated in Japan in the 1900s, and Japan has had a codified law of trusts since 1922. In Japan, trusts developed primarily through trust banks in the area of commercial trusts, particularly since the end of World War II. Since Japan is a fast-aging country, increasingly, needs have appeared in the area of family trusts for guardianship-substitute and will-substitute purposes. Accordingly, to meet the new demands, an amended Trust Act was enacted in 2006, which substantially amended the old Trust Act. It includes several improvements to facilitate the use of trusts for family or succession purposes, but the taxation of trusts, which takes a hostile view of trusts for estate planning, sometimes discourages people from using such trusts.

2004 Amendment of Trust Business Act
There has been a license requirement to engage in a trust business since 1922. Since all the trust companies had merged with ordinary banks to form trust banks by 1948, only trust banks have served as trustees in Japan until 2004. To meet the demands of the times, mainly in the area of commercial trusts, an amended Trust Business Act was enacted in 2004, allowing certain trust companies other than trust banks to engage in the trust business. For family or succession purposes, however, there are only a few trust companies which offer services. An attorney cannot become a trustee as a professional, since professionals providing trust services must be a joint stock company licensed by, or registered with, the Prime Minister of Japan (Articles 3 and 2 (Paragraphs 1 and 2) and Articles 5 and 7 of the Trust Business Act).

2.2 Local legislative and regulatory developments
Not applicable, because Japan has only a national law.

2.3 National case law developments
Not applicable, because Japan has adopted a civil law system, and codified statutes predominate.

2.4 Local case law developments
Not applicable, because Japan has only a national law.

2.5 Practice trends
Execution of the will made easier
The amendment of the Civil Code to change an heir's right to the legally reserved portion into a monetary claim against a devisee has made the execution of the will easier. Even if an heir claims their right, the will remains valid, and therefore the executor no longer needs to worry about whether to stop the execution of the will. Still, a trust bank, often designated as executor of a will in Japan, would

be nervous about being involved in a family dispute over the legally reserved portion, and thus encourages the testator to make a will not infringing such heir's right by devising certain assets to all the eligible heirs.

Practice of family trusts in Japan

Recently more people who own real properties have set up a trust for real properties to avoid a guardian appointed by a court and to let a family member as a trustee manage the real properties before/during the owner's mental incapacity. It is possible to change the owner's name into the trustee's name in the real property registry.

In contrast, regarding financial assets in Japan, it is practically very difficult to find a financial institution, including a bank, in Japan which will let a trustee open a trust account under the name of the trustee of a trust, even if it is a Japanese trust. Therefore, even if trusts can be legally created in Japan, it will be practically easier for a US citizen to transfer funds and stocks from their accounts in Japan to accounts under the name of the trustee of their US revocable trust in the US.

2.6 Pandemic related developments
No developments.

3. ESTATE AND TRUST LITIGATION AND CONTROVERSY

3.1 National legislative and regulatory developments

The 2011 Amendment of Code of Civil Procedure (CCP) added provisions regarding jurisdiction of courts in Japan for international cases including the following:
- For a lawsuit against an individual, Japanese courts will have jurisdiction if the defendant resides in Japan (Article 3-2 of CCP).
- For a lawsuit regarding inheritance rights, legally reserved portion, or bequests and other acts which will have effect by reason of death, Japanese courts will have jurisdiction if the decedent resided in Japan at the time of his death (Article 3-3, Item 12 of CCP).

3.2 Local legislative and regulatory developments

Not applicable, because Japan has only a national law.

3.3 National case law developments

Please note that Japan has adopted a civil law system, and codified statutes predominate.

Recent district court decisions include the following:
- Japanese courts will apply the legally reserved portion rules to the worldwide assets as well as the Japanese-*situs* assets. A Tokyo District Court Decision dated March 28, 2007 included a decedent's overseas assets such as a Cayman trust, joint accounts in the United States and a condominium in California among the basic assets to calculate the amount of the legally reserved portion.

FREQUENTLY ASKED QUESTIONS

1. When can a client avoid Japanese inheritance tax on their US-*situs* assets?

Here is the outline of the 2021 rule from the standpoint of a decedent:

- **Japanese Citizen.** Suppose the client is a Japanese citizen. The advice would be to stay alive (if possible) more than 10 years after leaving Japan. A beneficiary who is a Japanese citizen also needs to meet the same requirement.

- **Foreign Resident.** Suppose the client is a US citizen living and working in Japan. In this case their type of visa would matter. If they reside in Japan with a Table 1 visa under the Act (such as a work visa) at the time of death, Japanese worldwide taxation may not apply to the estate, depending on the status of the beneficiary. In contrast, if the client resides in Japan with a Table 2 visa under the Act (such as a spouse visa) at the time of death, Japanese worldwide taxation will apply to the estate, regardless of the status of the beneficiary. Any spouse can, however, claim the spousal credit.

- **Foreigners Who Have Left Japan.** Suppose the client is a US citizen with a US spouse who has resided in Japan for more than 10 years and will leave Japan to return to their home country. If they leave Japan, the client's US assets inherited by the US spouse will not be subject to Japanese inheritance tax. In contrast, if they have a Japanese spouse, assets inherited by them will remain subject to the Japanese inheritance tax for 10 years after the spouse leaves Japan.

- A Tokyo District Court Decision dated September 12, 2018 invalided a trust agreement between a decedent and his second son as trustee, because it was made to avoid another heir's right to the legally reserved portion and thus against the public policy of Japan.

3.4 Local case law developments
Not applicable, because Japan has only a national law.

3.5 Practice trends
A Japanese Notarial Deed Will is recommended. One reason is that an heir can challenge a will in Japan based on the decedent's mental capacity, but it is practically difficult to win a judgement invalidating a Japanese Notarial Deed Will, even with evidence of a testator's medical records at the time when the testator made the will.

The Japanese Notarial Deed Will is prepared by a notary who is a retired judge or prosecutor, and therefore, a credible person from a judge's perspective, and the notary tends to assert or testify in front of the judge that the testator had mental capacity. The notary does so because, if the will he prepared is declared invalid, it will disgrace the notary.

3.6 Pandemic related developments

The 2022 Amendment of Code of Civil Procedure was enacted in May 2022, which will take effect in 4 years, aimed at making civil court procedures online. Currently, a written complaint to file a lawsuit and a written brief need to be brought or sent to the court, but the amended law will allow such documents to be submitted online ("e-Filing"). Hearings and witness examinations now need to be held in a court room, but can be carried out in the form of online conferences under the amended law ("e-Court"). Plaintiffs, defendants and their attorneys will thus be able to complete procedures without visiting a court. Court decisions and other records are now kept in paper form at the court, but will be digitized and made available to be viewed and downloaded by involved parties through the internet ("e-Case Management").

AUTHOR BIOGRAPHY

Tomoko Nakada

Tomoko Nakada, attorney-at-law admitted in Japan and New York, is a founder of Tokyo Heritage Law Firm in Tokyo, Japan. Ms. Nakada focuses her practice on international estate planning and estate settlement. Ms. Nakada has been chosen as an International Fellow of the American College of Trust and Estate Counsel (ACTEC) since 2015, and is a member of its International Estate Planning Committee. She has been Academician of the International Academy of Estate and Trust Law (TIAETL) since 2017 as well.

Ms. Nakada is a graduate of the University of Tokyo (Bachelor of Laws 1995) and New York University (L.L.M. 2001) and worked as a visiting researcher at Harvard Law School (2001-2002). She was admitted to practice in NY in 2002. She began her legal career in Japan in 1997 as a Tokyo District Court judge, a member of the three judge panel, a special honor for a junior lawyer.

JERSEY

Sarajane Kempster
RBC Wealth Management

INTRODUCTION

Jersey is a British Crown Dependency, separate from the United Kingdom, allowing a high degree of autonomy, including its own fiscal and legal/judicial systems.

Jersey's customary law jurisdiction is long-established, which has been influenced, *inter alia*, by Norman customary law, English common law and modern French civil law. The financial and legal sectors are substantial, renowned for expertise in areas such as trusts, banking, wealth, fund & asset management and family offices.

Jersey is recognised as a well-regulated, leading international financial centre dedicated to meeting the highest international standards set by a number of worldwide organisations and international regulatory bodies (including the EU, OECD, IMF and MONEYVAL) through the continued development and implementation of robust regulation and legislation.

As a low tax jurisdiction with a strong and respected regulatory framework, residents and businesses in Jersey benefit from growth opportunities in the comfort of a secure and compliant jurisdiction, ensuring the protection of their assets.

1. TAX AND WEALTH PLANNING

1.1 National legislative and regulatory developments

See below Section 1.2. Although Jersey is not independent of the United Kingdom its status as a Crown Dependency gives it constitutional rights of self-government and judicial independence. Accordingly "national" and "local" developments will in this guide be treated as being the same.

1.2 Local legislative and regulatory developments

Jersey's tax system is relatively uncomplicated. The standard rate of tax for Jersey resident individuals is 20% and there is no capital gains tax. There is a goods and services tax (GST) of 5% on the majority of goods and services supplied in the island, the tax also being levied on imports worth more than JEP 135. High value residents who are granted permission to become resident in Jersey must demonstrate an annual worldwide income in excess of JEP 750,000 and the minimum tax that they must pay is JEP 145,000 per annum. In general terms they are taxed at a rate of 20% on the first JEP 725,000 of income and 1% on all income above that.

Jersey resident companies are liable to tax on their worldwide income but pay rates of 0%, 10% or 20% depending on the type of company. For example a Jersey financial services company will pay 10%, a Jersey-based utility company or large corporate retailer will pay 20% and the majority of other companies will pay 0%.

Jersey introduced economic substance legislation for accounting periods beginning on or after 1 January 2019 pursuant to which companies resident in Jersey carrying on certain relevant activities have to meet an economic substance test. The relevant activities are: banking; insurance; fund management; finance and leasing; headquarters; shipping; holding company; intellectual property holding; and distribution and service centres.

Jersey signed an Intergovernmental Agreement (IGA) with the United States in 2013 to implement the exchange of information under the Foreign Account Tax Compliance Act (FATCA) and adopted the Common Reporting Standard (CRS) in 2016 with the first reporting taking place in 2017.

1.3 National case law developments
See below Section 1.4.

1.4 Local case law developments
The Jersey legislature has shown itself adept at preserving beneficial case-law principles that have been restricted by foreign judicial decisions. An obvious example is the so-called rule in Hastings-Bass, whereby trustees who had made a mistake as to their dispositive powers were able to apply to the court to have their action declared void. This allowed any adverse consequences, which were often tax-related, to be ameliorated without the need for the beneficiaries to sue the trustees for negligence or breach of trust. The principle was significantly restricted by two decisions of the United Kingdom Supreme Court in 2013 (*Pitt v. Holt* and *Re Futter* [2013] UKSC 26). Jersey immediately acted to enshrine the pre-existing principles in an amendment to the Trusts (Jersey) Law 1984, an example which has been followed by a number of other offshore jurisdictions. The Jersey courts are therefore able to continue to apply the principle in its wider form, to the benefit of beneficiaries who would otherwise have to have resorted to more lengthy and less certain litigation against their trustees for any losses incurred.

1.5 Practice trends
Although Jersey provides a tax neutral location for international private client structures, the motivation for structuring is increasingly that of succession planning or asset protection rather than tax minimisation. Clients who live in countries where there is little respect for the rule of law tend to want to hold assets in a politically stable jurisdiction with a well-developed legal system and access to high quality professional advice. Although Jersey trusts are a popular structure there is increasing interest in alternatives such as foundations, particularly where clients come from jurisdictions where the trust is relatively unknown. There is also increasing interest in trust structures where families can continue to exercise a degree of control through mechanisms such as settlor reserved powers or prescribed directions.

1.6 Pandemic related developments
Jersey's financial institutions proved themselves to be suitably resilient when the first lockdown occurred. Jersey's Government has for some years pursued a strategy of making the island a centre of excellence in relation to its digital sector. For example, by 2019 fibre connections were rolled out across the whole island, delivering some of the highest broadband speeds anywhere in the world. As a result the majority of private wealth businesses were able to adapt speedily to the working from home model, thus minimising disruption to their clients.

2. ESTATE AND TRUST ADMINISTRATION

2.1 National legislative and regulatory developments

See Section 2.2 below. Although Jersey is not independent of the United Kingdom its status as a Crown Dependency gives it constitutional rights of self-government and judicial independence. Accordingly "national" and "local" developments will in this guide be treated as being the same.

2.2 Local legislative and regulatory developments

Financial services businesses, which includes trust and company administration providers, are regulated by the Jersey Financial Services Commission (JFSC). The JFSC's responsibilities are set out in the Financial Services Commission (Jersey) Law 1998. It is well-resourced and its Supervision Division, which adopts a risk-based approach, carries out frequent inspections of regulated businesses.

The statutory framework for Jersey trusts is the Trusts (Jersey) Law 1984. The Law is subject to regular review by a working party comprising leading trust industry practitioners and representatives of government and, as a result of their recommendations, is amended from time to time. The most recent amendment is the Trusts (Amendment No.7) (Jersey) Law 2018 which, amongst other amendments:

- clarified that the reservation or grant by a settlor of all of the powers listed in the Law would not invalidate the trust;
- provided that a trustee is entitled to refuse to comply with a beneficiary's request for information, if the trustee is satisfied that it is in the interests of any one or more, or of the whole of the beneficiaries to so refuse, subject to a beneficiary's right to apply to the court;
- made provision for an indemnity to be granted on the retirement of a trustee by the new trustee in favour of a wide class of persons engaged in the management of the trust (such as employees) without their being made party to the relevant contract;
- permits the terms of a trust to direct or authorise the accumulation of income without requiring it to be distributed or converted to capital within a particular time period; and
- enabled the court to approve variations of a trust not just on behalf of minors but also on behalf of persons who cannot be found despite reasonable effort or falling within a large class of beneficiaries where it is unreasonable to contact each member.

The administration of estates of deceased persons domiciled in Jersey or with assets in the island is governed by the Probate (Jersey) Law 1998 and falls under the supervisory jurisdiction of the Royal Court of Jersey. Applications for grants of probate are made to a court officer known as the Judicial Greffier.

2.3 National case law developments

See below, Section 2.4.

2.4 Local case law developments

Jersey's Royal Court produces a significant number of judgments that contribute to the jurisprudence in relation to trusts and estates and its judgments are frequently cited in courts outside Jersey. Recent cases of note have concerned the existence of the so-called "substratum" rule and the role of protectors.

In *Re Rysaffe Fiduciaries SARL* [2021] JRC230 the Royal Court had to consider a decision by trustees to add the settlor's widow as a beneficiary of a trust for the purposes of a reorganisation of a family's interest in the estate and two trusts. The addition of the widow was directly contrary to the settlor's intentions as expressed in his letter of wishes. The substratum rule, which originated in certain English cases concerning variations of trusts, suggested that an arrangement that changes the whole substratum of the trust cannot be regarded simply as a variation. The court held that there was no substratum rule in Jersey law, the test to be applied in relation to the trustees' decision being whether the proposed exercise of the trustees' power to add a beneficiary was permitted by the terms of the trust, whether the trustee had given adequate deliberation as to whether it should exercise the power and whether the use of the power was for a proper purpose. In the circumstances the court approved the exercise of the power to add the settlor's widow.

In *Re the Piedmont and Riviera Trusts* [2021] JRC 248 the Royal Court was asked to approve a trustee's decision as to the allocation of assets in termination of two trusts. The distribution required the consent of a protector, which had initially been refused but was subsequently given when the trustees reformulated their distribution allocation. Amongst other matters the court had to consider the role of a protector. The court held that the paramount duty of a protector is to act in good faith in the best interests of the beneficiaries. In doing so the protector was required to exercise its own judgment. Whilst the court's judgment was still in draft it was asked to consider a decision of the Supreme Court of Bermuda in *RE X Trusts* [2021] Sc (Bda) 72 Civ where the court had considered whether the consent provisions in a trust deed conferred an independent decision-making discretion on the protector (the Wider View) or merely a discretion to ensure that the trustee's substantive decision was a valid and rational one (the Narrower View). The Bermuda court had ruled in favour of the Narrower View. The Royal Court disagreed, saying that: "It seems inherently unlikely that settlors would go to the trouble of appointing themselves or trusted friends or advisors as protectors if they intended the role of protector to be limited to that of assessing rationality. If that were the case, the key requirement for a protector would be a legal qualification rather than knowledge of the settlor's wishes and sound judgment as to what is in the best interest of particular beneficiaries". The court did however qualify its view by pointing out that it had not heard full argument on the matter.

2.5 Practice trends

Although it is often suggested that the motive for setting up private wealth structures in jurisdictions such as Jersey is tax mitigation, the reality is that the majority of structures are set up for succession planning or asset protection. Wealth creators are increasingly concerned at the potential impact upon the next generation of inheriting substantial wealth. Increasingly cognisant of the old adage 'rags to riches to rags in three generations" they wish to ensure that the transfer of wealth to succeeding generations is carried out in a controlled manner. The use of

FREQUENTLY ASKED QUESTIONS

1. Why would an UHNW International family choose Jersey as the jurisdiction for their wealth structuring?

Jersey is often the jurisdiction of choice for UHNW families due to the quality of its legal system, its professional community, regulatory environment and proximity to London. It is very well-established as an International Finance Centre with a robust legislative and regulatory framework. In addition to this, given the large size of the financial services industry, there is a significant professional workforce on the island meaning access to top quality advice from industry-recognised individuals is readily available.

2. How nimble is the Jersey legal system/judiciary and are parties really given sufficient access to justice?

Jersey's court system is very efficient and provides real access to justice. As it has a particularly sophisticated Trust law regime, this has led to the implementation of agile court processes and the development of leading private client trust law practitioners, who are seen as global leaders in their field. What this has also meant is that the Jersey judiciary has been responsible for dealing with some of the most complex and high-value trust litigation in the world and produced industry-leading judgments as a result.

a trust or foundation structure in a well-regulated, tax neutral jurisdiction such as Jersey can assist in ensuring that future generations are provided for. In addition, in a world of increasing political uncertainty a structure located in a jurisdiction that respects the rule of law, has a well-respected judicial system to enforce it and ease of access to appropriate professional expertise are all attributes that help to protect the family's assets.

Philanthropic structures have also become more common following the introduction of a new Charities Law in 2014 and the establishment of a Jersey Charity Commissioner.

2.6 Pandemic related developments

During the pandemic Jersey enacted legislation temporarily relaxing the requirement for two witnesses to be physically present when a will is signed and instead permitting this to be completed by audio/video communication, as well as the requirement for an applicant to travel to Jersey in order to obtain a Grant of Administration.

3. ESTATE AND TRUST LITIGATION AND CONTROVERSY

3.1 National legislative and regulatory developments

See Section 3.2 below. Although Jersey is not independent of the United Kingdom its status as a Crown Dependency gives it constitutional rights of self-government and judicial independence. Accordingly "national" and "local" developments will in this guide be treated as being the same.

3.2 Local legislative and regulatory developments

The practice of Jersey law is regulated by the Law Society of Jersey pursuant to The Law Society of Jersey Law 2005, which provides that no person may practice law as an advocate or solicitor unless they are an ordinary member of the Law Society of Jersey. Only Jersey advocates may appear and have rights of audience in the Royal Court of Jersey. The constitution and procedure of the Royal Court in relation to civil matters is principally governed by the Royal Court (Jersey) Law 1948 and the Royal Court Rules 2004, as amended.

3.3 National case law developments

See Section 3.4 below.

3.4 Local case law developments

Described by one magazine journalist as a "veritable bloodbath of litigation and rancour" the litigation concerning the Crociani family and their trustees has occupied the attention of courts in Italy, Mauritius, the Bahamas, the U.S. and Jersey for more than 10 years, with a cast of princesses, film stars and allegations of missing works of art. The case concerned a trust set up by a mother principally for the benefit of her two daughters and an allegation by one daughter that the trustee had committed a breach of trust in appointing substantial assets to a trust of which the mother was a beneficiary. The daughter was ultimately successful (see *Crociani & ors. v. Crociani & ors.* [2017] JRC146) and the former trustees and the mother were ordered to reconstitute the trust fund. The litigation has continued into 2021 with the latest skirmish being an application by the successful daughter for an order requiring her sister to withdraw proceedings that her sister had brought against her in Paris, essentially trying to recoup the money that the Jersey Court had ordered her to pay. However, the Paris court sat the day before the Jersey court hearing and ordered the withdrawal of the Jersey court application. The claimant in the Jersey court had no option but to withdraw her application (see [2021]JRC279) given that she risked a daily fine by the Paris court if she did not do so. The Jersey court did, however, mark its displeasure by making an indemnity costs order against the sister for what it described as the "disrespectful and manipulative actions" taken by the sister in seeking the withdrawal order in the Paris proceedings. It would appear that real-life litigation can sometimes have as many twists and turns as fictional versions.

3.5 Practice trends

Although cases with the fact pattern exhibited by the Crociani litigation may be rare, the size of Jersey's finance industry means that trust and commercial cases will form a significant part of the work of the courts. The trust and commercial bars are significant in number and whilst only Jersey qualified advocates have rights of audience they are often assisted by representatives of London law firms and members of the English bar. Many of the cases coming before the Jersey courts are trust-related and, as a result, Jersey trust jurisprudence is substantial and frequently cited in courts of other jurisdictions. The ability of the courts to "bless" momentous decisions made by trustees has proved to be a useful resource for trustees administering large and complex trusts and can be a useful safeguard for beneficiaries of those trusts.

3.6 Pandemic related developments

The Jersey courts reacted swiftly to the restrictions imposed by lockdowns, with many hearings being conducted by video conference and papers that would ordinarily have been filed in hard copy being filed electronically. The largely positive experience has probably hastened the move by the courts towards electronic document management.

AUTHOR BIOGRAPHY

Sarajane Kempster

Sarajane Kempster is Head of Fiduciary Clients and Fiduciary Specialist Team Lead for RBC Wealth Management's fiduciary business in the British Isles. Based in Jersey, Sarajane leads a team of fiduciary specialists who have business development responsibility for the fiduciary business. She is also responsible for maintaining strong relationships with RBC's fiduciary clients and ensuring excellent client service delivery. In addition, Sarajane manages the interests of a portfolio of private clients. She specialises in establishing and managing offshore structures for high net worth individuals and their families, with a particular focus on those connected to the Middle East. She also has experience in addressing the wealth management and estate planning needs of clients from the UK and globally. Born and educated in Jersey, Sarajane spent 10 years managing the offshore dealing and registration operation of a prominent fund management company. In 1997 she became a director and member of the management team of Mourant Private Wealth, which was acquired by RBC in 2009. Outside of work, Sarajane enjoys dancing, choreography, theatre and spending time with her family.

LIECHTENSTEIN

Dr. Johannes Gasser

Gasser Partner

INTRODUCTION

Compared to Liechtenstein's population of roughly 38,000, the number of 24,000 corporations, foundations and trusts under management today is significant. With 10,000 foundations, the civil law "alter ego" of the common law trust is still the most frequent asset protection structure in use.

Corporate laws date back to 1926, when Liechtenstein also introduced, as a first continental European jurisdiction, the concept of the Anglo-Saxon trust. For almost 100 years, Liechtenstein's legal and fiduciary practice employs these legal instruments with in-depth experience and expertise.

Liechtenstein is a civil law jurisdiction, and, sandwiched between Switzerland and Austria in the heart of the Alps, often borrows from these two neighbouring jurisdictions both statutory and case law, along with professionals for roughly 120 trust companies and many esteemed members of the judiciary. Courts and regulatory authorities are known to work efficiently and timely, having the resources and the know-how to facilitate and ensure swift registration, licensing and the resolution of complex and often international cross-border disputes involving significant wealth in a confidential manner.

Liechtenstein is also an early adopter of international initiatives and laws seeking to enforce the exchange of tax information as well as anti-money laundering laws. As a member of the European Economy Area (EAA), the "little brother" of the EU, Liechtenstein is always at the pace of the European Union in implementing internationally harmonised standards and regulations, also offering EU-passporting to financial intermediaries, including investments funds, thus allowing them to provide services in the EU. Concurrently, Liechtenstein companies and trusts enjoy the same legal freedoms and privileges as EU equivalents, and they are protected from discrimination. Some of the laws, however, are not harmonised, which is on purpose. By way of example, the EU-laws on taxation are not relevant for Liechtenstein, and, most importantly, there are no multilateral treaties allowing for the enforcement of foreign judgements in Liechtenstein. Accordingly, legal disputes need to be fully retried in Liechtenstein courts, which many consider as a strong technique in favour of asset protection.

For many hundred years, the Principality was shaped and reigned by the Royal family who has shared with the people and the country its name, integrity, sovereignty and success. Today, the Royals own the largest bank in Liechtenstein, which also ensures that compliance, confidentiality and a stable currency and economy work for the whole financial industry and provide for a steady future.

1. TAX AND WEALTH PLANNING

Whenever companies or trusts are managed from within Liechtenstein, they are taxable in Liechtenstein. Generally, there is a 12.5% corporate tax, which, however, will not be levied in many circumstances. First, many corporations and foundations opt for a unique flat tax regime which is at CHF 1,800 annually only, if the circumstances so allow, and trusts enjoy such preferential tax regime at all times. Second, dividends and capital gains are not taxable at all (subject to the new anti-avoidance rules discussed below).

1.1 National legislative and regulatory developments

Liechtenstein is currently facing the implementation of the Organisation for Economic Co-operation and Development (OECD) requirements regarding the introduction of a **global minimum tax of 15% for companies** with a turnover of more than EUR 750 million. It must be assumed that the Liechtenstein legislator will implement the requirements of the G20/OECD Inclusive Framework into domestic Liechtenstein law at the beginning of 2024. Under the currently applicable tax regime in Liechtenstein, companies (legal entities) are subject to an annual income tax, which is levied in the form of a flat-tax rate of 12.5%. This corporate tax rate is thus significantly lower than the planned 15%. The trend towards reducing international tax competition is therefore also noticeable in Liechtenstein. However, Liechtenstein as a jurisdiction is able to shine with numerous local advantages: despite the elimination of tax competition, Liechtenstein continues to be an attractive jurisdiction for wealth planning, in particular due to its liberal and highly modern corporate law and the efficient rule of law.

1.2 Local legislative and regulatory developments

As from 1 January 2022, Liechtenstein also introduced **new anti-avoidance rules on dividend income and capital gains**. Dividend income and capital gains are, generally, tax-exempt for income tax purposes in Liechtenstein. However, those deriving from investments in foreign legal entities are no longer tax-exempt if more than 50% of the total income of the foreign legal entity consists of passive income and its taxable income is subject, directly or indirectly, to low taxation. For participations owned before 1 January 2019, the new rules did not apply if a dividend income or capital gain was realized before 31 December 2021. As of 1 January 2022, regular anti-avoidance rules apply to such participations.

1.3 National case law developments

In terms of wealth planning, there is new ground-breaking case law regarding **the special formal requirements for allographic wills**. In 2022, the case law once again confirmed that caution must be exercised when drawing up a will in the form of an allographic will, as special formal requirements must be observed. In the case of an allographic will, the text may also be electronically printed or drafted by a third party. However, an allographic will is invalid if the testator has signed on a loose sheet of paper without there being any physical connection or any connection in terms of content with the sheet containing the actual terms of the will. An allographic will consisting of several loose sheets requires a note, signed by the testator, on the additional sheet with reference to their testamentary disposition. In contrast, the mere continuation of the text in the case of a testamentary disposition made by a third party which is not handwritten is not sufficient to establish the internal unity of the document.

1.4 Local case law developments

Although Liechtenstein law acknowledges **forced heirship rules**, it is also established that such can be **avoided legitimately** by sophisticated wealth planning. As a general rule, if the founder or settlor survives for a period of two years, the creation of the trust or foundation (located in Liechtenstein) to which they bequest their assets (where there are no heirs with forced heirship claims as appointed beneficiaries, and further provided that they divest of reserved powers or any other means of control), become immune from the claw-back of forced heirs (and, mostly, all other potential creditors) in Liechtenstein. Recent case law deals with the level of control permitted in the circumstances to protect the foundation from the claw-back.

1.5 Practice trends

Increasingly, wealth planning will require paying attention to **gender, religion or similar discrimination** issues. The European Court of Human Rights case law appears to have bearings on structuring and wealth planning, where settlors seek to favor, by way of example, male over female beneficiaries. Liechtenstein practice notes that there is a groundbreaking Austrian Supreme Court case where provisions of a family dynasty agreement of a limited liability partnership were considered *contra bonos mores* and invalid as they provided that distributions to female beneficiaries required protector consent, whereas such to male beneficiaries did not (6 Ob 55/18h). The Austrian Supreme Court considered such provisions **discriminatory and unenforceable**, and Liechtenstein courts are likely to consider, and apply, such principles against gender or similar discrimination. However, given the international nexus of most of Liechtenstein wealth structures, including trusts and foundations, it will certainly matter where the settlor or founder came from. By way of example, if the settlor of a Liechtenstein trust was based in the middle-east and provided in the Liechtenstein trust deed for Sharia rules (which generally favor male over female heirs and beneficiaries of their estate), it is believed to not be considered discriminatory, as the culture and rules of the settlor's domicile are deemed to be overruling. Only in extreme circumstances, Liechtenstein rules against discriminatory treatment may be considered "public policy" and thus may prevail.

1.6 Pandemic related developments

Because in the course of the COVID-19 pandemic it was *de facto* impossible to consult a lawyer or notary due to the contact restrictions imposed by the authorities in many places, the will forms of the testator's own **handwritten will** and the so-called **emergency will** have regained more relevance. If a testator wishes to establish a will in writing and without witnesses, then they must write the will, on their own, in handwriting and sign it (§ 578 Civil Code). Although the date and place of the establishment of the will is not prescribed by law, it is strongly recommended for reasons of proof and to avoid later disputes. According to § 597 Civil Code, the emergency will can only be considered as an option if there is an imminent danger that the testator will die or lose the ability to testify before they can declare their last will in another way. In such cases, the testator may also testify orally or in writing with the assistance of two witnesses. However, a last will declared in this way loses its validity three months after the imminent danger in the aforementioned sense ceases to exist.

2. ESTATE AND TRUST ADMINISTRATION

2.1 National legislative and regulatory developments

In 2022, the Liechtenstein legislator explicitly clarified that board meetings can also be held in **hybrid or electronic form**. In a hybrid meeting, there is a meeting location where individual board members physically meet while the other board members join electronically. In a virtual meeting, on the other hand, discussions take place and resolutions are resolved exclusively by electronic means.

According to prevailing opinion, the holding of hybrid or electronic board meetings was already (implicitly) permissible under the current legal framework. However, as the issue of hybrid and/or electronic holding of board meetings gained relevance especially in the height of the COVID-19 pandemic, the Liechtenstein legislator decided to explicitly clarify in Art. 112 para. 4 Persons and Companies Act that, as of 1 August 2022, board meetings held in this form are permissible. Thus, it is now explicitly clarified that, for example, foundation board meetings can permissibly take place in hybrid or electronic form. The provision of Art. 112 para. 4 Persons and Companies Act is also applicable to trusts by way of analogy.

2.2 Local legislative and regulatory developments

New rules governing Liechtenstein fiduciaries and professional trustees seek to **ensure best practices standards** and the **avoidance of conflicts of interests**. If such conflicts occur, professional fiduciaries are obliged to disclose such conflicts to beneficiaries and seek to avoid or manage them diligently. Frequent audits of fiduciaries by independent auditors have also been introduced to assess whether and to which extent fiduciaries are fully compliant with these standards, including Anti-Money Laundering Rules. Certainly, such AML rules are one of the most serious and efficiently enforced of all international financial centres. Further, new rules ensure that directors of Liechtenstein companies are **fit and proper**. Persons convicted of certain (insolvency and monetary) criminal acts, in Liechtenstein or abroad, are not eligible to become board members of foundations or trustees of trusts (Art. 180b Persons and Companies Act).

2.3 National case law developments

Many cases of Liechtenstein courts deal with the liability of Liechtenstein fiduciaries. Generally, it is accepted that fiduciaries, trustees and directors may call to their defence the **Business Judgement Rule** (BJR). The BJR provides that they are immune from liability if in the preparation and proper act of decision making they follow certain technical procedures, mainly aimed at documenting a well-balanced weighing of pros and cons in the interest of the company and its stakeholders (e.g., beneficiaries of a trust), and provided that there is no conflict of interest (Art. 182 Persons and Companies Act).

2.4 Local case law developments

In recent case law, the rights of beneficiaries are in the focus. As a general trend, certainly in the context of foundations, **beneficiaries are entitled to receive information and apply in court for supervisory measures** if they have a discretionary beneficial interest only. However, in a trust setting, only beneficiaries with a fixed interest are considered to have those rights. Most recently, Liechtenstein courts are also considering whether the applicant beneficiaries (for example, when applying for the removal of foundation board members or the setting aside of board resolutions) have indeed a legitimate interest to do so.

2.5 Practice trends

If beneficiaries of trusts and foundations have fallen out with trustees or foundation board members, who did not follow the beneficiaries' request to resign, the **Liechtenstein Trustees Association** introduced a **new and very efficient mediation procedure for removal of recalcitrant fiduciaries and trustees**, following critical controversy over Liechtenstein professionals. If the mediation concludes that the existing trustee should resign in favour of the new one (who is being favoured by the beneficiaries) and if it did not, the trustee may become subject to disciplinary sanctions by Liechtenstein courts. In the absence of the "Saunders Vautier" rule, which under common law allows beneficiaries to require the trustee under certain circumstances to terminate the trust and request the distribution of all assets to them, such new proceedings will assist beneficiaries to a great extent to terminate Liechtenstein wealth structures.

2.6 Pandemic related developments

As mentioned above, Liechtenstein law allows for board meetings to be held in **hybrid or electronic form**, which is a prompt and adequate response to pandemic related restrictions in travels and thus physical meetings.

3. ESTATE AND TRUST LITIGATION AND CONTROVERSY

3.1 National legislative and regulatory developments

The latest legislative reform of the Liechtenstein procedural code stems from 2019. The Liechtenstein legislator used this reform to update and modernise procedural rules and to catch up with its Austrian model law.

In 2022, the Liechtenstein legislator introduced a **significant shortening of the Statute of Limitation period for damage claims** brought against trustees, foundation board members or other bodies of legal entities, which will become relevant in the future. As from 1 August 2022, claims for damages against foundation board members and trustees who, for example, commit a breach of trust, are in any case time-barred within a period of 10 years from the time of the damaging act, irrespective of the knowledge of the damage or the person of the damaging party. Prior to 1 August 2022, this absolute limitation period was situated significantly higher, at 30 years.

Regulatory developments closely followed European requirements. In 2021, the **UBO-register Act** was adapted to the 5th Anti-Money-Laundering-Directive standard including a reform of the access to UBO (i.e., Ultimate Beneficial Owners) data for third parties. However, access by the public to data still requires a legitimate interest and the approval of a UBO commission board. Further, discretionary beneficiaries are not subject to registration, and an applicant who demonstrated a legitimate interest may only obtain information from the register on beneficial owners who are deemed controlling.

3.2 Local legislative and regulatory developments

In trust and estate litigation, **supervisory court proceedings** started by beneficiaries to set aside board resolutions of foundations and trusts or to remove board members or trustees are more and more frequent in Liechtenstein. Some of the reported cases deal with the obvious trend of foundation governing bodies to vary the constituting documents and to opt for the foundation to be subjected to **compulsory government supervision**, an act often considered by beneficiaries as a hostile attempt to deprive them of their right to information. In many cases, the courts rejected such attempts as unlawful, as it could eliminate the checks and balances within the foundation governance.

3.3 National case law developments

Over the last years, the Liechtenstein Supreme Court backed asset tracing efforts in a widely recognised landmark decision (LES 2018, 270). In short, the Supreme Court strengthened the rights of **decanted** entities and allows them to **claw back their assets** from third parties if the asset transfer exceeded their purpose and the third party knew or ought to have known about it.

On a procedural note, the Supreme Court has held in several recent decisions that a founder or a **beneficiary cannot necessarily participate as side interveners** in disputes of 'their' foundation. They cannot deduce from their mere position as founder or beneficiary a legitimate interest, which, however, is a requirement to participate.

Most interestingly, in the context of proceedings where beneficiaries apply for the removal of trustees or fiduciaries, case law seems to be changing regarding **conflicts of interests**. Previously, a member of the foundation board or trustee had to abstain from voting only if a specific conflict of interest was present. In a recent decision, the Supreme Court held that such member must abstain from voting even in cases of a *prima facie* **conflict of interest**, failing which they became unfit to act and needed to be removed.

3.4 Local case law developments

If, in the context of estate planning, assets of a (later) decedent are transferred as endowments to legal entities which are to be legally separated from the decedent, such as foundations or trusts, it may be the case that those entitled to a **compulsory portion** of the decedent's estate (above all spouses and children) are reduced in their compulsory portions as a result of this transfer of assets and subsequently reverse this transfer of assets by asserting their compulsory portions (in court).

Pursuant to § 785 para. 3 Civil Code, however, endowments shall not be considered in the calculation of the compulsory portion claim if they were made earlier than two years before the death of the decedent to persons not entitled to a compulsory portion. However, according to the so-called Vermögensopfertheorie (Doctrine on "sacrificing" the assets) developed in case law, this two-year period does not begin to run until the decedent irrevocably and finally disposes of the assets transferred to a foundation/trust as an endowment.

In the context of endowments to foundations or trusts, the sacrifice of assets is not yet considered to have been made if the trust is revocable or the settlor can change the beneficiaries of the trust. Therefore, if the sacrifice of assets has been

FREQUENTLY ASKED QUESTIONS

1. Is the new Beneficial Owner Register in Liechtenstein public?

In practice, it is not. Only law enforcement authorities combatting money laundering are able to access the register. The general public will only be granted access if an applicant could demonstrate to a commission comprised of judges and data protection experts that they have a legitimate interest for AML purposes. Even if they could in exceptional circumstances, they would not see more than the name of the still living settlor or founder and persons exercising control, which, in the absence of any such controlling persons in a (standard) discretionary set-up of a trust or foundation, they would be provided with the identities of the fiduciaries of trustees only.

2. Will my children, as the future beneficiaries of my trust or foundation, be subject to registration to the BO Register?

Certainly not. Regularly, fiduciaries will not, as they do not have to, register the names of the beneficiaries and family members. It would be totally sufficient if they registered as beneficiaries "the descendants of the founder and other family members", without giving any names or other specifics.

3. How can I make sure that the assets in the trust are safe from the onslaught of creditors?

First, allow yourself as little control as possible, and distance yourself from the trust and foundation which is set up for you and/or your family. If you want to reserve some level of control, you may do so, but leave and defer it to an independent person you trust, which we call "protector". It is a separate body that oversees and controls the trustees and fiduciaries. Such protector may even be vested with the powers to "hire and fire" trustees and foundation board members. Second, the location of the respective assets held by the trust or foundation may be key in determining how solid the asset protection works.

4. Will such protector be subject to reporting under the Common Reporting Standard (CRS) regime?

Some clients wish to entrust such office of protector to a person who, however, may wish to avoid the net asset value of the trust or foundation being reported to their homeland revenue service (which may be the case if they were considered "beneficial owners" under CRS). It is the level and width of control that may vary from case to case and which will decide on whether a protector is a controlling person and will thus be reportable as "beneficial owner". In most circumstances, protectors are not reportable, if they have no absolute powers.

made by the decedent, after the expiration of two years from the transfer of assets to a foundation or trust, the endowment can no longer be challenged by invoking a shortened claim to a compulsory portion. By way of example (from recent case law), the sacrifice of assets in the case of an endowment of a property by the decedent to a foundation is deemed to have been made even if the **decedent has reserved a usufruct right to the property** in their favour.

3.5 Practice trends

In 2021, the Liechtenstein Supreme Court held that **information requests can be legitimate if the party was ordered by a foreign court to request** said information (even under threat of contempt of court). Until that decision, it was widely assumed that such attempt may be subject to criminal liability pursuant to the Liechtenstein State Protection Act, which is the "legal clone" of Article 271 Swiss Criminal Act.

3.6 Pandemic related developments

During the pandemic, the Liechtenstein courts and authorities showed remarkable flexibility when it came to **witness questioning via video conference**. Unfortunately, this has not (yet) led to a sustainable change in procedural rules. From our experience, judges have started requesting the personal appearance of witnesses again, which can be a problem for foreign witnesses and parties.

Due to the pandemic, a provision was included in the Liechtenstein procedural law, which was limited until 30 June 2022 and has since expired, which enabled courts and administrative authorities, with the consent of the parties, **to conduct oral proceedings and hearings without the personal presence of the parties or their representatives using technical means of communication**.

Further, arbitration hearings do not require face-to-face attendance, which has already been explicitly confirmed in case law. **Video conferencing**, real-time image and sound transmissions, serves the purpose equally well. This is a form of communication that has increasingly come into focus or gained relevance due to advancing digitalization and not least also as a result of the travel and contact restrictions caused by the COVID-19 pandemic.

Against this background, it should also be noted that physically held meetings will probably be increasingly pushed back in favor of more modern means of communication in the future, and not only in cross-border (arbitration) proceedings. **Trust disputes**, as well as most **foundation disputes**, are **arbitrable in Liechtenstein**.

AUTHOR BIOGRAPHY

Johannes Gasser

Johannes Gasser is senior partner of GASSER PARTNER Rechtsanwälte, formerly Batliner Gasser, one of the leading law firms in Liechtenstein and a Chambers Global top tier firm, which was established in 1954. Johannes Gasser is ranked by Chambers Global as a "leading individual" in Liechtenstein. He is admitted to the Liechtenstein and Austrian Bar and specializes in advising UHNWI in setting up, administrating and challenging and defending Liechtenstein foundations and trusts in international litigation and arbitration. Johannes is a frequent speaker at the Liechtenstein University and University of Innsbruck (Austria) on foundation and trust law issues and legal expert witness in UK and other courts on Liechtenstein law. He is a member (Trust Estate Practitioner/TEP) of the Society of Trust and Estate Practitioners (STEP), an academician of The International Academy of Estate and Trust Law (IAETL) and an International Fellow of the American College of Trust and Estate Counsel (ACTEC).

LUXEMBOURG

Guy Harles, Eric Fort,
Ellen Brullard & Bilal Ajabli
Arendt & Medernach

INTRODUCTION

The Grand Duchy of Luxembourg is a country in the heart of the European Union. It is a sovereign and independent state, and a parliamentary democracy in the form of a constitutional monarchy. Luxembourg's judicial system has its origins in Roman law and was based on the French Civil Code instituted by Napoleon Bonaparte. Its domestic law of succession has its source in the country's own Civil Code.

Regarding international law, with the creation of the European Union and the consequent desire to have and develop a zone of freedom, security and justice within which the free movement of persons is ensured, it was decided that measures should be adopted in the field of judicial cooperation in civil matters with a cross-border impact, in particular where this is made necessary by an increase in the number of trans-European families.

The vast majority of EU Member States (all except for Denmark and Ireland) have adopted Regulation (EU) No 650/2012 of the European Parliament and of the Council of 4 July 2012 on jurisdiction, applicable law, recognition and enforcement of decisions and acceptance and enforcement of authentic instruments in matters of succession and on the creation of a European Certificate of Succession (the EU Succession Regulation), in order to ensure the compatibility of the rules applicable in the EU Member States as regards matters of succession.

In addition, Luxembourg has a long tradition of private wealth activities and is positioned as a leading private wealth management centre. The country has always promoted a stable and flexible legal and political environment favourable to the preservation, enhancement and transmission of patrimonies.

As an AAA country, Luxembourg is one of the most attractive places to carry out business activities within the European Union. In finding the right balance between being EU law compliant and promoting stimulating economic policies, Luxembourg shows its strong determination to contribute to the development and prosperity of wealthy families.

Luxembourg provides a platform for asset protection, international investments and estate planning for families wishing to manage properly their wealth.

1. TAX AND WEALTH PLANNING

1.1 National legislative and regulatory developments

Luxembourg tax rules in relation to estate planning have not fundamentally changed over the last few years. Luxembourg remains stable for high-net-worth individuals wishing to manage their private wealth. See the following for an overview of tax considerations for Luxembourg tax residents.

Income tax

Luxembourg income tax is levied on the net taxable income, consisting of the aggregate gross income less deductible expenses, earned by the taxpayer during the tax year.

The individual income tax rates are progressive, ranging from 8% to 42%. An employment fund contribution is added to the above rates of income tax, which is set at 7% (and 9% for income exceeding EUR 150,000 in case of single taxpayers or EUR 300,000 for couples assessed jointly). The progressive income tax rates (including the employment fund contribution) range from 8.56% to 45.78%.

All taxpayers are divided into three tax classes: a tax class is a computation formula whereby the income tax burden is recalculated in order to take into account of family/personal circumstances.

Married individuals are, by default, jointly taxed. Since 2018, married individuals can opt for a separate taxation.

Gift taxes

A gift tax (droit de donation) will be levied on any donation if the gift is recorded in a Luxembourg notarial deed and/or submitted for registration in Luxembourg. The proportional gift tax is computed on the net fair market value of the asset transferred and the tax rates vary depending on the kinship between the donor and the donee (from 1.8% to 14.4%).

Inheritance taxes

An inheritance tax (droit de succession) is levied on the net fair market value of the worldwide estate of a Luxembourg tax resident at the moment of their death. However, inheritance of immovable property located abroad is expressly exempt from Luxembourg tax, even if this property is not subject to tax in the jurisdiction where it is located.

The inheritance tax rates vary depending on the kinship between the parties, on the amount of the transferred estate and on the question of whether the estate is received on the portion the heir is entitled to under intestacy rules (from 0% to 15% – there is no inheritance and succession tax on direct line descendants).

Any inheritance with a net value exceeding EUR 10,000 is subject to a surcharge tax varying between 1/10 and 22/10.

Wealth tax

There is no wealth tax for natural persons in Luxembourg.

Taxation of investment income

As a rule, dividend and interest income are taxed according to the progressive tax rates, irrespective of whether the distributing company is resident or non-resident.

- A 50% exemption is granted on the gross amount of dividends received by a Luxembourg resident shareholder under certain conditions.
- Interest income (or similar income) may – under certain conditions and formalities – be subject to a discharging withholding tax of 20%.

Capital gains on shares realised by a resident individual acting within the management of their private wealth are taxable if they qualify as either speculative gains or gains on substantial participation:

- **Speculative gains.** Any capital gains on shares realized within the first 6 months of their acquisition (or if their disposal precedes their acquisition) are taxed as miscellaneous income subject to the progressive income tax rates applicable to the individual.

- **Gains on substantial participation.** A participation is deemed to be substantial where a resident individual shareholder holds (either alone or together with their spouse/partner and/or minor children) directly or indirectly, at any time within the 5 years preceding the disposal, more than 10% of the share capital of the issuing company. A shareholder is also deemed to have disposed of a substantial participation if it was acquired for no consideration within the 5 years preceding the disposal, and if it constituted a substantial participation when held by the alienator (or alienators, in the case of successive transfers for no consideration within the same 5-year period). Capital gains realised on a substantial participation are subject to income tax by applying the half-global rate method (i.e. between 0% and 22.89% in 2022) and reduced by an allowance of EUR 50,000 (EUR 100,000 for spouses/partners filing jointly) every 10 years.

Besides, capital gains realised on non-substantial participation or on shares held for more than 6 months are not taxable in Luxembourg.

1.2 Local legislative and regulatory developments

There are no very recent legislative developments but – nonetheless – we would like to emphasise the following changes introduced into the Luxembourg tax landscape over the last few years which are relevant for private clients:

- Since the law of 18 December 2015, a step-up principle has been introduced with regard to securities forming part of a significant shareholding (i.e. more than 10% in the target company) in the assets of an individual upon the transfer of tax residence to Luxembourg. This domestic rule provides for a revaluation of the acquisition price of the above-mentioned securities at the fair market value as of the date of migration to Luxembourg without having any impact on their holding period.
- The Luxembourg law of 25 March 2020 has implemented the EU Directive 2018/822 dated 25 May 2018 (DAC 6) and introduced a mandatory reporting obligation for Luxembourg resident intermediaries, or relevant taxpayers, on cross-border arrangements and transactions involving Luxembourg entities with characteristics or features presenting an indication of potential risk of tax avoidance (according to listed hallmarks).

1.3 National case law developments

There has been no recent national case law relevant to private clients.

1.4 Local case law developments

There has been no recent local case law relevant to private clients.

1.5 Practice trends

Family members usually use Luxembourg limited partnerships to transfer the family business to the next generation, this can be combined with the subdivision of the ownership right (usufruct and bare-ownership schemes, see Section 2.5 Practice trends: Subdivision of proprietary rights). The contractual freedom provided by these investment vehicles allows the partners to draw up the contract in order to ensure the transmission of the inheritance in the best way.

1.6 Pandemic related developments

The special bilateral agreements signed between Luxembourg and the Belgian, French and German authorities concerning the taxation rules applying to cross-border workers in the context of the COVID-19 pandemic came to an end on 30 June 2022.

Consequently, from 1 July 2022, the general rules on the taxation of employment income received by Belgian, French and German cross-border commuters (i.e. employees residing in France, Germany or Belgium and commuting to Luxembourg to perform employment-related activities) apply.

2. ESTATE AND TRUST ADMINISTRATION

2.1 National legislative and regulatory developments

The Grand Duchy of Luxembourg is a civil law jurisdiction.

Title I of Book III of the Civil Code on the settlement of successions dates back to 1804. It has since been developed several times in order to adapt to changing customs, but without abandoning its main principles; for example, that of property passing to the closest heir (la mort saisit le vif) or that of forced heirship (réserve héréditaire).

Indeed, unlike in common law jurisdictions, death results in the automatic transfer of ownership of the property held by the deceased at death to the legal heirs (provided they accept the estate).

Thus, under Luxembourg law, there is no need to appoint an executor, as the accepting heirs can administer and manage the property, as well as dispose of it (although there are certain exceptions to this principle, particularly where the heirs are not legal heirs but rather legatees).

Moreover, Luxembourg domestic law does not contain the concept of the trust. It is therefore not possible to create a trust under Luxembourg law. However, Luxembourg has ratified the Hague Convention of 1 July 1985 on the Law Applicable to Trust and their Recognition, and the Law of 27 July 2003 approving the Hague Convention of 1 July 1985 on the Law applicable to Trusts and on their Recognition, as amended, therefore trusts that are validly established under foreign law will be recognised, and will thus be able to produce their effects and be executed on Luxembourg territory.

Note also that, since a bill creating a register of fiducies and trusts was adopted on 1 July 2020, foreign trusts have been obliged to complete disclosure formalities with the Luxembourg authorities if the trustee is established or domiciled in Luxembourg, or if they enter into a business relationship with a professional established in Luxembourg, or if they acquire real estate located in Luxembourg for the trust.

In this respect, there is, for example, an obligation for the trustee to keep an internal file listing the beneficial owners of the trust at the trust's registered place of business if it is administered from the Grand Duchy of Luxembourg. The file is accessible to national competent authorities and professionals with whom the trustees enter into a business relationship or carry out certain types of transactions.

Such information must also be shared with the Luxembourg authorities, by filing with the Luxembourg register of fiducies and trusts. Such information is therefore available to:

- national competent authorities such as the public prosecutor and the tax administration upon their request for the purpose of their supervisory duties; but also
- self-regulatory bodies (i.e. the Bar Council and the Chamber of Notaries); or
- professionals of the financial sector (such as credit institutions and insurance companies) in the context of their customer due diligence measures.

The public has no access to this register of fiducies and trusts.

Non-compliance with the obligations imposed on the trustees is punishable by administrative penalties such as fines of up to EUR 1,250,000.

2.2 Local legislative and regulatory developments

Luxembourg legislation is adopted by the Chamber of Deputies (who currently number 60), and comes into force after promulgation by the Grand Duke and publication in the Official Journal of the Grand Duchy of Luxembourg (see *https:// gouvernement.lu/fr/systeme-politique/chambre-deputes.html*).

As the country is not divided into federal states, it has only one legislature, at the national level.

2.3 National case law developments

Under Luxembourg law, it is not mandatory to have an executor to settle an estate. In fact, the vast majority of successions are settled without the intervention of an executor. As appointing one is optional, it is up to the testator to choose whether to do so, under the terms of the will.

The main role of the executor is to ensure the proper execution of the last will and testament, but also to release the legacies to the beneficiaries or to draw up an inventory of the estate's assets. They may also take legal action if the provisions of the will are not carried out.

In the performance of their duties the executor is liable to the testator's heirs, who may ask the executor to give an account of how the tasks were carried out.

Thus, the executor has a role to play in the settlement of the succession, but does not replace the heirs. Moreover, it has been ruled that the executor cannot decide on a resumption of proceedings initiated by the deceased because the executor is not called upon to succeed the deceased, as only the heirs have this power (Court of Appeal, 20 October 2010, roll number 31770).

The executor under Luxembourg law therefore has the role of a guardian, verifying that operations are carried out in accordance with the deceased's last wishes and having the power to protect them if necessary.

2.4 Local case law developments

For the reason stated in Section 2.2, Luxembourg does not have local case law (only national case law).

2.5 Practice trends

Succession management where the deceased was married

Under Luxembourg law, the succession of a married person cannot be settled without first considering their matrimonial property regime.

The assets of a married person are subject to the matrimonial regime under which that person was married. That is why it is essential to proceed to liquidate the matrimonial regime first, and only then to settle the estate.

There are four main matrimonial property regimes:

- The **legal regime** applied by default or by agreement: community of property acquired after marriage (communauté de biens réduite aux acquêts). Under this regime, all assets acquired from the marriage with fruits and income received during the marriage, are owned in common by both spouses, whereas property acquired before the marriage (or by inheritance or gift even during the marriage) remains the property of the spouse who acquired or received it. Thus, when a person married under the legal regime dies, it is necessary to liquidate the matrimonial regime to know the inheritance (in other words, to determine which assets belonged to the deceased in full ownership and which belonged half to them and half to their spouse).

- The **regime of joint ownership** of all property (communauté universelle) is one where the spouses choose to put all assets in common, whether they were acquired before or during the marriage, even as gifts or inheritance. This regime is often supplemented by a clause of full allocation to the surviving spouse (clause d'attribution intégrale), so that upon the death of the first spouse, all assets are transferred to the surviving spouse in their sole name. It should be noted that means of protection exist for descendants from previous unions to prevent them from being disinherited.

- The **separate property regime** (séparation des biens) is one under which each spouse remains the sole owner of the property they acquire or receive before and during the marriage. In this case there is no need to liquidate the matrimonial property regime, although there may still be claims between the spouses (loans from one to the other) to be taken into account in the settlement of the estate.

- The **regime of participation in matrimonial assets** (participation aux acquêts) is similar to a separate property regime during the marriage, but if the marriage is dissolved, it causes any increase in the assets of the spouses to be shared between them. Thus, at the time of marriage dissolution, it resembles a joint ownership regime. This hybrid regime must be liquidated as part of the succession settlement in order to determine the inheritance to be divided among the heirs.

Thus, estate planning inevitably involves matrimonial arrangements for future spouses or married couples. This is something that our clients understand, and for which demand is increasing.

Subdivision of proprietary rights

Another practice in Luxembourg law is the subdivision of proprietary rights (démembrement de propriété). This is where full ownership, which is composed of bare ownership (abusus) and usufruct (usus and fructus), is divided among multiple persons.

The usufructuary has the right to use the property and to receive the fruits of it (e.g. to live in a house or to rent it out and receive the rent), whereas the bare owner has a right to recover full ownership of the property when the usufruct ceases to exist.

The usufruct can be for a fixed period, or it can be for life (i.e. ending on the day the usufructuary dies).

Full ownership is established automatically at the end of the usufruct.

FREQUENTLY ASKED QUESTIONS

The questions our clients ask most routinely are about the possible forms for drawing up a valid will (see Section 3.3 National case law developments) and, for those who wish to marry, which matrimonial regime they should adopt (see Section 2.5 Practice trends: Subdivision of proprietary rights).

Our more senior clients are concerned with the transmission of their assets, and thus their requests tend to relate to gifts and donations. These entail immediate and irrevocable dispossession. However, they can, under certain conditions, also be made under foreign law, and will be in principle fully recognised in Luxembourg as long as they were made in accordance with the foreign legal requirements.

Finally, our clients who have family and assets in several countries often want to know which law applies to their succession, and whether this law will be recognised in the countries where their children reside or their assets are located. Thanks to the EU Succession Regulation, only one applicable law is recognised for a given succession: that of the deceased's last habitual residence or, if chosen, that of their country of nationality (even if not an EU Member State).

The appeal of this mechanism is that a person can, securely and with long-term effect, distribute assets during their lifetime by giving away the bare ownership or, for example, allocate assets to multiple generations when they die by bequeathing subdivided proprietary rights to different parties. This mechanism allows for flexibility in the organisation of clients' assets, and is much appreciated by them for its greater efficiency.

2.6 Pandemic related developments

Unlike neighbouring jurisdictions, Luxembourg did not experience any changes in how last wills and testaments were made or how powers of attorney were granted during the COVID-19 pandemic.

However, there were some temporary changes in company law on how general meetings of shareholders or boards of directors may be held, whether for companies or associations. These changes allowed participants to take part at a distance even when not provided for in the articles of association and decisions to be taken by means of written resolutions despite this sometimes being prohibited by law. Note that by the time this document is published, this temporary exceptional regime will most likely have ended.

3. ESTATE AND TRUST LITIGATION AND CONTROVERSY

3.1 National legislative and regulatory developments

Until recently, trusts did not have to be reported to any particular Luxembourg register, as they are not entities with a tradition in Luxembourg law.

However, this began to change with the law of 13 January 2019 establishing a register of beneficial owners (RBO). This law obliged companies and Luxembourg entities like non-profit organisations to list their beneficial owners in the national RBO. For anti-money laundering and counter terrorist financing purposes, they also have to keep an internal file containing the beneficial owners' information at their registered address. As a result, a foreign trust that owns a Luxembourg company through the trustee may be viewed as the beneficial owner of that company. In those cases, the RBO may need to contain information on the settlor, the trustee, the beneficiary and the protector (if any). The information in the RBO consists of names and surnames, nationalities, place and date of birth, country of residence and nature of the interests (settlor, trustee, beneficiary, protector, and so on) and was publicly accessible.

However, the judgment of November 22, 2022 by the Court of Justice of the European Union ruled in relation to Directive 2018/843 that the provision of the latter providing that information on the beneficial owners of companies incorporated in the territory of the Member States be accessible in all cases to any member of the general public was invalid. Following this judgment, the Ministry of Justice required Luxembourg Business Registers (LBR) to immediately suspend all public access to the RBO pending the introduction of access rights more in line with the conclusions of the Court's ruling.

As a first step, on 16 December 2022, the LBR announced a new procedure for obtaining access to the RBO, applicable solely to professionals that are subject to the amended law of 12 November 2004 on the fight against money laundering and terrorist financing.

The access to the RBO then has been enlarged under conditions to journalists following an agreement between LBR and the Press Council signed on 20 December 2022.

On 1 February 2023, the LBR announced that it has put into place a procedure for entities to access their own RBO data by means of a confidential code.

All data in the RBO database can be viewed except for personal data such as addresses and personal identification numbers. It is possible to request that access to certain beneficial ownership details be restricted, but these restrictions must be temporary and justified. Justifying circumstances might include, for example, a disproportionate risk of fraud, kidnapping, blackmail, extortion, harassment, violence or intimidation, or when the beneficial owner is a minor.

If the RBO approves a request to restrict access to beneficial ownership details, they will only be accessible to a certain category of professionals such as national authorities, lending institutions, financial institutions, bailiffs and notaries.

To our knowledge, the only such requests that have been granted to date have been for beneficial owners who are minors.

3.2 Local legislative and regulatory developments

Luxembourg legislation is adopted by the Chamber of Deputies (who currently number 60), and comes into force after promulgation by the Grand Duke and publication in the Official Journal of the Grand Duchy of Luxembourg (see *https://gouvernement.lu/en/systeme-politique/chambre-deputes.html*).

As the country is not divided into federal states, it has only one legislature, at the national level.

3.3 National case law developments

Under Luxembourg domestic law, a testator can express their last wishes and arrange for what will happen to their property after they die by means one of the following:

- an authentic will: one that must be drawn up by two notaries or by a notary in the presence of two witnesses; or
- a holographic will: one that is handwritten, signed and dated by the testator; or
- a mystic will: one that must be prepared in advance and presented in a closed envelope to the notary, who will seal it, and who must then draw up a special deed (acte de suscription) in the presence of two witnesses.

For many years, the question of how to revoke authentic wills was a controversial topic in both case law and legal scholarship.

The controversy stemmed from a specific interpretation of articles 980 and 1035 of the Civil Code, according to which an authentic will could only be validly revoked by means of another authentic deed.

However, the Court of Cassation eventually helped dispel the legal controversy surrounding the revocability of authentic wills by ruling that a testator can validly revoke an authentic will by means of a subsequent holographic will (decision of 5 July 2018, docket number 77/2018).

This welcome decision put an end to a long period of uncertainty in inheritance law.

3.4 Local case law developments

For the reason stated in Section 3.2, Luxembourg does not have local case law (only national case law).

3.5 Practice trends

The subjects of litigation in inheritance matters are as numerous as they are varied. Among other examples, disputes may arise over which law applies where a foreign element is involved or for the purpose of contesting a will's validity, or even over how to legally characterise an instance of inheritance fraud (where an heir appropriates an inheritance to the detriment of the other heirs).

3.6 Pandemic related developments

A number of measures have been agreed between the Courts and the Bar since the beginning of the pandemic in 2020 in order to be able to exit the crisis under favourable conditions.

To reduce lawyers' travel to a minimum, email accounts were set up to handle routine case management electronically. It was thus agreed that, except for the submission of documents (which must be done by post), exchanges should be done electronically by means of these special email addresses.

In addition, it was agreed that lawyers should request an appointment to argue a case, to avoid having too many people in the courtroom at once.

In general, all exchanges were kept to a minimum.

Although the health measures have been lifted now that the pandemic has died down and the situation has almost returned to normal, some other measures that proved beneficial remain in place. For example, the email accounts are still used, and some requests can still be made by email. In addition, the system of prior appointment for oral argument of scheduled cases remains compulsory in some courts.

AUTHOR BIOGRAPHIES

Guy Harles

Guy Harles is a Founding Partner and former Chairman of Arendt & Medernach. He specialises in corporate projects, advising multinational and domestic companies, as well as HNWIs on the structuring of international transactions, private equity investments, corporate reorganisations, mergers and acquisitions, corporate finance and private wealth management. As an entrepreneurial lawyer, Guy plays a major role in Arendt & Medernach's international development. He has acquired a very good knowledge of the international market and more specifically of Asia, where he regularly advises clients. Guy's international business experience and long-standing position as trusted advisor are underscored by a number of Board-level appointments. Guy also regularly serves as an arbitrator, designated by leading international arbitration centres.

Eric Fort

Eric Fort is a Partner in the Tax Law and Private Client practices of Arendt & Medernach. He advises on both national and international tax issues. He has substantial experience in real estate, private equity, private wealth structuring and finance transactions. Eric was Head of the firm's New York office from 2017 to 2021, where he gained deep knowledge of the US and greater North-American markets. He has been a member of the Luxembourg Bar since 1996. He was the chair of the Luxembourg branch of the International Fiscal Association, where he was appointed as national co-reporter for the annual congresses in 1997, 1999, 2003, 2006 and 2012.

Ellen Brullard

Ellen Brullard is a Senior Associate in the Private Client practice of Arendt & Medernach. She specialises in estate planning, international succession and private wealth structuring. She advises private clients, family offices and entrepreneurs, both national and international, on the global structuring of their wealth including but not limited to matrimonial, inheritance and civil matters as well as relocation. Ellen Brullard graduated in France as a notary and holds Master's degrees in both Business and Private law as well as an advanced degree in Asset and Wealth Management from the Université Robert Schuman de Strasbourg (Strasbourg III – France). She is also a board member of STEP BeNeLux.

Bilal Ajabli

Bilal Ajabli is a Senior Associate in the Private Client practice of Arendt & Medernach where he advises high net worth individuals and family offices on the global tax structuring of their private wealth. He holds a Master degree from the Université Catholique de Louvain (Belgium) and a Postgraduate degree in tax law from the Vrije Universiteit Brussel (Belgium). Bilal joined Arendt & Medernach in 2022 and is also a member of the Belgian Bar.

SCOTLAND

Paul Macaulay & Mark McKeown
Turcan Connell

INTRODUCTION

As a jurisdiction, Scotland forms part of the wider United Kingdom, the other constituent jurisdictions of which are England and Wales, and Northern Ireland. It has its own distinct system of laws, retained after the Act of Union in the eighteenth-century: this system is mixed, drawing on both Roman civil law tradition and English common law. Legislation which applies to Scotland is generated in both the UK Parliament, based in London, and a devolved Scottish Parliament, based in Edinburgh. Matters affecting tax and succession are considered by both parliaments, depending upon whether the relevant area of legislative competence rests at UK or Scottish level. The UK Supreme Court, the final civil Court of Appeal for all constituent parts of the UK, decides Scottish cases relating to tax and succession matters.

1. TAX AND WEALTH PLANNING

At the date of writing, certain limited taxation powers have been devolved from the UK Parliament to the Scottish Parliament (see below).

Where the Scottish Parliament has legislative power over taxation, however, this primarily relates to the taxation of income (limited) and land transactions. The process of devolution, begun under the Scotland Act 1998 and its successor statutes, conferred on the Scottish Parliament the ability to set different rates and bands of income tax to those of the rest of the United Kingdom, and to create a Land and Buildings Transaction Tax as well as a Scottish Landfill Tax. Responsibility for the collection of income tax rests with H M Revenue & Customs, the UK-wide revenue collection authority, but that of the Land and Buildings Transaction Tax and Scottish Landfill Tax rests with Revenue Scotland, an entity created under statute by the Scottish Parliament.

Legislative powers relating to capital taxation rest with the UK Parliament. Reference is made in the England & Wales chapter to the principles and rates of taxation.

Income Tax

In respect of the taxation of income, the Scottish rates and bands of income tax apply only to those taxpayers who are identified as Scottish in terms of the Scotland Act, and only then to their income (except for dividends and bank interest). From 2016, the Scottish Parliament was granted the limited power to set a 'Scottish Rate of Income Tax', which means that all rates and bands of income tax on non-savings and non-dividend interest are set by that body, although the tax-free 'personal allowance' is still set by the UK Parliament. See the England & Wales chapter for the rates of tax set by the UK Parliament. A Scottish taxpayer, as defined in statute, may only be a taxpayer who is resident in the United Kingdom for tax purposes for the relevant tax year, as determined by the United Kingdom statutory residence rules. The individual must be:
- a Scottish parliamentarian; or
- have a "close connection" with Scotland; or
- if there is no close connection with any part of the UK, the individual must spend more days in the tax year in Scotland than any other part of the UK.

Draft guidance exists as to how the taxpayer's "close connection" may be established, particularly where there is uncertainty as to the location of that taxpayer's main place of residence.

For tax year 2023/24 the rates and bands of income tax applicable for non-dividend or interest-related income, announced in the Scottish government's December 2022 budget statement, are as follows:

Taxable Income (GBP)	Tax Rate
Over 12,571 – 14,732	19%
Over 14,733 - 25,688	20%
Over 25,689 - 43,662	21%
Over 43,663 - 125,140	42%
Above 125,140	47%

At the time of writing, the Budget (Scotland) Bill had yet to be enacted, but since the current Scottish government enjoys a majority in the Scottish parliament, it seems likely that the tax rates and bands above, together with the change to the Land and Buildings Transaction Tax (LBTT) Additional Dwelling Supplement referred to below, will come into effect by 6th April 2023 when the new UK tax year begins.

Land Tax
Of the land taxes that have been devolved to the Scottish Parliament, private individuals will deal most often with LBTT given that it is payable on the acquisition, lease etc., of residential and commercial land and buildings.

LBTT is payable at different rates, depending on the purchase price of the property, or the value of the rent payable in a lease, within different tax bands. The residential LBTT rates and bands in tax year 2023/24 are as follows:

Purchase Price (GBP)	LBTT Rate
Up to 145,000	0%
145,001 - 250,000	2%
250,001 - 325,000	5%
325,001 - 750,000	10%
Over 750,000	12%

A relief for first time buyers is available, which increases the residential nil rate band of LBTT to GBP 175,000. Separate non-residential LBTT rates and bands exist in respect of commercial purchases and leases.

There is an Additional Dwelling Supplement which is payable on the purchase by a taxpayer of an additional dwelling in Scotland where the buyer already has an interest (widely defined to include a right in land which is enforceable against everyone, not just one person, or other interest in or over land in Scotland, including the benefit of an obligation, restriction or condition affecting the value of such a right or interest over land in Scotland) in residential property anywhere in the world. This could include, for example, a buy to let property, or a purchase for a student family member to live in, an interest in an inherited property (at the earlier of the point when the period of estate administration ends and the point at which the property is transferred to the beneficiary), or purchases by non-natural persons, such as trusts (although the acquisition by certain types of trusts can be assessed on individual beneficiaries, meaning that it is the individual rather than the trustee who is deemed to have acquired an interest). In tax year 2023/24, as announced in the Scottish government's December 2022 budget statement the supplement is charged at 6% of the total purchase price, where the purchase of the relevant property is over the value of GBP 40,000.

LBTT also applies to those leasing non-residential land and buildings in Scotland. The tax liability is calculated with reference to the net present value (NPV) of the rent payable over the term of the lease. At every three-year review of the lease, the NPV amount must be recalculated using the actual amount of rent paid during that period. The same calculation applies where the Lease is assigned or is terminated. This ensures that over the lifetime of the lease the tax paid reflects the actual rent payable rather than an estimated amount. The rates of LBTT in tax year 2023/24 for leases are as follows:

NPV of Rent Payable (GBP)	LBTT Rate
Up to 150,000	0%
150,001 - 250,000	1%
Above 250,000	5%

1.1 National legislative and regulatory developments
Other than changes in rates (see above) there have been no significant legislative or regulatory developments in Scotland. See the England and Wales chapter for other developments.

1.2 Local legislative and regulatory developments
Other than changes in rates (see above) there have been no significant legislative or regulatory developments in Scotland.

1.3 National case law developments
See the England and Wales chapter for case law developments which affect non-devolved taxes.

1.4 Local case law developments
There have been no recent significant local case law developments which affect devolved taxes.

1.5 Practice trends
See the England and Wales chapter for practice trends in relation to taxation issues which affect Scotland as part of the wider United Kingdom.

1.6 Pandemic related developments
See the England and Wales chapter for pandemic related developments in relation to taxation issues which affect Scotland as part of the wider United Kingdom.

2. ESTATE AND TRUST ADMINISTRATION
Wills and estate administration
In Scotland, the applicable law affecting the overall scheme of succession to an estate is decided by reference to the domicile of the deceased. In Scots law,

domicile for succession purposes is a broad concept which is decided by case law, rather than by statutory provision. That case law has derived from cases heard by both courts in Scotland and in other constituent parts of the United Kingdom.

Scotland has its own probate system and the authority to grant the Scottish equivalent of probate, known as 'Confirmation', is regulated by statute, having its basis in the nineteenth-century. Where the testator was domiciled in Scotland, the local (Sheriff) court has jurisdiction to confirm to the assets of the deceased in Scotland, England and Wales and Northern Ireland: it does not have any jurisdiction to grant the equivalent in respect of any assets held in any foreign jurisdiction. By virtue of the Administration of Estates Act 1971, Scottish Confirmation is recognised as the equivalent of Probate in the jurisdiction of England and Wales, ensuring that Executors applying for Confirmation in Scotland may use that grant to take title to assets in England and Wales, and vice versa. Where testators are not domiciled in Scotland but a grant of Confirmation is required to permit the succession to the Scottish estate held by non-Scottish-domiciled persons, an application may be made by Executors to the Sheriff Court in Edinburgh, which acts as a central point for such applications: in those circumstances, a separate Probate application would be required for any property owned by the deceased and situated in England and Wales.

In common with England, Wales and Northern Ireland, testators may nominate Executors under their Will, and those Executors are then responsible for the administration of the deceased's estate on death. Executors may also be appointed, but by the Court, where the deceased died intestate (see below).

After death, it is the duty of the deceased's Executors to gather in the assets within the deceased's estate. In order to do so, they must pay liabilities (including any UK inheritance tax) and seek Confirmation from the local Sheriff Court.

To be used in the probate process, a testamentary writing must be valid and probative (self-proving). This requires compliance with legal requirements set out in legislation (see below) and the testator must have capacity to make the testamentary writing. In Scotland, the testator must be over the age of 12, and there is a presumption as to the capacity of the testator when the testamentary writing is made.

The Requirements of Writing (Scotland) Act 1995 sets out the basis for executing a valid Will after 1st August 1995. To be self-proving, the Will must be made in writing, subscribed by the testator, signed on each separate page and witnessed by one person who is 16 years of age or over and has mental capacity, subject to our comments at Section 2.6 below. If the Will is not valid or self-proving, it might still be possible to improve the position by the provision of evidence to the court by way of affidavit or other document, and, in more complex cases, by a hearing in open court.

If a Will is valid on the face of it (having been signed correctly and witnessed), there are three grounds under which it could still be challenged:

- **Incapacity.** For incapacity, the test is that the person making the Will must:
  - understand the nature of the Will and its effect;
  - have some idea of the extent of the property of which they are disposing under the Will; and
  - be aware of the persons for whom they would usually be expected to provide and the claims that those people might have on their estate.

Testamentary capacity need not be permanent and may only be in place for the period that the person created their Will. The presumption is that each person has testamentary capacity.

- **Facility and circumvention.** To prove facility and circumvention, the testator must have a weakness such as old age or ill health which exposes them to influence and that weakness must have been exploited by a particular person. The greater the weakness, the less evidence is required to prove the exploitation.
- **Undue influence.** For a Will to be challenged as a result of undue influence, there must be a relationship between the parties that creates "a dominant or ascendant influence" involving confidence and trust. It must be established that a material or gratuitous benefit was received by the party with influence.

Testators domiciled in Scotland do not have complete freedom to dispose of their assets as they wish. Certain relatives of a deceased testator may claim 'legal rights' or legitim. These are a form of forced heirship, deriving from the civil law system, applicable to those who die domiciled in Scotland for succession purposes. Those who may claim legal rights are restricted to the testator's surviving civil partner or spouse and their natural or adopted children; children of pre-deceasing children may represent their parents. Legal rights apply whether there is a Will or not.

Where a spouse or civil partner is entitled to claim, they may claim a one-half share of the net moveable estate (that is, all assets apart from land and buildings) if there are no surviving children, but only a one-third share if there are surviving children. Those surviving children may be entitled, collectively, to claim a one-half share of the net moveable estate where there is no surviving civil partner or spouse, or a one third share if there is a surviving civil partner or spouse. In certain circumstances, some planning can be undertaken in lifetime to improve the position where there is a risk of a legal rights claim on death. Care should be taken where immoveable property is owned within a partnership structure, as Scots law could treat the asset as moveable, and therefore subject to a potential legal rights claim.

Legal rights claimants may not claim after twenty years from the date of the death of the deceased. An entitlement to claim legal rights may be discharged by the potential claimant during the testator's lifetime, or on the testator's death, by way of deed. Previous lifetime gifts are relevant: certain lifetime gifts can reduce the share of the legal rights fund to which a claimant may be entitled. This is known as "collation", and certain advances made by a deceased parent to a child during their lifetime could then be taken into account in calculating the legal rights fund.

Where the deceased did not make a valid Will, the laws of intestacy apply. The Succession (Scotland) Act 1964, as amended by further legislation in 2016, governs the distribution of an intestate estate.

Where the deceased was survived by a spouse or civil partner, those survivors are currently awarded:

- a right to the deceased's dwellinghouse, or a share of the deceased's dwellinghouse, up to a value of GBP 473,000;
- a right to the furniture and plenishings of the deceased's house, or a share of the furniture and plenishings, up to a value of GBP 29,000; and
- a cash right to a value of GBP 50,000 (where the deceased was survived by children), or up to GBP 89,000 (if the deceased was not survived by children).

The net moveable estate (i.e., the estate other than land and buildings, after settlement of debts and liabilities) is then subject to any legal rights claims.

The succession legislation sets out a list of those entitled to the remaining estate after settlement of the surviving spouse or civil partner's share, any legal rights claims and settlement of any debts. Those entitled to inherit are ranked in the following order: natural or adopted children (with representation by their own children); parents (one-half) and siblings (one-half); siblings (with representation by their own children); parents; spouse or civil partner; uncles and aunts, both maternal and paternal; grandparents; grandparents' brothers or sisters; and so on.

A surviving co-habitant is entitled to seek an award from the estate of their pre-deceasing co-habitant only where that co-habitant has died without making a testamentary writing. The Scottish courts have discretion as to what award may be made, if any. Any such claim must be made to the Scottish courts within six months of the death of the pre-deceasing co-habitant.

Trusts and trust administration

Under Scots law, a trust constitutes a legal relationship in which property is vested in one person: the trustee. That trustee is under a fiduciary obligation to apply the property for the benefit of another person: the beneficiary. That obligation is a qualification of the trustee's proprietary right to the trust property. There is, therefore, a tripartite relationship, which may at first appear familiar to those in common law systems, but the distinction between legal and equitable ownership, which exists in the common law countries, does not exist under Scots law. Whilst Scots law does not recognise the concept of a private foundation found elsewhere, trusts are commonly used for estate planning purposes either as *inter vivos* entities, or established under Wills. They are often used where assets may be intended to benefit minor beneficiaries, or those who lack capacity otherwise. They are also efficient vehicles for tax and/or asset protection planning purposes.

The most common types of trusts recognised by Scots law are:

- **Liferent Trusts.** The beneficiary, known as the liferenter, is conferred the right to the Trust income and to enjoy any non-income producing assets within the Trust Fund, and another beneficiary (the fiar or capital beneficiary) becomes entitled to the capital, either on the termination of the liferenter's interest by way of lifetime event or on their death.
- **Discretionary Trusts.** The trustees have discretion as to which beneficiary, from a defined class of beneficiaries, may receive a benefit from the Trust Fund. The Trustees have complete flexibility as to the nature and extent of the interest which such beneficiaries may receive: they may receive capital or income, at any point, in whatever shares the Trustees think appropriate. Beyond the accumulation period, which is currently a maximum of twenty one years from the establishment of the Trust, the Trustees may not accumulate the income of the Trust.
- **Bare Trusts.** This is effectively a nominee arrangement under which the Trustees are owners of the Trust assets in terms of the documents of title, but the underlying beneficiary is entitled to demand from the Trustees payment of the Trust Fund at any time.
- **Charitable Trusts.** The trustees of such trusts hold assets for charitable purposes, which must be for the benefit of the public. The criteria as to whether a trust benefits the public are set out in the Charities and Trustee Investment

(Scotland) Act 2005. An entity known as the Office of the Scottish Charity Regulator is responsible for the regulation of registered charities in Scotland.

Trusts are taxed as to income and capital under UK-wide legislation. This legislation is covered in the England & Wales chapter, and the residence of the Trust, if the Trustees are in Scotland, does not currently affect that taxation regime.

Asset Protection for Spouses and Co-habitants

Under Scots law, assets received by way of gift or inheritance during a marriage are generally not taken into account in the event of divorce or separation of the donee. If, however, the assets were to change in nature – for example if investments were sold – they may become matrimonial property, unless the donee can make a successful claim regarding the source of funds. In order to protect the position of such donees, they may enter into a pre- or post-nuptial agreement with their fiancé or spouse. The question as to whether prenuptial agreements are enforceable in Scotland has not yet been fully tested before the Scottish courts. As a matter of course, however, the Scottish courts are reluctant to interfere with an agreement entered into between two adults of sound mind and the widely held view is that a prenuptial agreement will be upheld provided that it was fair and reasonable at the time it was entered into. Many prenuptial agreements only seek to extend the protection already offered by Scots law to gifted/inherited assets and to assets acquired with non-matrimonial funds. Against this background, it is considered unlikely that most prenuptial agreements would be considered to be unfair in the majority of cases, provided that both parties had an opportunity to seek independent legal advice on the agreement, and sufficient time to consider its terms ahead of the marriage. Similar agreements may be put in place for (prospective) cohabitants.

2.1 National legislative and regulatory developments

The Economic Crime (Transparency and Enforcement) Act 2022, enacted by the UK Parliament in 2022, includes measures to counter money-laundering, including the creation of a beneficial ownership register for overseas entities holding UK real estate. Under these measures, offshore entities which own land and/or buildings in Scotland (or the wider UK) must register with Companies House. Although trusts are not immediately caught within the scope of the provisions, overseas entities which are registrable and which have trustees as shareholders may bring trusts into the ambit of the register.

2.2 Local legislative and regulatory developments

The Scottish Law Commission recently produced a draft bill updating the existing law of trusts in Scotland, following which, at the date of writing, the Scottish government had introduced its own version of the bill to the Scottish parliament, covering not only trust law but also succession law. The trust-related provisions of the Trusts and Succession (Scotland) Bill, as introduced, replace all existing trust legislation, other than that dealing specifically with charitable and public trusts (which are governed by separate legislation). Whilst the Bill replaces all existing Scottish trust legislation, it does not give a comprehensive statutory statement of trust law in Scotland. The common law of trusts in Scotland, where it is not altered by provision made in the Bill, will continue to have effect. The principal aim of the Bill is to modernise trust law in Scotland, including – amongst other areas – trustees' duty of care, their duty to provide information to beneficiaries and third parties, their investment powers, the power for them to resign or be removed, the powers of the Scottish courts in relation to trusts and a statutory power to allow the appointment of protectors (previously not present in any Scottish legislation). The Bill also contains a proposal to abolish the rule on accumulations referred to above. As regards succession law, amongst other provisions, the Bill clarifies the law in relation to special destinations, where individuals buy property jointly with a provision that their share in that property automatically passes to the surviving owner. The Bill sets out that if, under these circumstances, the owners were married, but later divorced, the property is not automatically inherited by the ex-spouse. It also reorders who is to inherit property when an individual dies intestate. As mentioned above, at present, spouses and children are entitled to a specific share of the property whether or not an individual has left a will. If the individual died intestate, the Bill proposes to list the deceased's spouse after children and grandchildren in the new statutory list of beneficiaries. It is anticipated that the Bill will be enacted during the 2023 calendar year, subject to a three-stage process of parliamentary scrutiny.

The Scottish government has indicated that it would review the laws on inheritance on intestacy and the legal rights rules as part of extensive succession law reforms and the Trusts and Succession (Scotland) Bill goes some way towards changing the rules on intestacy, but at the date of writing, there are no plans to reform the current law regarding legal rights where the distinction between immoveable and moveable assets is made.

Trustees in Scotland, as in the wider UK, are obliged, with few exceptions, to register with HMRC's Trust Registration Service, which was introduced by the UK government in 2017 after the adoption of the Fourth EU Anti-Money Laundering Directive.

Where trustees hold land in Scotland, they may also be obliged to join the Register of Persons Holding a Controlled Interest in Land, a Scottish government initiative introduced in 2022, which is administered by Registers of Scotland, and which was intended to increase transparency in relation to how title to real estate is held.

2.3 National case law developments

See the England and Wales chapter for case law developments affecting Scotland as part of the wider United Kingdom.

2.4 Local case law developments

There have been no recent significant local case law developments in Scotland.

2.5 Practice trends

See the England and Wales chapter for practice trends in relation to trust and succession issues which affect Scotland as part of the wider United Kingdom.

2.6 Pandemic related developments

For estate administration purposes, Executors and their agents in Scotland deal with entities both at UK and devolved levels: HM Revenue & Customs and the Scottish Courts and Tribunals Service. Changes in relation to the interaction with

FREQUENTLY ASKED QUESTIONS

1. What regard must Scottish courts have to the decisions of courts in the wider United Kingdom?

As mentioned above, Scotland forms a constituent part of the wider United Kingdom, but has retained its own distinct system of laws. Decisions of 'lower courts' in the wider United Kingdom (and indeed abroad) can be taken into account in the decisions of Scottish courts, where those may be useful in the decision-making process, though decisions of such courts are not binding. Decisions of the United Kingdom Supreme Court, which is the final civil court of appeal for all constituent parts of the UK, are binding on the Scottish courts. The Judges of the UK Supreme Court comprise lawyers qualified in England and Wales, Scotland and Northern Ireland.

2. To what extent is Scotland aligned to the rest of the United Kingdom on legal and tax matters?

As we note above, Scotland retained its distinct legal system when it formed a union with England in the eighteenth-century. The nature of the union has meant that an inevitable element of shared UK-wide legislation has harmonised the law across the constituent parts of the United Kingdom. As can be seen from the content of this chapter, the taxation of capital in Scotland is broadly implemented by UK-wide legislation, with the notable exception of taxes on the transfer of land referred to above. The taxation of income is, as we note, the responsibility of both the UK and Scottish governments depending on the nature of the income in question. Scotland has its own distinct laws of property, trusts and succession which reflect its status as a mixed legal system.

3. How does the law of property in Scotland differ from that of England and Wales?

The two property law systems in Scotland and England and Wales differ significantly although there are similarities between the two. Whilst the focus of this volume does not relate direct to property law, it is important for clients purchasing property in the United Kingdom to be aware that the principal difference is that in England and Wales, property ownership is split between leasehold (ownership of the property for a limited time) and freehold (ownership of the property and the underlying land, for an unlimited period); in Scotland, no such distinction exists.

4. What is the position in Scotland as regards the use of entities such as trusts and companies to purchase property?

The tax and legal implications of the purchase of property using an entity must be carefully considered, taking advice from Scottish tax and legal advisers prior to the purchase, as the tax and legal advantages in the purchaser's home jurisdiction may not be replicated in Scotland. The regulatory consequences of purchasing in this manner, such as registration in the beneficial ownership register for overseas entities holding UK real estate, if relevant, must also be borne in mind.

HMRC were experienced by agents across the UK during the COVID-19 pandemic. Requirement for 'wet' signatures on Inheritance Tax paperwork was removed for ease of administration, but whilst the Courts of England and Wales moved towards a more digital way of applying for Probate there, relevant Coronavirus legislation in Scotland did not extend the same changes to the Scottish Court system, where Applications for Confirmation were concerned. In that regard, Scottish Commissary business is a notable exception to a wider rule. Executors and their agents in Scotland are still required to submit principal testamentary writings, docketed appropriately, together with supporting documentation to the relevant Sheriff Court on paper. Although payment of Court fees may be made electronically using bank cards or other methods, the process remains distinctly analogue.

During the pandemic, the Coronavirus (2) (Scotland) Act 2020 removed the requirement that a solicitor or notary public in Scotland witnessing a document or taking an oath/making an affirmation or declaration was in the same room as the person signing/taking the oath, where it was otherwise a requirement that the solicitor or notary public was present. This allowed the helpful practice of notarising or signing documents by video call. The relevant provisions of the 2020 Act were appealed in 2022, but the Requirements of Writing (Scotland) Act 1995, which governs the execution of legal documents in Scotland, has been amended so as to permit solicitors, advocates and notaries public in Scotland to sign or notarise as the case may be even though they may not be physically in the same place as the person signing, taking an oath or making an affirmation or declaration.

3. ESTATE AND TRUST LITIGATION AND CONTROVERSY

Scotland does not tend to be a forum for a large body of trust and succession litigation. Major decisions affecting UK-wide matters, ultimately decided at Supreme Court level, tend to originate from the lower courts of England and Wales. Reference to these decisions are made in the England & Wales chapter of this volume.

AUTHOR BIOGRAPHIES

Paul Macaulay
Paul is a Partner at Turcan Connell and advises private individuals, entrepreneurs, family businesses and landowners on wealth, tax, succession and asset protection planning, often working with advisors in other jurisdictions on cross border solutions. Paul is a member of the International Academy of Trust and Estate Law and the Society of Trust and Estate Practitioners (STEP). He also holds the STEP Advanced Certificate in Family Business Advising.

Mark McKeown
Mark is a Legal Director at Turcan Connell, based in Edinburgh. Mark specialises in tax and estate planning for private clients, their families, trusts and partnerships, and has a particular interest in cross-border work. He also provides advice to private philanthropists and those involved in the charity sector. Mark chairs Turcan Connell's in-house Executry Practice Group. He is a member of STEP, the Charity Law Association and holds the STEP Advanced Certificate in Cross-border Estates.

SPAIN

Florentino Carreño
Cuatrecasas

INTRODUCTION

Spain's infrastructure, culture and climate make it one of the best destinations in which to live and work in the European Union. Also, the language and history Spain shares with Latin America make it the preferred gateway to Europe for Latin Americans. The country also continues to be a world-leading destination. Indeed, according to the World Tourism Organization, before the COVID-19 pandemic, Spain received 83.7 million international tourists, making it the world's second most popular tourist destination after France (and ahead of the United States). Spanish legislation has been improved to encourage this trend and attract talent, high-tech projects and wealthy families. Golden visa programs have been introduced, as well as tax incentives for those coming to Spain to work or manage projects.

This chapter is a comprehensive introduction to Spanish legislation relevant to private clients, with a focus on how Spanish legislation and tax authorities approach foreign legal institutions such as trusts.

1. TAX AND WEALTH PLANNING

As a basic principle, Spanish tax residents pay Personal Income Tax, or Wealth Tax where applicable, on their worldwide income or assets, while non-resident individuals are taxed regionally only on their income, assets and rights sourced or located in Spain. A resident taxpayer's income includes all earnings, profits, capital gains and losses, and attributed income established by law during the calendar year, regardless of where it is obtained. Income tax is due on June 30 of the subsequent year.

In Spain, powers over certain tax matters are partially or fully delegated to the autonomous communities (administrative territories). Personal Income Tax is partially collected by the autonomous communities, while Inheritance and Gift Tax and Wealth Tax are fully collected by them. The autonomous communities can also modify the corresponding share of the tax delegated. Consequently, an individual's place of residence within Spain requires special attention, as it will directly affect their taxation.

Non-residents apply the tax legislation of the Spanish autonomous community where their highest value assets are located. The Personal Income Tax base is broken down into two categories with different tax rates:

- The saving tax base, which mainly includes (i) income from movable capital (dividends and interest); (ii) positive and negative capital gains, which arise on transfers of assets. The maximum tax rate for 2023 would be 28% for income above EUR 300,000.
- The general tax base includes employment, business and professional income, imputed income from unrented real estate, imputed income from controlled foreign corporation when applicable.,

Wealth Tax is a direct and personal tax imposed on a taxpayer's assets and rights as at December 31. Non-residents are taxed on assets located in Spain and rights that can be exercised there. The autonomous communities apply this tax, so it will depend on where an individual is a resident. Madrid and Andalusia have a tax credit of 100% against gross wealth tax (i.e., no wealth tax). In autonomous communities where wealth tax is applied, special attention should be paid to deductions on family-owned business and to the cap on joint Personal Income Tax and Wealth tax, which cannot exceed 60% of income subject to the personal income tax, both in the general and savings tax base, without considering capital gains from assets held for more than one year. When the total sum payable (Wealth tax plus Personal Income Tax) exceeds 60% of the tax base, the wealth tax payable can be reduced by 80% to reach that 60%, so that 20% of the Wealth Tax is always payable.

On 28 December 2022 the Extraordinary High Net Worth Individuals Tax, complementary to the Wealth Tax, was published. It is a tax of a personal nature and complementary to Net Weath Tax (NWT), which is levied on net wealth in excess of EUR 3,700,000 for tax resident individuals and for non-resident individuals in excess of EUR 3,000,000 of assets located in Spain and/or rights that can be exercised in Spain. This tax is a temporary tax with a duration of two years from its entry into force (2022 and 2023). The rules contained in the Wealth Tax, and described above, shall be applicable for the determination of the taxable base of this Extraordinary Tax.

The tax rates are as follows:
- a tax rate of 1.7% between EUR 3,000,000 and EUR 5,347,998.03;
- a tax rate of 2.1% between EUR 5,347,998.03 and EUR 10,695,996.06; and
- a tax rate of 3.5% above EUR 10,695,996.06.

Again, the joint limit described above for Wealth Tax will also be applicable to this Extraordinary Tax. For these purposes, the amount to be paid under the Extraordinary Tax, together with the amounts to be paid for Personal Income Tax and Wealth Tax and the Extraordinary Tax, cannot not exceed, for Spanish resident taxpayers, 60% of the sum of the taxable bases of Personal Income Tax, without taking into consideration capital gains from assets held for more than one year.

This tax has raised great legal concerns based on:
- **The lack of parliamentary procedures.** While affecting the legal framework relating to the financing of the Spanish Regions, the Government has not modified the Law of Financing of the Regions subject to reinforced parliamentary procedures (i.e., specific reports, public information, etc.).
- **Constitutional breach.** The new tax has been introduced as an amendment to a Law not relating to the tax, which was introduced once the original Law had already been subject to parliamentary discussion. By doing so the political parties supporting the government impede the remaining members of the Parliament from discussing, proposing amendments to etc., the proposed extraordinary tax. Accordingly, their constitutional rights as legislators have not been respected.
- **Legal uncertainty.** The fact that the new tax was approved and officially published on December 28th 2022, three days before it became due, surprisingly, running over taxpayers and without allowing the taxpayer the opportunity to prepare or adapt (there is an element of retroactivity) affects a very basic principle contemplated in the Spanish constitution – the right to "legal certainty". By acting as it has done, the Spanish legislator has breached the legitimate expectations of taxpayers with regards to the tax treatment they could expect.
- **Potential breach of EU fundamental freedoms.** This new tax may affect the freedom of movement of persons and capitals within the European Union, affecting the internal market. As a consequence of these legal concerns, a great level of litigation is expected once the corresponding tax is declared and paid through the month of July.

The government has also introduced legislation aimed at promoting startups, with significant changes affecting the venture capital industry, entrepreneurs and impatriates. Under the impatriate regime, individuals are taxed in Spain only on their Spanish-source income and capital gains, except for income from employment and entrepreneurial activities, which is taxed on a worldwide basis.

This regime applies in the tax period in which the taxpayer acquires tax residence in Spain and for the following five tax periods (i.e., for a total of six years), unless the taxpayer is excluded from the regime or waives its application. This regime also extends — under certain conditions — to impatriates' spouses and children up to 25 years of age or to children of any age who have disabilities.

The basic requirements to apply this regime are:

- Not being a tax resident in Spain in the last five years.
- Moving to Spain for work reasons, which are:
  - having an employment contract;
  - people working for a foreign company rendering their services remotely (digital nomads);
  - being the director of a company (if the company is considered a passive company, the company cannot be a related party to the director; i.e., the director must have a shareholding below 25%);
  - carrying out an entrepreneurial activity in Spain (any activity that is innovative or of special economic interest and obtains a favorable report issued by the state-owned innovation company Empresa Nacional de Innovación SA (ENISA)); and
  - being a highly qualified professional who moves to Spain to carry out an economic activity that involves providing services to startups or to carry out training, research, development, and innovation activities for which the individual receives remuneration that makes up over 40% of their income from work and economic activities.
- Not to obtain income to be qualified as obtained through a permanent establishment located in Spanish territory.
- Filing Form 149 to notify the Spanish tax authorities of the decision to apply this regime within six months from the date of starting the activity listed in the social security registration in Spain or in the documentation that allows the individual to maintain the social security legislation of the country of origin.

If the impatriate regime applies, the basic principle is that individuals who become tax residents in Spain are only taxed on their Spanish-source income — as defined in the regulations applicable to non-residents — rather than on a worldwide basis, and they do not pay taxes on foreign-source income, except income from labor or professional activities, which is taxed at 24% on the first EUR 600,000 and, above this figure, at the marginal tax rate of the autonomous community where the individual is a tax resident.

Exit Tax applies when the individual leaving Spain has been considered a tax resident in Spain for at least 10 out of the 15 tax periods before the last tax period in which the individual was subject to personal income tax. For taxpayers who have chosen to apply the impatriate regime, this period will start running from the first tax period in which the impatriate regime is no longer applicable.

With regards to Inheritance and Gift tax, individuals are subject to the legislation of the autonomous community where they reside.

Finally, they will be subject to Wealth Tax only on the assets and rights that are located or that can be exercised in Spain.

1.1 National legislative and regulatory developments

The Spanish legal system, figures and institutions all follow the tradition and principles of civil law. Within this framework, Spain is a European Union Member State so European legislation directly influences or has preferential application to Spanish international private law. This means that Spanish international private law, as stated in the Spanish Civil Code, has been modified or must be interpreted according to the European Union regulations, directives and its other legislation, even when applied to non-European citizens (sometimes also under the scope of these regulations). This is particularly relevant in cases of dual or multiple citizenship.

In addition, Spain is divided into 17 administrative territories, regions or autonomous regions (comunidades autónomas). Some of the regions have the sovereign authority to regulate civil matters, but this is limited to personal relationships (i.e., family and inheritance law) in those regions and does not affect the regulation of contracts. In relation to internal civil law, we can differentiate between the so called "foral regions" (territorios forales), which include the regions of Catalonia, Basque Country, Navarre, Galicia, Balearic islands and Aragón, and the "common law regions" (so-called "territorios de derecho común") that corresponds to the rest of Spain including the Canary Islands. These differences are due to historical reasons and medieval traditions that have coexisted. Accordingly, the Region within Spain in which a person lives, or dies, will have a direct impact on the applicable law and regulations. The region in which a person is resident within Spain will, therefore, have an impact on the applicable civil law.

From a Wealth planning perspective, the main issues with regards to business related participations are the limits for Family owned business to have access to the different exemptions and substantial deductions that are applicable under Spanish Wealth Tax. If the family business meets the requirements to be exempted for Wealth Tax purposes in principle there is a general 95% reduction, which is even higher in some regions, for transfers of participations in family businesses under Spanish Inheritance and Gift Tax both at national and regional levels. With regards to financial investments, the main issue is obtaining the rollover exemption. Under certain circumstances, divestments in collective investment institutions (CIIs) are exempt when the proceeds obtained are reinvested in other CIIs, with the new participation maintaining either the original acquisition cost or the participation being transmitted.

Following the current wording, the amount obtained by a Spanish tax resident individual as a result of the reimbursement or transfer of shares in Collective Investment Institutions (CIIs) being commercialized in Spain, is used, in accordance with the procedure established by Personal Income Tax Regulations, for the acquisition or subscription of other shares in CIIs, the capital gain or loss shall not be taken into account for Personal Income Tax purposes, and the new shares subscribed for shall retain the value and the date of acquisition of the shares transferred or reimbursed, in the following cases:
- redemptions of units in CIIs which are regarded as investment funds; or
- on transfers of shares in CIIs with corporate form (SICAV), provided that both of the following conditions are met:
  - the number of shareholders of the CII whose shares are transferred exceeds 500;
  - the taxpayer has not held, at any time during the 12 months prior to the date of the transfer, more than 5% of the capital of the CII.

Finally, a new anti-abuse clause has been introduced under the Wealth Tax, applicable from tax year 2022, according to which securities representing equity interests in any type of entity, not traded on organized markets, of which at least 50% of its assets are directly or indirectly made up of real estate situated in Spanish territory, shall be deemed to be situated in Spanish territory for the purposes of applying this tax. Accordingly, non-residents holding equity in companies whose assets consist directly or indirectly of over 50% of immovable property situated in Spanish regions where the Wealth tax applies will be subject to Wealth Tax. The applications of Tax Treaties in force with Spain should be analysed as they may limit the application of this new provision.

1.2 Local legislative and regulatory developments

Regional authorities have the sovereignty to administrate certain taxes. For Tax and Wealth planning for individuals the relevant taxes would be Wealth Tax and the Inheritance and Gift Tax. These taxes are regulated at national level but administrated by the Regions. Wealthy individuals that generate income derived from shares or financial assets (i.e., dividend income, interest income or capital gains), are subject to tax at a maximum tax rate of 28%, applicable to all income above EUR 300,000.

It is important to mention that, with regards to Inheritance and Gift Taxes, significant allowances apply at the national and regional levels, as well as special tax relief in some Autonomous Regions, mostly for *mortis causa* or *inter vivos* transfers between close relatives or inheritance of family owned businesses. These allowance can significantly reduce the taxation, applying a 99% deduction to inheritance between direct relatives, which is the case for the Autonomous regions of Madrid and Andalusia. With regards to Wealth Tax, both resident and non-resident individuals are subject to Wealth Tax, applying the regulations of the Region in which the individual is resident, or in which the majority of the assets in Spain are located. The Region of Madrid decided not impose the tax and approved a tax deduction of up to 100% of the quota. Therefore Wealth Tax is not applicable in the Madrid Region. The Region of Andalusia has announced that will also limit the application of this tax.

1.3 National case law developments

There have been important case law developments in Spain with regards to the concept of residency and when an individual is to be considered as a Spanish resident for tax purposes. The Spanish Supreme court has taken a stricter position, benefiting tax payers, than the Spanish Authorities challenging specific cases.

With regard to reporting obligations, Spanish residents are obliged to annually declare their assets located abroad by filling out Form 720. Therefore, as the assets a Spanish resident settlor transfers to an offshore trust are still considered the settlor's property, and because the trust should be disregarded, the settlor is obliged to include in Form 720 the assets transferred to the trust as well as, under certain circumstances, the trust's tax residents' beneficiaries,

Previously, there were significant penalties for incorrect, incomplete or late reporting. In addition, rights and assets abroad that had not been reported to the authorities in time could be treated as unjustified capital gains, which would be added to general taxable income and subject to the progressive tax rates discussed above in the earliest tax period among those that are open to a tax audit and subject to a potential 150% penalty. Even if the taxpayer was able to prove that those assets or rights derive from a statute barred year, the taxpayer was not be able to avoid these severe tax implications for personal income tax unless the taxpayer proved that those assets and rights were acquired with disclosed income or with income earned in years the taxpayer was not resident in Spain.

However, the Court of Justice of the European Union issued a judgment on January 27, 2022 (Case C-788/2019) concluding that Spanish legislation regulating tax Form 720 (form regulating the declaration of assets held abroad by Spanish tax residents) is contrary to EU law. Specifically, it found that restrictions on the free movement of capital are disproportionate with regard to the three issues raised in the proceedings:

- No possibility of benefiting from limitation.
- The fine of 150% linked to the tax resulting from unjustified capital gains imposed on taxpayers that fail to comply with reporting obligations.
- The flat-rate fines imposed for failure to submit tax Form 720, for submitting it late, and for providing incorrect information.

Nevertheless, the obligation to provide information on assets and rights located abroad has not been declared contrary to EU law. Therefore, it remains fully in force.

1.4 Local case law developments
No relevant local case law developments have taken place in the recent past.

1.5 Practice trends
Spain is perceived as a country of high taxes. However, Spanish legislation is also aimed at favouring the development of international activity relating to real businesses and at attracting talent. In addition, its extensive tax treaty network and bilateral investment protection treaties, especially, due to historical reasons, with Latin-American countries, makes Spain a country of choice for establishing international platforms that Spanish multinational companies have enjoyed and that is also available to anyone effectively establishing residence in the country.

A good example is the exemption of the requirement of 10 or 5 years of effective residency prior to initiating the administrative process for obtaining a Spanish passport or citizenship — reduced to two years for nationals of Spanish spoken Ibero-American countries, Andorra, Portugal, the Philippines, Equatorial Guinea and Sephardi Jews.

Investors in Latin-American countries also consider Spain in order to benefit from its special regime for holding companies (Entidad de Tenencia de Valores Extranjeros (ETVE)). The ETVE is defined as a resident company whose corporate purpose is to manage participation in companies that are non-resident in the Spanish territory and that have human and physical means. The Spanish holding regime lies on the following main principles:

- Dividends obtained and capital gains derived in the sale of shares in subsidiaries by the Spanish ETVE are 95% tax exempt if the general requirements for the Spanish participation exemption regime are met.
- Dividends and capital gains obtained by non-resident shareholders of the ETVE are not subject to tax in Spain, to the extent that both originate from foreign-sourced dividends or capital gains that were exempt at the level of the ETVE.

Thus, as to the shares in foreign subsidiaries that develop business activities, this special tax regime allows an almost neutral tax treatment to both the Spanish holding company and its non-resident shareholders. Moreover, the ETVE has access to Spain's extensive network of double tax treaties and benefits from a consolidated and stable regime. This explains Spain's attractiveness as a holding company jurisdiction. Finally, the application of Investment protection treaties signed by Spain will also be relevant, especially with Latin-American countries. Spain has the most extensive Tax and Investment Protection Treaty network with countries in Latin-America.

From a practical perspective, an individual tax resident in Madrid, would be subject to taxation on savings income above EUR 300,000 at a flat rate of 28%; will not be subject to taxation under Wealth Tax and will benefit from a 99% deduction on Inheritance and Gift Tax between spouses and direct line of descendants and ascendants.

1.6 Pandemic related developments

Legislation has been disclosed aimed at promoting start-ups that introduce significant changes affecting the venture capital industry, entrepreneurs and impatriates with the purposes of incentivising investment and attracting the development of new activities in Spain.

2. ESTATE AND TRUST ADMINISTRATION

2.1 National legislative and regulatory developments

The concept of trust does not exist under Spanish legislation. Spanish legislation does not recognise trusts and has not signed nor ratified the Hague Convention of 1 July 1985 on the Law Applicable to Trusts and on their Recognition.

In addition, where the term "trust" is used in Spanish legislation it is to clarify the Spanish word 'fideicomiso' (fiduciary agreement) in the list of legal agreements to be closely followed, and which would be subject to special scrutiny when used.

As a trust cannot be incorporated under Spanish legislation, in principle, Spanish legislation would be applicable only where, under private international law, the law applicable to the assets within a trust is Spanish legislation or Spanish tax resident individuals are involved, causing uncertainty relating to tax conclusions when analysing particular trust arrangements.

For the Spanish legal system, a trust cannot have rights or obligations, nor can it own assets. This is because the Spanish legal system considers property to be an unlimited right, which cannot be divided into "formal ownership" and "economic ownership" unless a partial disposal of said right takes place. The specific trust arrangement will have to be analysed, and potential tax consequences will follow from the classification of the transactions agreed by the parties under Spanish civil law.

In general, under Spanish legislation, the legal owner is also the beneficial owner unless a transfer has taken place. Under a simplistic approach, a conclusion might be that in case of a trust, the trustee (as legal owner) is treated as beneficial owner; however, it can also be interpreted that as long as no transfer (presumably to the beneficiary) has taken place it is the settlor who is considered as the beneficial owner. As there is very little administrative doctrine on the taxation of trusts and what exists is inconclusive, Spanish taxation of a trust can be controversial, depending on the regulation and the type of income obtained by the trust. According to the Spanish tax authorities' current interpretation, trusts should be disregarded for tax purposes:

the relationships established through this figure are considered to take place directly between the individuals involved. Due to this principle, and as a general rule, Trusts, as such, are not subject to taxation in Spain and are not considered taxpayers.

The Spanish tax authorities have traditionally interpreted the trust's assets as being directly owned by the settlors until their death and considered that distributions made by the trustee to the beneficiaries while the grantor remains alive are a gift from the settlors to the beneficiaries and, if made upon death of the settlor, constitute an inheritance. According to this interpretation, non-resident trustees are generally treated as mere administrators of the trust funds.

However, recent tax rulings issued by the Spanish tax authorities have drawn attention to the clauses, facts and circumstances of each trust to determine which of the parties in the trust should be deemed the owner of the assets. In this regard, the Spanish tax authorities have recently considered that the assets in a trust may already belong to the beneficiaries when, for instance, the beneficiaries:
- have a clear right to dispose of the assets in the trust and to request them from the trustees; and
- are also the trustees and have broad powers to dispose of and distribute the assets.

Therefore, particular attention should be paid to the clauses of the trust deed and the actual actions of the settlors, protectors, trustees and beneficiaries to determine who should be considered the owner of the assets in trust.

2.2 Local legislative and regulatory developments
There have been no significant local legislative and regulatory developments.

2.3 National case law developments
The only case law to date is the Spanish Supreme Court decision of 30/04/2008, according to which the trust constitutes a legal institution that establishes a fiduciary relationship both *inter vivos* and *mortis causa. The* High court established that this institution is not foreseen under Spanish legislation. The case goes on and recognized that in the case under analysis following International conflict law applicable in the Spanish legal system, the foreign law would have been of application. However, such foreign law was not proved and, accordingly, Spanish law was the one applicable. This statement opens the door for scholars to consider that, if properly proved, the foreign law would have been of application and with the foreign law the trust would have been recognized, provided the specific trust does not go against the Spanish public order (public policy) or constitute a legal fraud. In addition, Act 29/2015, of July 30, on international legal cooperation in civil matters, forces the Spanish courts to:
- recognize an unknown legal institution (e.g., a trust); and
- adapt its effects to those of an institution under the Spanish legal system.

The EU Succession Regulation (EU 650/2012) contains a similar rule. However, the application and legal development of these regulations remains to be seen.

2.4 Local case law developments
There have been no local case law developments.

2.5 Practice trends
It is worth mentioning life insurance contracts of the unit linked type under

FREQUENTLY ASKED QUESTIONS

1. Spain is a member of the European Union and has signed the Schengen agreement under which 27 European countries have abolished their borders. Does Spain offer a golden visa program?
Yes, Spain offers residence permits for investors to non-European Union citizens who invest in Spanish territory and have sufficient means to sustain their living in Spain. This residence permit does not require actual residence in Spain and entitles the holder to work as an employee, be self-employed and hire third parties. The investment required is one of the following:

- real estate in Spain with a value equal to or greater than EUR 500,000, free of taxes, liens and encumbrances;
- EUR 1 million in bank deposits in Spain;
- EUR 1 million in shares in Spanish companies with a real business activity;
- EUR 1 million in investment funds, closed-end investment funds or venture capital funds incorporated in Spain; or
- EUR 2 million in Spanish public debt.

This permit does not require actual residency and allows the holder to choose between residing in Spain, becoming a Spanish tax resident or using the permit as a multiple-entry visa.

2. Is the golden visa program a pathway to Spanish citizenship?
Individuals who are residents in Spain can apply for Spanish citizenship. The general requirement is 10 years of continuous residency before applying, although this requirement is reduced to two years for individuals from Latin America, Andorra, Philippines, Equatorial Guinea, and Portugal, as well as for Sephardic descendants. This possibility is one of the reasons Spain is such a popular European destination for Latin Americans.

3. Is Spain still an attractive jurisdiction for tax purposes in the international environment?
Spain's culture, infrastructure, health system, and climate make it an attractive destination, as do its golden visa programs, citizenship legislation, impatriate regime, regional inheritance tax regime, tax regime for holding companies, and investment protection agreements with Latin American countries. However, each case must be analyzed on an individual basis.

which the policy holders bear the risk of the investments under the policy as are extensively being used as an alternative to trusts and private foundations for the structuring and administration of a person's assets.

Spanish Inheritance and Gift Tax provides that the amounts received by individuals (both Spanish-residents or, under certain conditions, non-residents) who are beneficiaries of life insurance contracts are taxable under Inheritance and Gift Tax, either as a gift or as an inheritance (depending on the circumstances), if the beneficiary is a person different from the policyholder.

For Personal Income Tax purposes, income deriving from life insurance contracts and obtained by Spanish tax-resident individuals is considered to be "movable capital" and is included in the "savings income taxable base" and taxed at the marginal rate of 28% for income above EUR 300,000.

2.6 Pandemic related developments
There have been no developments relating to the COVID-19 pandemic.

3. ESTATE AND TRUST LITIGATION AND CONTROVERSY

As trusts are disregarded under Spanish law, there is no trust litigation and controversy in Spain. The general approach from a tax perspective to disregard the arrangements under the trust, although the tax authorities are increasingly paying attention to the clauses, facts and circumstances of each trust to determine the party in the trust that should be considered the owner of the assets and to ascertain the tax implications deriving therefrom.

3.1 National legislative and regulatory developments

Spanish regulation on the legal capacity of persons with disabilities have been amended extensively. The aim of the new legislation is for people with disabilities to make their own decisions. For this purpose, the law establishes support systems that aim to respect their will and preferences. This legislation is changing the approach of legal advice when dealing with persons with disabilities, particularly in civil, corporate or litigation matters.

3.2 Local legislative and regulatory developments

There have been no relevant local legislative and regulatory developments.

3.3 National case law developments

There have been no relevant national case law developments.

3.4 Local case law developments

There have been no relevant local case law developments.

3.5 Practice trends

None.

3.6 Pandemic related developments

There have been no developments relating to the COVID-19 pandemic.

AUTHOR BIOGRAPHY

Florentino Carreño

Florentino Carreño is a lawyer based in Madrid, Spain, partner at Cuatrecasas. He is a private client lawyer and an expert in asset structuring between countries and generations. He also advises on structuring of family offices, private equity, hedge funds and insurance. An academician of The International Academy of Estate and Trust Law, currently member of its Executive Committee. He is also an elected international fellow of the American College of Trust and Estate Counsel. He opened the London office of Cuatrecasas where he worked for three years. This experience has enabled him to acquire in-depth knowledge of common law wealth structures while advising national and international clients, especially British, US, Canadian and Latin-American. He lectures Tax Law and European tax harmonization at the University of Navarra and at the University Carlos III.

SWITZERLAND

Tina Wüstemann & Ruth Bloch-Riemer

Bär & Karrer AG

INTRODUCTION

Politically and economically, Switzerland is one of the most stable countries in the world. It is a federal republic made up of 26 cantons, each of which has considerable autonomy in the areas of taxation, healthcare, social welfare, law enforcement and education; this creates a number of differences in local governance.

Switzerland has a population of almost 8.5 million. The country has four official languages (German, French, Italian and Romansh) and English is also widely spoken.

As is the case with most European countries, Switzerland is a civil law jurisdiction. The judiciary comprises of federal and cantonal courts. Each canton has its own courts of first instance and a second instance of appeal. The highest judicial authority is the Federal Supreme Court located in Lausanne, which is the final instance of appeal against decisions of:

- the cantonal courts of appeal;
- the Federal Criminal Court, located in Ticino;
- the Federal Administrative Court in St. Gallen; and
- the Federal Patent Court, also located in St. Gallen.

1. TAX AND WEALTH PLANNING

The question of whether a person is obliged to pay taxes in Switzerland depends on whether they meet the requirements of tax residence. This applies if they have had an uninterrupted stay of at least 30 days in the country with professional activity or a stay of at least 90 days without professional activity. Unless a double taxation treaty specifically allocates the person's tax residence to another state, they will then become subject to unlimited tax liability in Switzerland. This means that their worldwide income and wealth become subject to income tax at the federal, cantonal and municipal levels, and to wealth tax on the cantonal and municipal levels.

For Swiss tax residents, income tax is generally levied on all forms of income, for example, from employment, investment, pension or real estate (exceptions apply for income deriving from foreign real estate or business, capital gains on privately held assets (for example shares) and income constituting a repayment of nominal capital or qualifying capital contribution reserves in companies). The applicable tax rate depends on a number of factors. Income tax rates are progressive and vary depending on the canton and, within a canton, on the specific municipality of residence.

Further to the taxation of income and moveable and immoveable assets, Swiss tax residents are also subject to wealth taxation at the cantonal and municipal (but not federal) level. For taxation purposes, gross wealth may also be reduced by various deductions, such as for debt (e.g. mortgages) or, depending on the canton, certain tax-free amounts (e.g. social deductions).

As an alternative to the ordinary regime of income and wealth taxation, most cantons provide taxpayers the option of being taxed on their worldwide living expenses by way of lump sum taxation. Lump sum taxation is only available to persons who are not Swiss nationals, who do not exercise a professional activity in Switzerland and who have recently relocated to Switzerland or have not lived here during the past ten years. In a lump sum regime, the income tax basis is determined by a tax ruling that must be obtained from the cantonal tax authorities.

Persons not resident in Switzerland for tax purposes may nonetheless be subject to limited tax liability here if they have a specific economic nexus to the country (for example: permanent establishments in Switzerland; brokering in or ownership of Swiss real estate; exercising professional activities in Switzerland and so on). If limited tax liability applies, only a certain portion of income will be taxable in Switzerland. At a minimum, this will include the revenue earned from Swiss sources. However, as a general rule, a person's global revenue will be used to calculate the applicable tax rate.

Other relevant taxes are inheritance tax and gift tax, which are levied at the cantonal and municipal level but not federally. The applicable tax rates and tax-exempt amounts vary between the cantons and depend on the relationship between the deceased/donor and the heir/donee. As a result, wealth and succession planning structures, such as trusts and foundations, still require individual assessment for tax purposes. For such structures, it would typically be appropriate to obtain a tax ruling from the competent cantonal tax authorities.

1.1 National legislative and regulatory developments
Revision of Swiss inheritance law
One of the most significant legislative developments is the revision of the Swiss inheritance law. The provisions of the first part of the revision came into force on 1 January 2023. The first part of the revision focused on increasing the testator's freedom of disposition by reducing the minimum share in the estate guaranteed by law to certain persons close to the deceased, the so-called forced heirship share. According to the new law, the descendants' forced heirship share is reduced to one half of their statutory share (instead of 3/4 as it currently stands), while the parents share was abolished completely. The entitlement of spouses and registered partners has remained unchanged. Due to this reduction or abolition of the compulsory shares, a testator can now freely dispose of at least half of the estate. Hence, there is more flexibility for favouring life partners or other persons or for allocating a larger share to specific heirs, whereby the relevant cantonal inheritance tax consequences must be considered when benefiting non-relatives.

A further change in Swiss succession law relates to the testator's freedom to dispose of their assets by way of lifetime gifts where the testator has concluded an inheritance pact. Under the new rules, testamentary dispositions and lifetime gifts – with the exception of occasional customary gifts – can be challenged by the contractual party to the inheritance pact if they are incompatible with the undertakings in the inheritance pact and such dispositions have not explicitly been reserved.

Moreover, since the revision, in cases where a spouse dies during ongoing divorce proceedings, the surviving spouse is no longer entitled to their forced heirship share, provided the proceedings have been initiated at the spouses' joint request or if they have been living separately for two years. Furthermore, spouses no longer have any inheritance claims during pending divorce proceedings based on former testamentary dispositions in last wills or succession pacts unless this has explicitly been stated. The spouses will, however, keep their statutory inheritance rights until the divorce is final. Therefore, a respective testamentary disposition is required if the testator no longer wants their spouse to benefit from the estate.

The ongoing comprehensive reform of Swiss succession law may also have significant impact on trusts and foundations. The Swiss legislator has indicated reforms with regard to information requests of heirs and other interested persons towards foundations and trusts.

The reduction of the forced heirship shares of descendants means greater freedom to dispose of assets, which may make succession planning easier, for example, for entrepreneurs – particularly in situations where a family business constitutes either the largest portion of the estate, or at least a significant element of it. In a further step, the Federal Council plans to facilitate the succession for family businesses. The new rules should apply to a broad range of "companies", i.e., to all forms of legal entities except pure investment companies and listed companies. The Federal Council signed off the dispatch on the new law for discussion in Parliament in June 2022.

In light of the new provisions which entered into force on 1 January 2023, existing wills and succession pacts should be reviewed, also given the new planning opportunities in the event of a divorce.

Same-sex marriage

Another recent change in Swiss legislation concerns the provisions on same-sex relationships. Until 1 July, 2022, same-sex couples could only enter into a registered partnership, but not get married. The registered partnership confers certain rights that are comparable to marriage (for example, right to share a surname, right to inherit from their partner, right to be protected from termination in rental agreements, and so on) but differs with regard to important aspects such as the default marital property regime or the right to adopt.

As of July 1, 2022, same-sex couples are able to get married or have their registered partnership converted into a marriage. Since that date, same-sex couples can no longer enter into new registered partnerships. However, existing partnerships may continue to exist without any specific declaration.

This development has far-reaching consequences for the wealth planning of same-sex couples, as the rules concerning the matrimonial property regime changed. The previous ordinary matrimonial property regime of the registered partnership – the separation of property – is no longer applicable should the partners decide to convert their partnership into a marriage. From the time of conversion into marriage, the ordinary matrimonial property regime of the participation in acquired property applies. If the couple wishes to convert their registered partnership into a marriage but retain the regime of separation of property, a respective marital agreement must be concluded. If such an agreement already exists, it remains valid following the conversion of the registered partnership into a marriage. The registered partnership is, to a large extent, treated in a similar way to marriage from a tax perspective. Same-sex marriage is treated like traditional marriage from a Swiss tax perspective.

Registration of Swiss family foundations

Existing Swiss family foundations had to register with the commercial register by the end of 2020, and new ones are considered validly set up only if duly registered. Swiss family foundations remain, however, exempt from supervision and there is no statutory requirement for an auditor. The new registration requirement in Switzerland might be regarded as a further impediment for Swiss family foundations since their confidentiality privilege has now been removed. That said, Swiss law prevents Swiss family foundations from granting unconditional maintenance payments to members of a family over generations. Therefore, Swiss family foundations are not often used in the context of wealth and estate planning.

Revision of Swiss foundation law

Swiss foundation law has recently been reformed by a Parliamentary Initiative to strengthen the Swiss foundation sector. Originally intended as a moderate modernization dealing with particular issues (e.g., tax exemption for charitable foundations with remuneration for the members of the foundation board, collection of data of charitable foundations, simplifications to amend the organization after the establishment of the foundation), the consultation process quickly demonstrated the interest of the sector to initiate a broader reform, especially when taking into account the parallel intentions to create a genuine Swiss trust law. However, only a few provisions have been revised. Most notably, it will be possible to reserve the right to amend the foundation's organization and minor amendments of the foundation deed shall be possible if they "appear justifiable on reasonable grounds". These new provisions will enter into force on 1 January 2024.

Supervision of Swiss trustees

Switzerland is host to many trusts and many trustees operate in Switzerland. In recent years, and as a result of international trends towards transparency, the regulatory environment for trusts and trustees has significantly changed. The introduction of the Financial Institutions Act brought a new supervisory regime for trustees, portfolio managers, managers of collective assets, fund management companies and securities firms (see Section 2.1 below).

1.2 Local legislative and regulatory developments

As is the case with most continental European countries, Switzerland is a civil law jurisdiction. One of the most important pieces of Swiss legislation is the codification of private law in the Civil Code and Code of Obligations. Since all important issues are codified at the national level (for example, succession and family law), there are no noteworthy local legislative or regulatory developments to report.

1.3 National case law developments

Taxation

Apart from the impact of CRS reporting (see Section 1.5 below), there have been court decisions relating to the place of effective management of foreign (often offshore) companies being in Switzerland due to the key decision-maker's place of residence and activity for the structure in Switzerland. With the place of effective management in Switzerland, Switzerland claimed taxation rights on the companies (e.g., underlying companies in trust structures).

Recognition of foreign family foundations

In a decision concerning a Liechtenstein family foundation from 2009, the Swiss Federal Supreme Court ruled that a foundation is recognized in Switzerland as long as it has been established in accordance with the applicable (in this case: Liechtenstein) law. The paradoxical result of this decision is that it is possible for a Swiss resident client to establish a Liechtenstein (dynastic) family foundation which allows for distributions to enhance the living standards of the beneficiaries, while a Swiss family foundation has to obey the strict rules. This situation has been criticized by some authors and it is anticipated that these aspects may be dealt with in upcoming reforms of Swiss foundation law.

Swiss divorce law

In a landmark decision of the Swiss Federal Tribunal of February 2021, the Federal Supreme Court abandoned the application of the so-called "45 rule". This rule meant that a spouse could no longer be expected to take up gainful employment if they had not worked during the marriage and had already reached the age of 45 at the time of the divorce. Now, it must always be assumed that gainful employment is reasonable, provided that such a possibility actually exists and there are no impediments, such as the care of small children. Parents who mainly took care of the children during the marriage and therefore did not pursue gainful employment are therefore forced to take up employment after the dissolution of the marriage, even at an advanced age.

Another recent decision of the Swiss Federal Tribunal of March 2022 also addresses the issue of post-marital maintenance. The Federal Supreme Court has ruled that – contrary to previous case law – the existence of joint children does not necessarily lead to a life-shaping marriage justifying post-marital maintenance.

Recent case law of the Swiss Federal Supreme Court further clarified the question of the binding nature of post-divorce maintenance payments agreed in prenuptial agreements. Swiss divorce courts are now bound to approve a respective agreement by the spouses, provided it is clear, complete and not manifestly unreasonable in light of the circumstances at the time of divorce.

1.4 Local case law developments

The judiciary comprises federal and cantonal courts. Each canton has its own courts of first instance and a second instance of appeal. The highest judicial authority is the Federal Supreme Court located in Lausanne, which is the final instance of appeal against decisions of:

- the cantonal courts of appeal;
- the Federal Criminal Court, located in Ticino;
- the Federal Administrative Court; and
- the Federal Patent Court, both located in St. Gallen.

Therefore, similar to legislation, the important and fundamental decisions are to be found at the national level.

1.5 Practice trends

Relocation to Switzerland

Switzerland has a stable economy thanks to its highly developed professional services sector and thriving manufacturing and pharmaceutical industries. Competitive taxation levels both for individuals and corporations help to stimulate business and migration. The trend to move to Switzerland has increased during the pandemic. The reason for this increase in immigration seems to be that Switzerland took a liberal approach to the pandemic and tried to restrict citizens' rights as little as possible. Therefore, Switzerland seems to provide what the wealthy in particular are looking for: mobility as well as legal and financial security.

Tax litigation

While the Swiss tax landscape with its tax ruling system provides for a strong tool to avoid litigation and to increase legal certainty for taxpayers, tax litigation has slightly increased in recent years, mainly as a consequence of the transparency rules introduced globally. The same rules also fostered onshoring activities, to render the planning and handling of structures less complex.

1.6 Pandemic related developments

The impacts of the COVID-19 pandemic are wide-ranging and created not only social but also legal and commercial challenges. Due to Switzerland's approach to fighting the pandemic, coupled with the conditions already in place, more and more people are moving their center of life to Switzerland. This relocation to Switzerland is also favored by the trend to work remotely. Due to the pandemic, there has been a significant and sustained increase in employers' acceptance of remote working. Accordingly, there is no longer a need to live where one works.

2. ESTATE AND TRUST ADMINISTRATION

2.1 National legislative and regulatory developments

Discussions are currently underway as to whether a new legal concept – the Swiss trust – should be introduced. However, the legislative process is still at an early stage. On 12 January 2022, the Federal Council opened the consultation on a first draft for a Swiss trust law. The proposal of the Federal Council provided that under certain circumstances a trust could be taxed as a foundation, i.e., as a separate legal entity. During the consultation it became clear that the proposed tax rules were met with criticism as they would eliminate both the established practice of the federal tax authorities as well as the discretion of cantonal tax

FREQUENTLY ASKED QUESTIONS

1. What are recent trends and developments you see in the market from a tax perspective?

We see a growing interest in relocation to Switzerland for (U)HNWI and their family members, among others due to the stable economic, fiscal and political environment and the solid infrastructure. Switzerland is perceived as a reliable hub to structure and plan family wealth and succession, with planning security in particular due to the possibility of discussing cases with the tax authorities and securing tax treatment within the framework of advance tax rulings.

2. Is it essential for an owner of assets in your jurisdiction to make a will in your jurisdiction? Does the will have to be governed by the laws of your jurisdiction?

When a Swiss-domiciled individual dies intestate, Swiss courts claim jurisdiction and apply Swiss inheritance law to the worldwide estate (except in relation to real estate located abroad, when the foreign state claims exclusive jurisdiction over real estate within its territory).

Under Swiss inheritance law, the deceased's intestate estate passes to their statutory heirs. If an individual wishes to deviate from the intestacy rules, or if they want to appoint an executor, they should make a will. Foreigners living in Switzerland, can opt for the law of the state of their citizenship to govern their worldwide estate.

If the deceased's last domicile (as defined under Swiss law, i.e. the deceased had their vital interests in Switzerland) was not in Switzerland, the competent foreign courts have, in general, jurisdiction over the entire estate, including assets in Switzerland. However, if the foreign authorities do not deal with the deceased's estate of a Swiss citizen living abroad, Swiss courts are competent to deal with the deceased's estate and will apply Swiss succession law. Additionally, if a foreign national dies with their last domicile being abroad and leaves Swiss assets, the Swiss authorities are competent in relation to such Swiss assets if the foreign authorities do not deal with the Swiss assets. In such a case, the Swiss courts will apply the succession law designated under the conflict of law rules of the deceased's last domicile.

Therefore, although it is generally not necessary (and sometimes also not recommended, depending on the case in question) from a Swiss law perspective to make a separate will specifically for assets located in Switzerland, depending on the law at the place of the last domicile of the deceased, there may be situations where a specific will is necessary.

authorities in a specific case at hand. From the authors' points of view, discussions over the introduction of a Swiss trust should also include the current treatment of Swiss family foundations. It is yet unclear if, and how, Switzerland will introduce the concept of a Swiss trust.

Another development that will impact estate and trust administration is the newly introduced obligation to register trustees. On 1 January 2020, the new Financial Institutions Act (FinIA) came into force and with it the new supervisory regime for asset managers and trustees. The FinIA provides that anyone who acts as a trustee on a commercial basis must be licensed by FINMA. This only applies if various financial, organizational as well as personal terms are met. Trustees who have started their activities before 1 January 2020 should have applied for a license by the end of 2022. Those who started their activity as trustees in 2020 had to do so by 6 July 2021.

2.2 Local legislative and regulatory developments
As already mentioned, the important issues are regulated at the national level. Accordingly, reference can be made to Section 2.1 above.

2.3 National case law developments
Over the last few years, practice has also confirmed the importance for executors and trustees to diligently handle their tax-related duties. Particularly in cross-border situations, not only the proper handling of Swiss filing obligations for income and wealth tax as well as inheritance and gift tax purposes is crucial but also the adequate liquidity planning and handling of tax payments from the estate as well as by heirs in Switzerland and abroad has shown to be increasingly relevant. In this context, executors and trustees are required to issue suitable documentation for heirs and beneficiaries in order for them to meet their local reporting obligations.

2.4 Local case law developments
There have been no noteworthy local case law developments.

2.5 Practice trends
Cross-border estates and structures
A quarter of the Swiss population are not Swiss nationals and half of all marriages are binational. Due to this increasing internationalization, a clear trend towards cross-border estates is emerging, which in turn makes more comprehensive estate planning necessary.

Review of "older structures"
The Automatic Exchange of Information (Common Reporting Standard (CRS)) and other cross-border reporting obligations imposed within the European Union (EU Council Directive 2011/16 in relation to cross-border tax arrangements (DAC6)) have become important driving forces, as cross-border structures in many cases are subject to reporting. Older and more complex structures have shown to be more exposed to suffer incorrect or multiple reporting within the automatic exchange of information.

2.6 Pandemic related developments
From a Swiss succession and tax planning perspective, the pandemic has increased the trend to plan residency and relocation more consciously and to consider aspects of infrastructure (e.g., medical system, schooling), environmental (e.g., access to recreational areas) and general systematic (e.g., stability, approach of government to crisis).

3. ESTATE AND TRUST LITIGATION AND CONTROVERSY

3.1 National legislative and regulatory developments

The concept of trusts is (as yet) alien to Swiss civil law. However, properly established trusts under foreign law are generally recognized in Switzerland as a matter of Swiss private international law (Switzerland is a signatory state of the Hague Trusts Convention). Nevertheless, the treatment of trusts in Switzerland continues to be defined by case law. However there has not yet been any precedent of the Swiss Supreme Court as regards the treatments of trusts in the context of Swiss succession.

3.2 Local legislative and regulatory developments

There have been no noteworthy local developments.

3.3 National case law developments

A difficult undertaking for heirs of settlors who pass away in Switzerland leaving assets in a trust that is unknown to the heirs is the information gathering process. In a decision of the Swiss Supreme Court in 2020, the Court clarified that heirs requesting information from Swiss banks with regard to trust accounts of which the deceased was a beneficial owner can only do so on the basis of Swiss succession law, but not contract law. This means that the heirs must show that the information is relevant for their inheritance claims (e.g., to determine forced heirship claims). In practice, this is often a cumbersome undertaking, as the heir is obviously lacking the necessary information to show the court why the sought information is relevant for their inheritance claim.

3.4 Local case law developments

There have been no noteworthy local developments.

3.5 Practice trends

In the context of cross-border estates planning, foreign trusts increasingly play a role, given that many testators are relocating to Switzerland with trust structures. Swiss law does not mention the concept of trusts and at the moment, they cannot be created under Swiss law. However, foreign trusts are fully recognised (see Section 3.1 above). As a result, trust-related disputes are on the rise. When disputes arise from situations involving trusts, they frequently involve the trustees. They are often the target of aggrieved beneficiaries or ex-spouses and can become involved in Swiss trust-related disputes, in particular in divorce and inheritance proceedings.

3.6 Pandemic related developments

The suspension of social life during the COVID-19 pandemic would suggest that there was less litigation due to fewer social contacts. However, the opposite is true. The frequency of disputes in private law has increased by about five percent overall in Switzerland during the last two years.

AUTHOR BIOGRAPHIES

Tina Wüstemann

Tina Wüstemann heads Bär & Karrer's private client team. She has over 20 years of experience in private client matters and is regarded as a leading practitioner in this field. She serves as board member in several charitable organizations, as member of the advisory board of the Department of Economics, University of Zurich and as board member of the ETH Zurich Foundation. Tina Wüstemann is a fellow of the American College of Trust and Estate Counsel (ACTEC), a member of STEP and the International Academy of Estate and Trust Law (TIAETL).

In Chambers and Partners HNW 2021, Tina Wüstemann is listed in Tier 1 for Private Wealth Law in Switzerland. In 2022 she has been awarded by STEP Private Clients as "Trusted Advisor of the Year" and by Who's Who Legal as Private Client Lawyer of the Year 2021 (global) and Lawyer of the Year 2019 (Switzerland). She is listed as Thought Leader in Global Elite 2021 (Private Client), Global Leader 2021 and National Leader Switzerland 2021 (Private Client). In 2022, Tina Wüstemann was also awarded with the Europe Women in Business Law Award 2022 as 'Best in trusts & estates', marking the sixth time she has received this recognition following 2021, 2020, 2019, 2017 and 2014.

Ruth Bloch-Riemer

Ruth Bloch-Riemer is a Partner in the tax department of Bär & Karrer AG. Her practice focuses on domestic and international tax law. She regularly advises Swiss and foreign high net worth individuals in all taxation matters. In particular, she supports clients with regard to wealth and succession planning, the structuring of charitable contributions, questions in the context of the taxation of art and artists, and questions within the field of the domestic and international structuring and coordination of their pension and social security.

Ruth Bloch-Riemer serves as an expert for the oral Swiss tax expert examinations. She frequently teaches and speaks at national and international conferences and publishes regularly in her field. She is a member of various bodies, including the international Fiscal Association Swiss Branch and the STEP Society of Trust and Estate Practitioners. Ruth Bloch-Riemer was awarded Gold as 'Lawyer of the Year, Switzerland' at the IFC Awards 2023 as well as the Rising Star Award 2019 by Euromoney Legal Media Group and listed as a Rising Star in Tax in the Legal Media Group's Expert Guides 2021 and 2022. She has been acknowledged by Chambers High Net Worth (HNW) 2020 and 2021 as "Up and Coming", ranking her as a driver of the firms growth and working towards an established reputation in the market and has been ranked Band 4 in private wealth law by Chambers High Net Worth (HNW) 2022.

UNITED STATES

Joshua S. Rubenstein & Jonathan Byer
Katten Muchin Rosenman

INTRODUCTION

The United States imposes taxes and has legislatures and courts at the national, state and local levels. While there are a large number of taxes to consider, the taxes with which this chapter is predominantly concerned are income taxes (which are paid by individuals, estates, trusts, business and other entities, etc. at the federal, state and local levels) and transfer taxes (i.e., estate, gift and generation-skipping transfer taxes, which are paid by individuals, trusts and estates at the federal and state levels). Rates of taxation, depending upon whether one lives (or is an estate, trust or entity located in) in a state or city that imposes the relevant taxes, can vary dramatically (as will be illustrated in the separate sections below). The laws of estates, trusts and property are largely (though not exclusively) imposed at the state level. The federal legislature is in session and passes new laws every year. Some state legislatures are in session every year, and others meet episodically. Private client litigations can be heard, depending upon the facts and circumstances, in either Federal or state level courts. All lawyers in the United States are permitted to appear in court, though generally only those lawyers who specialize in litigation do.

1. TAX AND WEALTH PLANNING

1.1 National legislative and regulatory developments

Overview

During 2022, COVID-19, the war in Ukraine, global inflation, the Tax Cuts and Jobs Act (TCJA), the uncertainty about the Build Back Better Act (BBBA), the Corporate Transparency Act (CTA), and the Inflation Reduction Act (IRA) dominated the planning landscape.

In our 2021 Year-End Estate Planning Advisory, there was a lot of uncertainty about whether the BBBA would be enacted and, if so, whether it would bring about a change in the estate, gift and generation-skipping transfer (GST) tax exemptions. At the end of the day, while a form of the BBBA passed the House (which form did not include a change to the aforementioned exemption amounts), the BBBA ended up being dead on arrival in the Senate.

The TCJA made significant changes to individual and corporate income taxes, restructured international tax rules, provided a deduction for pass-through income and eliminated many itemized deductions. Most significantly for estate planning purposes, the TCJA temporarily doubled the estate, gift and generation-skipping transfer (GST) tax exemptions. Absent legislative action by Congress, many of the changes imposed under the TCJA — including the increased exemptions — will sunset after December 31, 2025, with the laws currently scheduled to revert back to those that existed prior to the TCJA. Given the uncertain political landscape, practitioners continue to view this temporary increase in exemption amounts as an unprecedented opportunity for valuable estate planning.

While the permanency of the TCJA's provisions still remains uncertain, the current environment provides a great deal of opportunity for new planning. As the existing tax landscape is still in effect as of the date of submitting this chapter, and looks unlikely to change before the end of 2022, particularly in light of the results of the midterm elections, the following are some key income and transfer tax exemption and rate changes under the TCJA, including inflation adjusted amounts for 2022 and 2023:

- **Federal estate, GST and gift tax rates.** For 2022, the federal estate, gift and GST applicable exclusion amounts are USD 12.06 million. The maximum rate for federal estate, gift and GST taxes is 40%. For 2023, the federal estate, gift and GST applicable exclusion amounts will be USD 12.92 million. Absent any change by Congress, the maximum rate for federal estate, gift and GST taxes will remain at 40%.
- **Annual gift tax exemption.** Each year individuals are entitled to make gifts using the "Annual Exclusion Amount" without incurring gift tax or using any of their lifetime applicable exclusion amount against estate and gift tax. The Annual Exclusion Amount is USD 16,000 per donee in 2022. Thus, this year a married couple together can gift USD 32,000 to each donee without gift tax consequences. In 2023, the annual exclusion for gifts will increase to USD 17,000. The limitation on tax-free annual gifts made to noncitizen spouses will increase from USD 164,000 in 2022 to USD 175,000 in 2023.
- **Federal income tax rates:**
  - The TCJA provides for seven (7) individual income tax brackets, with a maximum rate of 37%. The 37% tax rate will affect single taxpayers whose income exceeds USD 518,400 (indexed for inflation, and USD 578,125 in 2023) and married taxpayers filing jointly whose income exceeds USD 622,050 (indexed for inflation and USD 693,750 in 2023). Estates and trusts will reach the maximum rate with taxable income of more than USD 12,950 (indexed for inflation, and USD 14,450 in 2023).
  - A 0% capital gains rate applies for single taxpayers with income up to USD 40,000 (indexed for inflation, and USD 44,625 for 2023) or married taxpayers filing jointly with income up to USD 80,000 (indexed for inflation, and USD 89,250 in 2023). A 15% capital gains rate applies for income above this threshold up to USD 441,450 for single taxpayers (indexed for inflation, and USD 492,300 in 2023) and USD 496,600 for married taxpayers filing jointly (indexed for inflation, and USD 553,850 in 2023). The 20% capital gains rate applies above these thresholds.
  - The standard deduction was increased to USD 12,000 for single taxpayers (indexed for inflation, and USD 13,850 for 2023) and USD 24,000 for married taxpayers filing jointly (indexed for inflation, and USD 27,700 in 2023).
  - The threshold for the imposition of the 3.8% Medicare surtax on investment income and 0.9% Medicare surtax on earned income is USD 200,000 for single taxpayers, USD 250,000 for married taxpayers filing jointly and USD 12,500 for trusts and estates (adjusted for inflation).
- **Tax Cuts and Jobs Act.** The TCJA, which was signed into law on December 22, 2017 and most of which became effective on January 1, 2018, has proven to have many implications for domestic corporate and individual income tax, as well as federal gift, estate and GST tax, fiduciary income tax and international tax. Since the TCJA's enactment, various technical corrections have been issued, as has the Internal Revenue Service's (IRS) guidance on certain aspects of the new tax regime. In light of the TCJA and recent IRS guidance, it is

important to review existing estate plans, consider future planning to take advantage of the increased exemption amounts, and maintain flexibility to allow for future strategic planning. Because of the continued importance of the TCJA's new tax laws, the most significant changes and recent guidance are summarized below.

○ *Gift, estate and GST exemptions, rates and stepped-up basis.* The TCJA retained the federal estate, gift and GST tax rates at a top rate of 40%, as well as the marked-to-market income tax basis for assets includible in a decedent's taxable estate at death.

While the federal gift, estate and GST taxes were not repealed by the TCJA, fewer taxpayers will be subject to these transfer taxes due to the TCJA's increase of the related exemption amounts. Under the TCJA, the base federal gift, estate and GST tax exemptions doubled from USD 5 million per person to USD 10 million per person, indexed for inflation. As noted above, the relevant exemption amount for 2022 is USD 12.06 million per person, resulting in a married couple's ability to pass USD 24.12 million worth of assets free of federal estate, gift and GST taxes. These amounts will increase each year until the end of 2025, with inflation adjustments to be determined by the chained Consumer Price Index (CPI) (which will lead to smaller increases in the relevant exemption amounts in future years than would have resulted from the previously used traditional CPI). The exemption amount in 2023 will be USD 12.92 million per individual, or USD 25.84 million per married couple. Without further legislative action, the increased exemption amounts will sunset, and the prior exemption amounts (indexed for inflation, using the chained CPI figure) will be restored beginning in 2026.

While the federal estate tax exemption amount has increased, note that multiple US states impose a state-level estate or inheritance tax. The estate tax exemption amount in some of these states matches, or will match, the increased federal estate tax exemption amount. However, in other states, such as Illinois and New York, the state estate tax exemption amount will not increase with the federal estate tax exemption amount, absent a change in relevant state law. Additionally, states may have their own laws that impact planning in that state.

The federal estate tax exemption that applies to non-resident aliens was not increased under the TCJA. Under current law, the exemption for non-resident aliens remains at USD 60,000 (absent the application of an estate tax treaty).

○ *"Anti-clawback" regulations.* While there is uncertainty about whether future legislation will address the sunset, either by extending the new exemption amounts beyond 2025 or changing the exemption amounts further, the IRS has issued guidance on how it will address differences between the exemption amounts at the date of a gift and exemption amounts at the date of a taxpayer's death (often referred to as a "clawback"). In Proposed Regulations REG-106706-18, the IRS clarified that a taxpayer who takes advantage of the current lifetime gift tax exemption will not be penalized, if the exemption amount is lower at the taxpayer's death. If a taxpayer dies on or after January 1, 2026, having used more than the statutory USD 5 million basic exclusion (indexed for inflation) but less than the USD 10 million basic exclusion (indexed for inflation), the taxpayer will be allowed a basic exclusion equal to the amount of the basic exclusion the taxpayer had used. However, any exemption unused during a period of higher basic exclusion amounts will not be allowed as an additional basic exclusion upon death. Additionally, the IRS clarified that if a taxpayer exhausted their basic exclusion amount with pre-2018 gifts and paid gift tax, then made additional gifts or died during a period of high basic exclusion amounts, the higher exclusion will not be reduced by a prior gift on which gift tax was paid.

The IRS issued further proposed regulations in April 2022. In REG-118913-21, the IRS provided an exception to the anti-clawback rule that preserves the benefits of the temporarily higher basic exclusion amount for certain transfers that are includable, or treated as includable, in a decedent's gross estate under Internal Revenue Code (IRC) Section 2001(b).

- ○ *Income taxation of trusts and estates.* The TCJA added new IRC Section 67(g), which applies to trusts, estates, and individuals, and provides that no miscellaneous itemized deductions (all deductions other than those specifically listed in IRC Section 67(b)) are available until the TCJA sunsets after December 31, 2025. While the TCJA doubled the standard deduction for individuals, taxpayers that are trusts and estates are not provided a standard deduction. Under the TCJA, trust investment management fees are no longer deductible. After the enactment of the TCJA, there was uncertainty about the deductibility of fees directly related to the administration of a trust or estate (e.g., fiduciary compensation, legal fees, appraisals, accountings, etc.). Historically, these fees had been deductible under IRC Section 67(e) and without regard to whether they were miscellaneous itemized deductions or not. In Notice 2018-61, the Treasury Department (Treasury) issued guidance on whether new IRC Section 67(g) eliminates these deductions. This notice provides that expenses under IRC Section 67(e) are not itemized deductions and therefore are not suspended under new IRC Section 67(g). Note that only expenses incurred solely because the property is held in an estate or trust will be deductible. While the notice was effective July 13, 2018, estates and non-grantor trusts may rely on its guidance for the entire taxable year beginning after December 31, 2017.

  New IRC Section 67(g) may also impact a beneficiary's ability to deduct excess deductions or losses of an estate or trust upon termination. Prior to the TCJA, it was common tax planning to carry out unused deductions of a trust or estate to the beneficiary upon termination, so the deductions could be used on the beneficiary's personal income tax return. Under new IRC Section 67(g), these deductions are arguably miscellaneous itemized deductions and therefore would no longer be deductible by the beneficiary. Notice 2018-61 notes that the IRS and Treasury recognize that Section 67(g) may impact a beneficiary's ability to deduct unused deductions upon the termination of a trust or an estate, and the IRS and Treasury intend to issue regulations in this area and request comments on this issue. In the interim, taxpayers should consult with their advisors about whether it would be prudent to engage in planning to utilize (to the extent permissible) these deductions at the trust or estate level.

Finally, the TCJA made a number of taxpayer-friendly changes to the taxation of electing small business trusts (ESBTs). Non-resident aliens are now permissible potential beneficiaries of ESBTs. Also, the charitable deduction rules for ESBTs are now governed by IRC Section 170 instead of IRC Section 642(c), which means that several restrictions imposed by IRC Section 642(c) (e.g., that the charitable donation be paid out of income and pursuant to the terms of the trust) no longer apply. Additionally, an ESBT's excess charitable deductions can now be carried forward five years, but the percentage limitations and substantiation requirements will now apply.

- *Income tax.* The TCJA also has implications for married couples who are divorcing or contemplating a divorce. The TCJA changed prior law to provide that alimony payments will not be deductible by the payor and will not be deemed to be income to the recipient. The TCJA also repealed IRC Section 682, which generally provided that if a taxpayer created a grantor trust for the benefit of their spouse, the trust income would not be taxed as a grantor trust as to the grantor-spouse after divorce to the extent of any fiduciary accounting income the recipient-spouse is entitled to receive. Due to the repeal of Section 682, a former spouse's beneficial interest in a trust may cause the trust to be taxed as a grantor trust as to the grantor-spouse even after divorce. These changes to the taxation of alimony and the repeal of IRC Section 682 do not sunset after 2025; they apply to any divorce or separation instrument executed after December 31, 2018, or any divorce or separation instrument executed before that date but later modified, if the modification expressly provides that changes made by the TCJA should apply to the modification.

- *Charitable deduction.* The TCJA increases the percentage limitation on cash contributions to public charities from 50% of the donor's contribution base (generally, the donor's adjusted gross income) to 60%. This 60% limitation applies if only cash gifts are made to public charities. The deduction limitations remain the same for donations of other assets, such as stock, real estate, and tangible property.

- *Business entities.* The TCJA reduced the top corporate income tax rate to 21%. To decrease the discrepancy in the tax rates between C corporations and pass-through entities, the TCJA also addressed taxation of pass-through entities (partnerships, limited liability companies, S corporations or sole proprietorships) that would typically be taxed at the rate of the individual owners. Generally, new Section 199A provides a deduction for the individual owner of 20% of the owner's qualified business income (QBI). This deduction has the effect of reducing the effective income tax rate for an owner in the highest tax bracket from 37% to 29.6%. The deduction is subject to numerous limitations and exceptions. Notably, the deduction may be limited for taxpayers over a certain taxable income threshold, USD 163,000 for single taxpayers (indexed for inflation, and USD 182,100 for 2023) and USD 326,000 for married taxpayers filing jointly (indexed for inflation, and USD 364,200 in 2023). For these taxpayers, the deduction may be subject to limitations based on whether the entity is a "specified service trade or business" (an SSTB, which is generally a trade or business involving the performance of services in health, law, accounting, actuarial science, performing arts, consulting, athletics, financial services, investing and investment management, trading, or where the principal asset is the reputation or skill of one or more employees), the W-2 wages paid by the business entity, and the unadjusted basis immediately after acquisition (UBIA) of qualified property held by the trade or business. The IRS issued Final Regulations on Section 199A on January 18, 2019, followed by a slightly corrected version on February 1, 2019. The IRS also issued Rev. Proc. 2019-11 providing guidance on calculating W-2 wages for the purposes of Section 199A, and Notice 2019-07 providing a safe harbor for when a rental real estate enterprise will qualify as a business for purposes of Section 199A. The rules surrounding the deduction, as well as the Final Regulations, are very complex, and taxpayers should consult with their tax advisors to determine the implications of the Section 199A deduction. Section 199A is effective until December 31, 2025.

- *Qualified Opportunity Zones.* The TCJA provides federal income tax benefits for investing in businesses located in "Qualified Opportunity Zones." Opportunity zones are designed to spur economic development and job creation in distressed low-income communities in all 50 states, the District of Columbia, and US possessions. By investing eligible capital in a Qualified Opportunity Fund (a corporation or partnership that has at least 90% of its assets invested in qualified opportunity zone property on two measuring dates each year) that has invested in qualified opportunity zone property in any of these communities, and meeting certain other requirements, investors can gain certain tax benefits, including the deferral or exclusion of existing gain or non-recognition of gain. The IRS issued proposed regulations and Rev. Rul. 2018-29 on October 19, 2018, and a second set of proposed regulations on April 17, 2019 which addressed, among other issues, what transactions would trigger recognition of previously deferred gains. The Qualified Opportunity Zone regime is complex and may impact the tax and estate planning of investors. Taxpayers should consult with their tax and estate planning advisors to discuss the potential tax benefits and implications.

- **Corporate Transparency Act (CTA).** Passed into law in 2021, the CTA set out to create a beneficial ownership registry for certain domestic entities and foreign entities doing business in the U.S (i.e., entities that are either created by a filing with a secretary of state in the United States or are required to file a document to do business in a state in the United States). The goal behind the new beneficial ownership registry is to combat tax evasion, money laundering, and other unsavory acts perpetuated through dealings in the United States. Specifically, the CTA requires a Reporting Company (defined below) to file information regarding itself, its Beneficial Owners (defined below), and its Company Applicant (defined below). While enacted on January 1, 2021, practitioners waited for over a year and a half for the Financial Crimes Enforcement Network of the US Department of the Treasury (FinCEN) to publish final regulations regarding the CTA and its reporting requirements. On September 30, 2022, FinCEN issued such final regulations implementing the CTA's beneficial ownership reporting requirements.

Reporting Companies formed <u>before</u> January 1, 2024 must file their initial reports with FinCEN by January 1, 2025, <u>provided</u>, that such Reporting Companies shall not be required to submit information regarding their initial Company Applicant. Reporting Companies formed <u>on or after</u> January 1, 2024 must file their initial reports with FinCEN within 30 days of formation. Any changes to a Reporting Company's Beneficial Owners must be reported within 30 days of such change. Failure to comply with the CTA's requirements may result in stern penalties.

- **Setting Every Community Up for Retirement Enhancement Act of 2019 (SECURE Act).** The SECURE Act was signed into law by President Trump on December 20, 2019 as part of the Consolidated Appropriations Act. Under the prior law, an IRA owner had to begin withdrawing required minimum distributions (RMDs) from a traditional IRA by April 1 of the year following the year the account owner turned 70-1/2. The SECURE Act increased the required minimum distribution age for taking RMDs from traditional IRAs from 70 1/2 to 72. This change is effective for distributions required to be made after December 31, 2019, for individuals who attain age 70 1/2 after that date.

  Additionally, the SECURE Act changed the distributions of retirement accounts after the death of an IRA account owner.

- **The Inflation Reduction Act (IRA).** On August 16, 2022, President Biden signed the IRA into law. In the estate-planning context, the IRA is significant more for what did not end up in the finalized version, rather than what did. For additional context, it is important to first note what was contained in the BBBA, which passed the House in November 2021. The BBBA contained provisions that would have: (i) decreased the estate, gift and GST tax exemptions; (ii) changed the grantor trust rules to significantly limit the wealth transfer technique of selling assets to an intentionally defective grantor trust; and (iii) eliminated valuation discounts for non-operating business property when valuing ownership interests in privately held companies. The BBBA also had provisions increasing the top marginal income tax rate and the top long-term capital gains rate. None of these proposals made it into the IRA. Additionally, another item missing from the IRA is the elimination of the current SALT limit. The current federal deduction of USD 10,000 for SALT was left in place, but it is important to be reminded that the limit is scheduled to sunset at the end of 2025.

  Although estate planners and clients alike are able to breathe a little easier considering what was not in the IRA, it is important to keep in mind that the absence of certain proposals from the IRA does not foreclose the possibility of the next Congress trying to bring provisions similar to the BBBA in future tax-focused legislation.

- **Treasury Priority Guidance.** On November 4, 2022, Treasury released its 2022-2023 Priority Guidance Plan, which contains 205 guidance projects that are priorities for allocating Treasury and IRS resources during the 12-month period from July 1, 2022 through June 30, 2023. Of these 205 projects, the following 11 were included in the gifts and estates and trusts section:

- Final regulations under §§1014(f) and 6035 regarding basis consistency between estate and person acquiring property from decedent. Proposed and temporary regulations were published on March 4, 2016.
- Guidance regarding availability of §1014 basis adjustment at the death of the owner of a grantor trust described in §671 when the trust assets are not included in the owner's gross estate for estate tax purposes.
- Regulations under §2010 addressing whether gifts that are includible in the gross estate should be excepted from the special rule of § 20.2010-1(c). Proposed regulations were published on April 27, 2022.
- Guidance on portability regulatory elections under §2010(c)(5)(A).
- Regulations under §2032(a) regarding imposition of restrictions on estate assets during the six-month alternate valuation period. Proposed regulations were published on November 18, 2011.
- Final regulations under §2053 regarding the deductibility of certain interest expenses and amounts paid under a personal guarantee, certain substantiation requirements, and the applicability of present value concepts in determining the amount deductible. Proposed regulations were published on June 28, 2022.
- Regulations under §20.2056A-2 for qualified domestic trust elections on estate tax returns, updating obsolete references.
- Regulations under §2632 providing guidance governing the allocation of GST exemption in the event the IRS grants relief under §2642(g), as well as addressing the definition of a GST trust under §2632(c), and providing ordering rules when GST exemption is allocated in excess of the transferor's remaining exemption.
- Final regulations under §2642(g) describing the circumstances and procedures under which an extension of time will be granted to allocate GST exemption. Proposed regulations were published on April 17, 2008.
- Final regulations under §2801 regarding the tax imposed on U.S. citizens and residents who receive gifts or bequests from certain expatriates. Proposed regulations were published on September 10, 2015.
- Regulations under §7520 regarding the use of actuarial tables in valuing annuities, interests for life or terms of years, and remainder or reversionary interests. Proposed regulations were published on May 5, 2022.

1.2 Local legislative and regulatory developments

Income tax

The TCJA made significant changes to the federal income tax, including by limiting the state and local taxes deduction (the "SALT" deduction) to USD 10,000 for jointly filing taxpayers, unmarried taxpayers, and trusts. In response to the cap on the SALT deduction, a number of states implemented workarounds to the SALT deduction limit by allowing residents to "contribute" to state-controlled charitable funds in exchange for SALT credits. Other states began to allow qualifying entities required to file tax returns within the state to make an election to pay a pass-through entity tax (PTET), as opposed to the income tax being passed through to the individuals who own the entity.

This chapter does not provide a detailed, state-by-state analysis of the PTET election or workaround, but rather provides guidance as to the complexity of this now widely accepted strategy. As the PTET appears, for now, to be the sole workaround to the TCJA's SALT deduction cap, it is crucial for each individual taxpayer and entity to discuss the benefits and potential pitfalls of the election with experienced counsel prior to electing to opt in or out of this tax regime.

Illinois Notary Public Act – implementation still pending

Changes to the Illinois Notary Public Act (the "Notary Act") were signed into law in July of 2021 as Public Act 102-160.

Electronic Wills and Remote Witnesses Act – Illinois an Early Adopter

On July 26, 2021, Governor Pritzker signed into law the Electronic Wills and Remote Witnesses Act (the "EWRWA"). In contrast to the Notary Act, the EWRWA became effective immediately upon signing. The EWRWA has two main purposes: (i) to allow electronic Wills to be executed in Illinois; and (ii) to provide a mechanism in Illinois for remotely witnessing Wills and other documents.

Illinois Real Property Transfer on Death Instrument Act

As of January 1, 2022, the amended Illinois Residential Real Property Transfer on Death Instrument Act (the "Act") became effective. The amended Act most significantly expands the scope of the Act to incorporate commercial real estate within the class of real estate that can be transferred via a transfer on death instrument (TODI), as well as provides several updates related to the construction and implantation of TODIs.

Trailer bill for Illinois Trust Code

The Illinois Trust Code (ITC), as modified by the proposed "trailer bill" which was present in 2021, became effective January 1, 2022.

New York State estate taxation

For individuals dying on or after January 1, 2023, the basic exclusion amount will be equal to the federal basic exclusion amount indexed annually, but without regard to the passage of the Tax Cuts and Jobs Act of 2017.

Changes to New York Statutory Short Form Power of Attorney

As of June 13, 2021, New York's Statutory Short Form Power of Attorney took on a different form. One of several changes that were enacted added a requirement that the principal's signature be witnessed by two disinterested persons in addition to being notarized.

New York elective pass-through entity tax

Last year, an addition to the New York State Tax Law provided for an elective pass-through entity tax to allow eligible partnerships (including LLCs taxed as partnerships) and S corporations to make an annual election to be subject to taxes at rates equivalent to the current New York State personal income tax rates. Through making this election, a qualifying pass-through entity allows its owners to avoid the USD 10,000 limitation on state and local tax (SALT) deductions and such owners may fully deduct their New York State income taxes on their federal income tax return.

New York not-for-profit organization donor disclosure

In August of 2021, the New York Attorney General suspended the state requirement to collect donor disclosure information in annual filings of not-for-profit corporations. This decision followed the United States Supreme Court striking down a similar statute regarding California donor disclosure requirements.

In November of 2021, an amendment to the New York Executive Law was signed by Governor Hochul changing the donor disclosure requirements of not-for-profit organizations. The amendment prohibits the disclosure to the public of the names, addresses and telephone numbers of contributors to a not-for-profit organization and the amounts contributed by such contributors that are typically reported on financial disclosure reports of certain not-for-profit organizations.

Remote notarization

- **New York — permanent regime.** Remote online notarization (RON) is set to go into effect on January 31, 2023. The New York Secretary of State is expected to issue regulations on acceptable methods for authenticating the identity of a remote principal.
- **New York — temporary regime.** Prior to January 31, 2023 and ceasing upon such date, any Notary Public currently registered with the New York Secretary of State may conduct remote ink notarization (RIN).
- **North Carolina.** S.L. 2022-54, signed into law on July 8, 2022, creates a new permanent remote online notarization (RON) law in North Carolina. The law also restored emergency video notarization and remote witnessing, which had previously expired on December 31, 2021, as a stop-gap measure until the RON law is effective.

Texas

The year 2022 was lucrative for the Lone Star State. As of August, Texas has enjoyed USD 77.2 billion in tax revenue, a 25.6% increase from the same period last year, attributable to economic growth and record-high inflation. In addition, receipts remitted by the oil and gas mining sector saw an 80% increase due to increased energy prices resulting from inflation and the war in Ukraine. However, with a growing economy and a rapidly expanding job market, voters have begun to feel an economic burden. The housing market is surging, and many residents fear that so too will their already-high property taxes. As such, on May 7, 2022, Texan voters overwhelmingly approved two amendments to the state constitution aimed at lowering the cost of living. Proposition 1 imposed adjustments to school district tax limitations based on school district tax rate compression schedule, cutting school district property taxes for elderly homeowners and disabled homeowners. Proposition 2, which will take effect on January 1, 2023, permanently increased the residence homestead exemption for school districts from USD 25,000 to USD 40,000. Lawmakers estimate a savings of approximately USD175 per year for the average homeowner. Besides Proposition 1 and Proposition 2, 2022 has been largely uneventful by way of legislative updates.

Texas rule against perpetuities

Within the realm of trusts and estates, it is worth noting that last year, in 2021, Texas made sweeping reforms to its statutory rule against perpetuities. Previously, Texas employed the traditional rule (lives in being plus 21 years). Now, however, Texas Trust Code §112.036(c) provides that an interest in a trust must vest "not later than 300 years after the effective date of the trust, if the effective date of the trust is on or after September 1, 2021." The effective date is the date the trust becomes irrevocable.

1.3 National case law developments
Estate of Levine v. Comm'r, T.C. Memo 2022-158
On February 28, 2022, the Tax Court issued a decision in *Estate of Levine v. Comm'r*, T.C. Memo 2022-158, which determined the viability of an economic benefit split-dollar transaction that reduced the size of the taxpayer's gross estate. A split-dollar transaction generally involves two parties who come to an agreement regarding a life insurance policy with such agreement containing the details as to how the parties will pay for the premiums on the life insurance policy and how the insurance benefits will be enjoyed. Ultimately, in an opinion that relied heavily on the specific facts of the case, the Tax Court ruled in favor of the taxpayer on issues regarding IRC Sections 2036, 2038 and 2703.

1.4 Local case law developments
New York State residency - *Matter of Obus v. New York State Tax Appeals Trib.* 2022, N.Y. Slip. Op. 04206, June 30, 2022
Generally, an individual is a New York resident for tax purposes if that individual: (a) maintains a permanent place of abode in New York; and (b) is present in New York for at least 183 days during the tax year. In *Matter of Obus v. New York State Tax Appeals Trib.* 2022, N.Y. Slip. Op. 04206, June 30, 2022, a case before the Third Department of New York's Appellate Division, the Court held that an individual who was domiciled in New Jersey and had a vacation home in New York was not a New York resident for tax purposes even though he spent more than 183 days in New York during the tax year.

Change to audit guidelines. In ascertaining whether an individual has a permanent place of abode in New York for purposes of determining whether a tax filing may be required, the requirement is that such permanent place of abode must have been maintained by the taxpayer for "substantially all of the taxable year." The previous requirement was a period of at least 11 months. For tax years starting January 1, 2022, "substantially all of the year" will generally mean a period exceeding 10 months, thus shortening the trigger period for a tax filing.

1.5 Practice trends
As can be seen from the preceding and following sections of this chapter, estate planning has become so complicated that it is increasingly being done not just by planners alone, but in conjunction with those who have deep experience in estate and trust administration and in estate and trust litigation.

1.6 Pandemic related developments
The Coronavirus Aid, Relief and Economic Security Act (the "CARES" Act), the Consolidated Appropriations Act, and the American Rescue Plan of 2021
- The CARES Act — signed into law on March 27, 2020 — was a USD 2.2 trillion economic stimulus to counter the adverse economic impacts of COVID-19.

The bill provided relief to businesses in the form of loans and tax benefits, and relief to individuals in the form of stimulus checks, unemployment benefits and tax benefits.
- The Consolidated Appropriations Act — a USD 2.3 trillion spending bill (made up of a USD 900 billion fiscal stimulus package and a USD 1.4 trillion government funding deal) — signed into law on December 27, 2020, building on the CARES Act.
- The American Rescue Plan Act of 2021 — a USD 1.9 trillion economic stimulus bill — signed into law on March 11, 2021, building on both the CARES Act and the Consolidated Appropriations Act.
- The Infrastructure Investment and Jobs Act – a USD 1.2 trillion bill (USD 550 billion in new spending) signed by President Biden on November 15, 2021.

Many such provisions have already expired but some of them remain.

Business relief
Deferment of social security taxes. The CARES Act allowed an employer to defer paying the employer's portion of an employee's social security taxes from March 27, 2020 through the end of 2020. Half of the deferred taxes were due December 31, 2021 (extended to the next business day on Monday, January 3, 2022) and the remaining half is due on December 31, 2022 (again extended to January 3, 2023).

Individual relief
- **Charitable deductions.** The CARES Act and then the Consolidated Appropriations Act temporarily allowed taxpayers claiming the standard deduction to also deduct (as an above-the-line deduction) USD 300 of cash contributions made to qualifying charitable organizations each year (USD 600 for those married filing jointly), but such charitable deductions by taxpayers claiming the standard deduction are no longer allowed beginning in tax year 2022.
- **Excess business loss limitation.** The excess business loss limitation of IRC Section 461(l) prevents taxpayers, such as individuals, trusts and estates, from deducting a business loss in excess of certain threshold amounts, indexed for inflation. This limitation was temporarily repealed by the CARES Act, but returned January 1, 2021. The threshold amounts for the 2022 tax year (for purposes of the excess business loss limitation) are USD 270,000 for single filers or USD 540,000 for those married filing jointly.
- **Retirement plans and accounts.** The CARES Act allowed qualified individuals (including those diagnosed with COVID-19 or experiencing adverse financial effects due to COVID-19) to withdraw up to USD 100,000 from qualified retirement plans in 2020, giving such individuals three years to recontribute the distribution (sometimes referred to as a "coronavirus-related distribution") to the qualified plan to unwind the taxability of the distribution. The Consolidated Appropriations Act provided a similar withdrawal exemption through June 25, 2021. Accordingly, anyone who received a coronavirus-related distribution is still within the window to recontribute such distribution.

Otherwise, if a qualified individual does not recontribute the distribution to the qualified plan, the distribution is subject to federal income tax, which may be paid ratably over a three-year period or included entirely in income in the year of the distribution. To the extent that any part or all of the distribution is recontributed to the qualified plan during the three-year period, the income to the taxpayer (from the distribution) for the taxable year of the recontribution will be offset, to the extent possible, and any excess may be carried forward to a subsequent taxable year or carried back to a prior year by filing an amended return for that prior year.

2. ESTATE AND TRUST ADMINISTRATION

2.1 National legislative and regulatory developments

Estate and trust administration in the United States is generally not handled at the national level.

2.2 Local legislative and regulatory developments

Duty in California to notify beneficiaries upon incompetency of last person holding power to revoke trust

Under California law, during the period of time when a trust is revocable, the trustee must provide periodic accountings to anyone who has the power to revoke the trust. In most circumstances, only the settlor holds the power to revoke, in which case the trustee has a duty to account solely to the settlor. During the incompetency of the settlor, prior law was unclear as to whom the trustee was obligated to provide accountings and information.

Effective January 1, 2022, California Probate Code sections 15800 and 16069 were amended to impose a new duty on a trustee to provide periodic accountings to each beneficiary who would be entitled to receive distributions of income or principal after the death of the settlor when either the settlor or the last person holding the power to revoke the trust is "incompetent".

Revision to California Partition Action

The Uniform Partition of Heirs Property Act (the "Act") became effective January 1, 2022 and added new sections to the California Code of Civil Procedure governing partition actions for real property held by tenants-in-common under specific circumstances.

Revisions to revocable transfer on death deed requirements and clarification of existing law

Revocable transfer on death deeds are governed by California Probate Code sections 5600 – 5698 and allow a transferor to transfer ownership of real property to a designated beneficiary upon the transferor's death, while avoiding the probate process and without needing to execute a will or trust. The transfer on death deed is a relatively recent statutory creation, coming into existence in January 2016. While revocable transfer on death deeds are inherently appealing due to the apparent easy avoidance of a costly and time-consuming probate administration or the costs associated with creating a revocable trust, since its enactment, critics of California's transfer on death deed statutory scheme have argued that the statutory procedures, which did not initially require witnesses or contain notice requirements, were ripe for abuse. The statute also failed to include provisions for correcting mistakes discovered after the death of the transferor. In response to these criticisms, the California Law Revision Commission reviewed the statutes, made recommendations and proposed substantive changes, which passed into law and became effective as of January 1, 2022.

Revisions to Spendthrift Trust Provisions

Assembly Bill No. 1866 (AB 1866) was signed into law on June 21, 2022 and will add a new section to the California Probate Code effective January 1, 2023, clarifying that a trustee's discretionary authority to reimburse a settlor for income taxes paid by the settlor does not allow a creditor to reach into the trust. The bill adds section 15304 subsection (c) to the California Probate Code, which provides "for purposes of this chapter the settlor shall not be considered to be a beneficiary of an irrevocable trust created by the settlor solely by reason of a discretionary authority vested in the trustee to pay directly or reimburse the settlor for any federal or state income tax on trust income or principal that is payable by the settlor, and a transferee or creditor of the settlor shall not be entitled to reach any amount solely by a reason of that discretionary authority."

Increase to small estate probate procedures

Assembly Bill 473 added section 890 to the California Probate Code which requires the Judicial Council, beginning April 1, 2022, and every three years thereafter, to adjust the statutory amounts of the property values used to determine eligibility for various procedures to succeed to a decedent's interest in property without administration.

Amendment of Powers Of Attorney For Health Care Article of the Illinois POA Act

On May 13, 2022, Governor Pritzker signed into law an amended Powers Of Attorney For Health Care Article of the Illinois Power of Attorney Act, to be effective January 1, 2023. The primary change that the amended Article enacts is that, in the amended Illinois statutory short form power of attorney for health care (Form Health Care POA), there is a new provision allowing electronic presentation of a Form Health Care POA as proof of agency.

2.3 National case law developments

Estate and trust administration in the United States is generally not handled at the national level.

2.4 Local case law developments

The applicable cases are also relevant for litigation developments so are included in Section 2.2 of this chapter.

2.5 Practice trends

As can be seen from the preceding and following sections of this chapter, estate and trust administration has become so complicated that it is increasingly being done not just by administrators alone, but in conjunction with those who have deep experience in estate planning and in estate and trust litigation.

2.6 Pandemic related developments

Refer to the local legislative developments of this chapter (Section 1.2) for new laws on remote witnessing and remote notarization, all of which were prompted by the pandemic.

3. ESTATE AND TRUST LITIGATION AND CONTROVERSY

3.1 National legislative and regulatory developments

Because estate and trust administration in the United States is generally not handled at the national level, litigation tends not to be at the national level.

3.2 Local legislative and regulatory developments

None of note on the litigation front.

3.3 National case law developments

Because estate and trust administration in the United States is generally not handled at the national level, litigation tends not to be at the national level.

3.4 Local case law developments

Circuit split concerning procedure for trust modification

The California legislature created California Probate Code sections 15401 and 15402 in 1986, codifying common law procedures for revocation and modification of California trusts. Prior to the enactment of these sections, California's common law doctrine held that the power to amend a trust was not a standalone power but rather was derived from the power to revoke a trust, which inherently included a power to modify a trust. Following the enactment of Sections 15401 and 15402, each power has its own statutory authority. However, notwithstanding the seemingly straightforward provision of section 15402, a dispute has developed among California appellate courts concerning the procedure for modifying revocable trusts. It is expected that this split will be resolved by a pending appeal to the California Supreme Court.

United States v. Allison, **No. 120CV00269DADHBK, 2022 WL 583573 (E.D. Cal. 2022)**

In *Allison*, decedent created a revocable *inter vivos* trust approximately two weeks before his death. Defendants, as co-trustees of decedent's trust, transferred certain assets totaling USD 518,750 to the trust. On or about February 27, 2007, defendants filed an estate tax return on behalf of decedent's estate. The estate tax return reported that the total gross estate value at the date of decedent's death was USD 1,663,242. Defendants subsequently transferred and/or distributed all the property of the trust and the estate, and the tax liability reported on the estate tax return — amounting to USD 192,425 — was paid in full.

Three years later, on or about February 9, 2010, defendants, acting as the estate's representatives and as trustees, executed a Waiver of Restrictions on Assessments agreeing to an immediate assessment of USD 96,808 in additional tax on the estate (the "additional assessment").

The additional tax assessments related to disallowed deductions or a recharacterization of a payment as a non-deductible transfer. The court found the defendants personally liable under IRC section 6324(a)(2) for the unpaid estate tax liabilities up to the value of property held in decedent's trust <u>at the time of his death</u>, even though the trust was fully distributed.

Corcoran v. Rotheimer, 2022 IL App (1st) 201374 (June 9, 2022)

In this case, a father ("Father") owning a beneficial interest in a parcel of land (held by an Illinois land trust) had amended the planned succession of such beneficial interest multiple times over his decades of ownership (most notably changing it from 100% passing to two of his children as joint tenants with rights of survivorship to 100% passing to a limited liability company (an "LLC") where Father's revocable trust was the sole member). Importantly, Father's revocable trust included all three of his children as beneficiaries (rather than just the two children, above) and named the third child as successor Trustee after Father.

Father passed in 2015, and the third child (i.e., the child that receives assets under Father's revocable trust but not under the previously executed beneficiary designation described above), as Trustee, brought an action for declaratory judgment in favor of Father's assignment to the LLC. The two children originally designated as beneficiaries ("Original Beneficiaries") contested this, arguing that the assignment was not in compliance with the land trust's requirements for valid transfers, including that Father did not file (or "lodge") such assignment with the land trustee. The trial court granted Trustee's motion and denied Original Beneficiaries' motion. Original Beneficiaries appealed.

The appellate court affirmed the Trustee's motion for summary judgment. The appellate court held that the assignment was not invalidated by Father's failure to lodge the assignment with the land trustee.

Palm v. Sergi, 2022 IL App (2d) 210057 (June 13, 2022)

In *Palm*, two spouses each created a revocable trust of which the respective grantor was the sole beneficiary during their lifetime. Under the terms of the two reciprocal trusts, upon the grantor's death, the surviving spouse was entitled to receive distributions during the surviving spouse's lifetime, with the remainder to be distributed equally among the grantors' two children upon the surviving spouse's death. The spouses' trusts both named the non-grantor spouse as an initial CoTrustee with the grantor spouse.

Husband's Trust was the owner of shares of stock and eventually sold said shares in exchange for a promissory note in the amount of USD 6,400,000 (the "Note"). Husband, as Co-Trustee of Husband's Trust, assigned a 20% interest in the Note to Wife's Trust and payments on the Note were initially deposited 80% to a separate bank account for Husband's Trust and 20% to a separate bank account for Wife's Trust.

Subsequently, Husband, unilaterally and in his capacity as a Co-Trustee of Wife's Trust, redirected the monthly payments on the Note so that 100% of the payments on the Note were deposited into Husband's personal bank account, including the 20% that formerly went to the Wife's Trust account. Husband then divested the Wife's Trust's interest in the Note to purchase a business interest, without written authorization from Wife as Co-Trustee of Wife's Trust.

On appeal, the appellate court found that the trial court erred when it found that Husband was authorized to take unilateral actions to divert and use trust assets. The appellate court remanded the case back to the trial court based on lack of evidence in the record to show that Wife had any knowledge of Husband's unilateral actions and suggested the discovery rule would apply to the date when Wife's sister and other beneficiaries of Wife's Trust learned of Husband's actions.

The appellate court also found Wife's sister (acting as agent to Wife's Trust and eventually Co-Trustee) did, at all times, have standing to sue a former trustee as Wife's Trust was always the real party in interest. The appellate court indicated that in this case, Wife's sister as an agent and Trustee, was always acting on behalf of Wife's Trust and the trust's beneficiaries.

In *re Estate of John W. McDonald III*, 2022 IL 126956 (April 21, 2022)

In *McDonald*, the Decedent prior to his death had been adjudicated disabled and the Decedent's brother was appointed as the Decedent's plenary guardian. Following the adjudication and five months prior to the Decedent's death, the Decedent engaged in a marriage ceremony with Decedent's alleged spouse. Upon Decedent's brother filing a petition for letters of administration upon Decedent's death, the Decedent's alleged spouse intervened. The Decedent's brother served as the Decedent's plenary guardian at the time the claimed marriage occurred, and the Decedent's brother disputed the legitimacy of the marriage (and therefore, the Decedent's alleged spouse's claims to the Decedent's estate) based on the fact that the marriage was entered into without the Decedent's brother's knowledge as guardian, or the knowledge of the probate court under which the Decedent was a ward. The Decedent's brother argued the marriage was void from its inception because the Decedent was a ward under a plenary guardianship at the time of the ceremony and lacked the capacity to enter into a valid marriage because the probate court never determined the marriage to be in the Decedent's "best interest" as required by Section 11a-17(a-10) of the Probate Act of 1975 (the "Probate Act").

The Supreme Court reversed the appellate court's ruling, holding that under the Probate Act, a ward who wishes to enter into a marriage may do so only with the consent of his guardian.

Providence Bank and Trust Company v. Raoul, 2022 IL App (3d) 210037 (March 4, 2022)

In this case, an appellate court affirmed a trial court's ruling in favor of the Executor of an estate, who sought to make an Illinois qualified terminable interest property election (QTIP election) on behalf of the estate. The primary points of contention were, in the context of filing an amended Illinois estate tax return: (i) whether a QTIP election first made on an original estate tax return can be modified in an amended return; and (ii) if so, whether such a modified QTIP election is effective when made after the (extended) deadline for the original estate tax return.

FREQUENTLY ASKED QUESTIONS

1. What is the substantial presence test for the purposes of avoiding worldwide U.S. income taxation?

Individuals satisfy the substantial presence test if they are present in the U.S. for a period of 183 days or more in any given year. If the individual is not physically present in the U.S. for 183 days or more in any given year, but is present in a given year for at least 31 days and the individual's presence in that year and the two preceding years equals a weighted aggregate of 183 days or more, then the individual is also deemed a resident for that year and is subject to U.S. income tax for such year. An individual will be subject to U.S. income tax on the first day of the year in which the individual meets the 183 days test.

For the purposes of this calculation: (1) each day in the first preceding year counts as only 1/3 of a day and each day in the second preceding year counts as only 1/6 of a day; and (2) partial days in the U.S., such as travel days, count as full days.

By way of example, the following calculation will apply to an individual who has spent 10 days in the U.S. during Year 1, 40 days during Year 2, and 25 days during Year 3:

By year:	Total day count:	Days left:
Year 1: 1/6 × 10 = 1.66 days. Year 2: 1/3 × 40 = 13.33 days. Year 3: 25 days,	1.66 + 13.33 + 25 = 39.99	183 – 40 = 143

Thus, the individual can return to the U.S. in Year 3 and remain for up to 142 days without becoming a U.S. resident for income tax purposes. If the individual returns to the U.S. in Year 3 and stays for more than 142 days, the individual's residency starting date will be the first day during Year 3 in which the individual

Texas

On the judicial front, the Texas Supreme Court ruled on whether beneficiaries of a class trust automatically have standing to sue the trustees. In the case of *Berry v. Berry* (65 Tex. Sup. Ct. J. 997 (2022)), if the beneficiaries are unnamed class beneficiaries, *Berry* reminds us that such beneficiaries do not have carte blanche standing to sue. Rather, counsel must be sure to specifically lay out the particular purpose for which the beneficiary is suing, as well as the specific interest the beneficiary has in the suit.

3.5 Practice trends

As can be seen from the preceding and following sections of this chapter, estate and trust litigation has become so complicated that it is increasingly being done entered the U.S. As a general rule of thumb, provided one does not spend more than 122 days in the U.S. in any given year, one will not meet the substantial presence test.

2. How long do I have to give up my green card without expatriation exposure?
Individuals who terminate their long-term permanent residency status (a green card held for at least eight of the 15 tax years preceding expatriation) after June 17, 2008, and who are "covered expatriates", are treated like citizens who give up their citizenship and are subject to a mark-to-market exit tax on their worldwide property, and certain gifts and bequests that they make after expatriating will also be subject to taxes.

It is therefore of crucial importance for green card holders who are considering giving up their green card to do so effectively before holding the green card for eight years in order to avoid being subject to the onerous expatriation rules, discussed below.

For purposes of determining the eight-year period, any portion of a tax year is considered a full year. By way of example, if an individual obtained a green card on December 1, 2016, and relinquishes the green card on January 1, 2023, the individual will have held the green card for a portion of eight tax years and will therefore be considered a long-term resident. It should be noted that there may or may not be re-immigration consequences to surrendering one's green card after eight years.

Notably, residence in the U.S. under any other immigration status, such as a work visa, does not count towards establishing one's long-term resident status for purposes of the expatriation rules.

Moreover, in order to no longer be considered a domiciliary of the U.S., it is not enough to relinquish one's green card. One must also establish a domicile elsewhere.

not just by fiduciary litigators alone, but in conjunction with those who have deep experience in estate and tax planning and in estate and trust administration.

3.6 Pandemic related developments
The federal and 50 states court systems addressed the pandemic in radically different ways. Some closed, and some never closed. Some functioned, remotely, some continue to function remotely, some were always in person, and some have resumed being in person. Almost all are severely backlogged as a result of the pandemic.

For further information, see Katten's extensive client advisory at
www.katten.com/2022-year-end-estate-planning-advisory.

AUTHOR BIOGRAPHIES

Joshua S. Rubenstein

Joshua S. Rubenstein is national chair of the firm's Private Wealth practice. He is also President Elect of the International Academy of Estate and Trust Law, the immediate past chair of the International Estate Planning Committee of the American College of Trusts and Estates Counsel, and an officer of the Family Law Section of the International Bar Association. Josh advises closely-held businesses, family offices and private individuals, including high net worth individuals, senior executives, professionals, entrepreneurs, artists and others with unique intellectual property interests. He handles a wide variety of private matters for these clients on a local, national and international level, including personal and estate planning, the administration of estates and trusts, and contested Surrogate's Court and tax proceedings. He has counseled clients in trust and estates matters for more than 35 years, building relationships with those who value and rely upon his advice. He focuses on creating sophisticated, yet uncomplicated, solutions for clients. Josh finds unforeseen problems and uses an interdisciplinary approach to resolve those problems, bringing in members of teams that deal with taxes, real estate or corporate and other transactional areas of the law, as necessary.

A link to Joshua's full biography: *http://katten.com/Joshua-S-Rubenstein*.

Practices: Private Wealth, Business Succession Planning, Charitable Planning, Philanthropy and Nonprofit Organizations, Fiduciary and Private Client Litigation, and International Private Wealth. **Industries:** Family Offices and Private Client Services. **Education:** JD, Columbia Law School, Harlan Fiske Stone Scholar and BA, Columbia University, magna cum laude, Phi Beta Kappa. **Bar Admissions:** New Jersey and New York. **Court Admissions:** US District Court, District of New Jersey US District Court, Eastern District of New York, US District Court, Southern District of New York and US Tax Court. **Community Involvements:** American Law Institute, Estate Planning Advisory Board, Central Park Conservancy, Advisory Council, Chess in Schools and Citywealth, Editorial Board.

Jonathan Byer

Jonathan Byer concentrates his practice in estate and tax planning for individuals and families, the representation of fiduciaries and the administration of estates and trusts. He frequently designs plans for high-net-worth individuals to help them both achieve personal goals and leverage their gift, estate and generation-skipping transfer (GST) tax exemptions to preserve and protect family wealth. He also works with young individuals and families to address their current estate planning needs and to plan for future inherited or earned wealth.

A link to Jonathan's full biography: *https://katten.com/jonathan-byer*.

Recognitions: Empire State Counsel® Pro Bono Honoree, 2016. **Practices:** Private Wealth, Business Succession Planning, Charitable Planning, Philanthropy and Nonprofit Organizations and International Private Wealth. **Industries:** Private Client Services. **Education:** JD, Brooklyn Law School, BA, Colgate University. **Bar Admissions:** New York. **Community Involvements:** New York State Bar Association, Estate and Trust Administration Committee.